2002

HIGH RESOLUTION

HIGH RESOLUTION
Critical Theory and the
Problem of Literacy

HENRY S. SUSSMAN

New York   Oxford
OXFORD UNIVERSITY PRESS
1989

OXFORD UNIVERSITY PRESS

Oxford   New York   Toronto
Delhi   Bombay   Calcutta   Madras   Karachi
Petaling Jaya   Singapore   Hong Kong   Tokyo
Nairobi   Dar es Salaam   Cape Town
Melbourne   Auckland
and associated companies in
Berlin   Ibadan

Copyright © 1989 by Oxford University Press, Inc.

Published by Oxford University Press, Inc.,
200 Madison Avenue, New York 10016

Oxford is a registered trademark of Oxford University Press

Library of Congress Cataloging-in-Publication Data

Sussman, Henry
High resolution: critical theory and the problem
of literacy/ Henry Stephen Sussman.
p.   cm.   Bibliography: p.   Includes index.
ISBN 0-19-505503-9
1. American, literature—History and criticism—Theory, etc.
2. Criticism—United States.   3. Literacy—United States.
4. Critical theory.   I. Title.
PS25.S87   1989   810'.9—dc19
88-14820
CIP

All or parts of the following material appear in this volume by permission:

Wallace Stevens, "The Man on the Dump," in *The Collected Poems of Wallace Stevens*. Copyright © 1942, 1954
by Wallace Stevens. Reprinted by permission of Alfred A. Knopf, Inc.

Ezra Pound, *The Cantos of Ezra Pound*. Copyright © 1934, 1937, 1940, 1948, 1956, 1959, 1962, 1963, 1968 by
Ezra Pound. Reprinted by permission of New Directions Publishing Corporation and Faber & Faber, Ltd.

William Carlos Williams, *Paterson*. Copyright © 1946, 1948, 1949, 1951, 1958 by William Carlos Williams. Reprinted by permission of New Directions Publishing Corporation and Penguin Books, Ltd.

Andrew A. Rooney, Letter to the Editor, *New York Times Magazine* (March 16, 1986). Reprinted by permission
of Andrew A. Rooney.

Printing (last digit): 9 8 7 6 5 4 3 2 1

Printed in the United States of America
on acid-free paper

To the Memory of
Rosalie Ruth Glickman Sussman
Ford City–Lewistown–Philadelphia, Pennsylvania

Preface

The following book attempts, through literary interpretation and by drawing upon the splendid improvisations of critical theory over the past three decades, to address and hopefully illuminate what is at all times a pressing cultural and intellectual problem: the status of literacy in the contemporary world. This is, I believe, an absolutely decisive endeavor. By virtue of the nature of its objects and field, however, it is as difficult as it is necessary.

The core of this book consists of readings of several literary works—by Hawthorne, Melville, Pound, and William Carlos Williams, among others—that have, by critical and cultural convention, not only become important but also indicate and dramatize the literate options—"present" and future—available to their public. On the other hand, twentieth-century theory, criticism, and philosophy strongly militate for us to treat these works purely as artifacts of language, to focus any account of them on the radical discrepancy between what they claim to do and what they actually do and what this implies for interpretative theory. Ultimately, the statements, representations, or systems that the literary works treated in this book claim to crystallize all dismantle themselves, because it is in the nature of language to forfeit its claims in the same gesture with which it advances them. The authors whose works we will be considering, Calvino and Kundera as well as the above-mentioned, demonstrate acute awareness of the elusiveness of language. If the works we read point to any world, it is one in a constant state of flux and reversal, where structures and meanings supplant one another as they proliferate.

By the same token, the time has perhaps arrived for us as readers to address certain concrete implications that emerge from the state of literacy itself and to acknowledge that literate conditions comprise a vital, even material element within the sociopolitical ecology. In directing his attention to what he termed the material conditions underlying economics, Marx observed a parallelism between the dominance of idealism in philosophy and the ideology of the ruling classes. Marx reacted to the Hegelian scenario of the revelation of consciousness in history by inverting the relationship between history and consciousness. History is not at the service of consciousness, argued Marx, but consciousness is determined by, is the product of, the material conditions of history.

> In direct contrast to German philosophy which descends from heaven to earth, here we ascend from earth to heaven. That is to say, we do not set out from what men say, imagine, conceive, nor from men as narrated, thought of, imagined, conceived, in order to arrive at men in the flesh. We set out from real, active men. . . . The phantoms formed in the human brain are also, necessarily, sublimates of their material life-process. . . . Life is not determined by consciousness, but consciousness by life.

These lines, from the opening pages of *The German Ideology,* both underscore Marx's methodological debt to Hegel and reverse the thrust of a particular dialectic. Yet contemporary mass culture, with its unprecedented technological facility and centralization, compels us to pursue Marx's dialectic one turn further, until we arrive at the material conditions and implications of cultural life, until we recognize the degree to which "consciousness" has imposed itself upon our tangible possibilities.

It is especially difficult, in light of the linguistic complexity that has been our own century's particular contribution to elucidate, to deploy artifacts of language, whether works of literature or theory, in approaching a set of very concrete problems and conditions. Indeed, Hegel's reading of Greek tragedies pivoted upon the agonizing conflict between the multiplicity of thought, for which we may substitute language, and the unity and purpose of action. Kant was particularly acute in pursuing the contradictions that emerge in the interaction between such disparate realms; and the following study, situated as it is between the possibilities of contemporary literature and theory and the state of literacy, is not exempt from its own antinomies. It defines literacy, for instance, as the wider skills of articulation and differentiation, yet it calls for an improved conversation between the various endeavors and institutions dedicated to literacy's dissemination. It bemoans the submersion by which the interest of literacy is effaced, yet it takes issue with certain well-intentioned approaches to the problem that happen to be different from its own.

Such contradictions have become ingrained in the field that the following chapters demarcate. To circumvent them in the name of conceptual neatness would be to avoid the issues: How can educational and cultural institutions be more efficient in disseminating the wider skills of reading and writing? What are these skills anyway? What is the role played by the electronic media in the transfer of information and cultural artifacts? Is there some implicit strategy by which these media, while inherently linguistic and informational, restrict at the same time that they convey their messages?

I began to ponder such questions when, as my vocation as a literature teacher emerged, I became aware of the peculiar conventions surrounding the depiction of professors and other intellectuals in the cinema and on television. These issues were brought even closer to home when, for several years, I assumed certain administrative responsibilities at my university. On the one hand, I was touched and gratified by the dedication to quality education demonstrated by a diverse array of teachers, civil servants, administrators, and technicians. I learned, however, that the university is hardly immune from the conflicts surrounding literacy in the society at large. In its ongoing infrastructural processes, such as the mounting of a curriculum and the determination of requirements, the university must constantly negotiate between the demands of rapidly advancing technical fields, such as engineering and computer science, and the plea to suspend or reduce specialization in the name of "General Education." This tension is exacerbated by its lack of clarity: "Technological" disciplines have much to offer to "General Education," while the social sciences and humanities have, in some respects, contributed to their own professionalization. Existing resolutions to these pressures are invariably provisional: The sciences and technologies are evolving too quickly, the heritage of general culture too rich for comprehensiveness during a four-year or at most five-year undergraduate career. The university is anything but an ivory tower existing at a remove from the debate on cultural values in contemporary society; it is at the very crux of the issues implicated by this conflict.

I was privileged to be involved in such tangible extensions of my literary work at a time when my university, the State University of New York at Buffalo, was engaged in profound introspection preparatory to the initiation of a new undergraduate college that would facilitate a better-integrated education and would reinforce the values of general verbal and mathematical literacy. Although this process continues at the university, every preliminary sign indicates that extremely variegated interests and disciplines will have succeeded in pooling their intellectual resources to institute a better-integrated and sequentially more thoughtful curriculum than previously existed. If my university succeeds in its aims, it will be because, at a crucial moment in its history, it promoted a nonreductive integration of often skewed scientific, humanistic, technological, and professional endeavors. It placed planning for the college in the hands of an aware semiotician, Professor James H. Bunn, who had at one time served as Dean of the Arts and Letters at the university and who now set out to improve the translation and transfer of the codes comprising current knowledge. If my university reaps the rewards it deserves for its efforts, it will be as a result of undertaking the integrative—Kant would say synthetic—effort whose rarity I bemoan in Chapter 1. It nurtured a productive interface between the intellectuals it engaged in the process and the sometimes stubborn practicalities of educational delivery. Indeed, the following book would have been impossible were it not for the ongoing intellectual vitality in the Faculty of Arts and Letters at the university.

Since I completed this project, the overall cultural climate in the United States has become better attuned to the values of literacy and the costs of its neglect. It has been particularly encouraging to me that a number of distinguished academicians, among them E. D. Hirsch and Allan Bloom, have shared this concern in their recent contributions to the debate. Their works, although quite different, agree with my basic premise: that literacy constitutes the primary interface and access prevailing between advanced knowledge and sociopolitical conditions, between seminal work accomplished in the arts and sciences and the public. In *Cultural Literacy*

(Boston: Houghton Mifflin, 1987), E. D. Hirsch goes so far as to address specifically "what every American needs to know." In assuming this difficult task, he applies his scholarly skills as widely as possible: He consults social scientific data to support his observation that cultural literacy is declining; he reconstructs the tendencies toward unity and diversity in American cultural history and education; and he explores the impact of nationalism both on the cultural offerings available to a public and on the conventions mediating access to those resources.

Hirsch circumvents some of the thornier philosophical problems involved in definitions of such terms as "literacy" and "culture" by pinpointing both the cultural repository and the vocabulary which a literate individual in contemporary American society can easily deploy. He also preempts charges of canonization by providing an appreciation of literate cultural pluralism. The difficult task of assembling a literate curriculum for a public—here the rigors of academic life are not as remote from the community at large as might seem to be the case—enables Hirsch's approach to cultural literacy to remain broad, as I feel that constructive contributions must be. Enlightened approaches to literacy in the contemporary world need somehow to mark the tortuous trail between standardized knowledge and the local difference distinguishing specific cultural communities and artifacts. The most gratifying aspect of Hirsch's work may well be the consistency between the mode of his scholarship and his grasp of the issue of literacy. His study powerfully demonstrates that scholarship may creatively address the conditions of its public, reception, and dissemination—at the same time that it offers a contribution "in field."

Allan Bloom's *The Closing of the American Mind* (New York: Simon and Schuster, 1987) may be a bit jaundiced, but it is infiltrated through and through by a profound concern regarding the current quality of cultural offerings. Bloom furnishes a powerful antidote to uncritical avatars of cultural and technological innovation. Through him emanates the voice, the very recriminations of the Great Tradition itself with its agencies (the family and the state) and its political and ideological extensions. Bloom's practical strategy would involve not so much the achievement of certain literate goals, whether measured in terms of quality or range, as a reinstatement of values once deemed irreproachable, an undoing of contemporary bastardizations or defilements. Bloom is a purist. His reaction to the problems raised, in different ways, by feminism, the Frankfurt School, and deconstruction is at best skeptical. At the same time, he invokes several of the most enduring and productive models and precedents for cultural articulation that are possible: Hobbes, Locke, Hegel, and Rousseau.

As this book goes to press, a fair amount of attention is being devoted to the wartime journalism of Paul de Man, a major figure of critical theory, on the basis of a single anti-Semitic article, counterbalanced by many others, that he contributed to the Belgian daily, *Le Soir*. In some journalistic and academic quarters, it is becoming fashionable to account for de Man's later work by virtue of his at best ambiguous wartime position, assumed under nearly incomprehensible circumstances by someone who emerged as one of critical theory's most inventive and ethical practitioners. Any capitulation to fascist ideology should be duly exposed and publicized. At the same time, the current discrediting of critical theory in de Man's name belongs more to the sociology of academic competitiveness and backbiting than to the extension and refinement of theoretical debate.

While the present refusal to read would situate critical theory at an unresponsive site on the political spectrum, the major premise of this book is that the political implications of deconstruction and other theoretical contributions strike out in quite another direction. The literary and discursive works that this book incorporates strongly suggest that a discerning and broadly disseminated literacy constitutes a fundamental defense against the reductions and generalizations of totalitarianism and kitsch. The body of de Man's criticism constitutes a vital and important contribution to literacy and its theoretical understanding and to the productive critique of totalitarianism in its conceptual forms. There is every indication that the current debate regarding de Man will spur critical theorists on to more extended meditations on the relationship between reading and the political than have thus far been produced. At the same time, neither attacking nor defending de Man can supplant rigorous literary or philosophical exploration, a fact that gets quickly lost in the excitement ignited when the light of public concern radiates toward the underground of scholarship. The need for tools and approaches to counteract the totalization that the mass media and technological refinement make possible will continue beyond current fashions in scholarship, beyond the careers that stand to be aggrandized or stalled by the debate. The field of contemporary critical theory is not a creation of the past fifteen or twenty years. It is the result of a meditation on the status of language in human art, thought, and social activity that has attained a distinctive quality at least since the beginning of this century. Within this purview, although in different ways, the work of all the major theoretical models for the present volume—Wittgenstein, Heidegger, Lévi-Strauss, Barthes, de Man, and Derrida—can be deployed in the upgrading and dissemination of literacy, in the release of the conceptual underpinnings that ossify ideological thought.

Chapter 4 began many years ago as a reading of Pound's *Canto LXXIV* when I studied English at the Johns Hopkins University. Its reader then, J. Hillis Miller, has been an endless source of receptivity, generosity, and support ever since. Chapters 2 and 3 emerged from a course I developed as a Mellon Postdoctoral Fellow at the same university. I am particularly indebted to Richard Macksey of the Humanities Center for the encouragement and latitude that enabled me to pursue that course, "American Culture as a Literary Problem."

Chapter 4 was considerably enlarged and the volume's theoretical framework—Chapters 1 and 5—was written during 1985–86, when I was the most fortunate recipient of a Rockefeller Fellowship in the Humanities. The Rockefeller Foundation not only offered indispensable support; it also kindly enabled me beforehand to complete my administrative assignment at SUNY-Buffalo. My year's leave was spent in Cassis, France, part of it at the Camargo Foundation, whose directors, Michael Pretina and Jean-François Gagneux, furnished every possible scholarly support and personal comfort. The educators and inhabitants of Cassis surpassed my every hope and expectation with the welcome and assistance they provided for my family and myself. This project has benefited considerably from the resources and services of the Lockwood Library at the State University of New York at Buffalo. Both the project, during its final stages, and the discipline of Comparative Literature at the university have received considerable support from the Dean of Arts and Letters, Dr. Jon Whitmore, and the Department of English. It has been particularly gratifying to work on the book with William

P. Sisler and Oxford University Press; the patience and generosity of both have approached inexhaustibility.

There is no more tangible proof of the centrality and vitality of the issue of literacy than the plurality of the approaches currently mustered in its elucidation. This volume begins and ends in appreciation for the educators, artists, curators, journalists, and freelance writers who, in a wide range of endeavors, sustain the wonder of language and languages.

Mrs. Sharon Schiller, Johann Pillai, and Maria Teresa Vicens of the Program of Comparative Literature at SUNY-Buffalo were enormously helpful in the preparation of this manuscript.

Williamsville, N.Y.   *H. S. S.*
March 1988

Contents

HIGH RESOLUTION

1

Toward Differential Literacy: The Pursuit of Rigor in the Age of Kitsch

Myth, Kitsch, and Television

It is now possible to complete the semiological definition of myth in a bourgeois society: *myth is depoliticized speech*. One must naturally understand *political* in its deeper meaning, as describing the whole of human relations in their real, social structure, in their power of making the world; one must above all give an active value to the prefix *de-*: here it represents an operational movement, it permanently embodies a defaulting. In the case of the soldier-Negro, for instance, what is got rid of is certainly not French imperiality (on the contrary, since what must be actualized is its presence); it is the contingent, historical, in one word: *fabricated*, quality of colonialism. Myth does not deny things, on the contrary, its function is to talk about them; simply, it purifies them, it makes them innocent, it gives them a natural and eternal justification, it gives them a clarity which is not that of an explanation but that of a statement of fact. If I *state the fact* of French imperiality without explaining it, I am very near to finding that it is natural and *goes without saying:* I am reassured. In passing from history to nature, myth acts economically: it abolishes the complexity of human acts, it gives them the simplicity of essences, it does away with all dialectics, with

3

any going back beyond what is immediately visible, it organizes a world
which is without contradictions because it is without depth, a world
wide open and wallowing in the evident, it establishes a blissful clarity:
things appear to mean something by themselves.

—ROLAND BARTHES, "Myth Today" (1957)

* * *

It follows, then, that the aesthetic ideal of the categorical agreement
with being is a world in which shit is denied and everyone acts as though
it did not exist. This aesthetic ideal is called *kitsch.*

"Kitsch" is a German word born in the middle of the sentimental
nineteenth century, and from German it entered all Western languages.
Repeated use, however, has obliterated its original metaphysical meaning: kitsch is the absolute denial of shit, in both the literal and the fig-
urative senses of the word; kitsch excludes everything from its purview
which is essentially unacceptable in human existence. . . .

And no one knows this better than politicians. Whenever a camera
is in the offing, they immediately run to the nearest child, lift it in the
air, kiss it on the cheek. Kitsch is the aesthetic ideal of all politicians
and all political parties and movements. . . .

When I say "totalitarian," what I mean is that everything that infr-
inges on kitsch must be banished for life: every display of individualism
(because a deviation from the collective is a spit in the eye of the smiling
brotherhood); every doubt (because anyone who starts doubting details
will end by doubting life itself); all irony (because in the realm of kitsch
everything must be taken quite seriously); and the mother who abandons
her family or the man who prefers men to women, thereby calling into
question the holy decree "Be fruitful and multiply."

In this light, we can regard the gulag as a septic tank used by totalitarian kitsch to dispose of its refuse. . . .

In the realm of totalitarian kitsch, all answers are given in advance and
preclude any questions. It follows, then, that the true opponent of totalitarian kitsch is the person who asks questions. A question is like a
knife that slices through the stage backdrop and gives us a look at what
lies hidden behind it.

—MILAN KUNDERA, *The Unbearable Lightness of Being* (1984)

Our current intellectual age is bracketed by a bemused despair at the bluntness of its messages. In the decade following the Second World War, Roland Barthes wrote of the denuded images with which tranquility had become asserted and business conducted in the consumption-driven economies of the West. Barthes' myth maintains a resolving function that has continued throughout the duration of memorable time, since the advent of social organization. The myth is an icon, itself subject to change, distilled out of everyday transactions proceeding at a far faster pace. Located at the junction where the everyday usage of language intersects with its far statelier forms (e.g., its grammar), the myth furnishes the dreams, wishes, and self-conceptions of a community with a *weight* otherwise lacking, with a measure of stability and continuity. The myth comprises a tangible residue of events proceeding so quickly they might otherwise disappear. It evolves and changes by its own internal linguistic principles, perhaps best articulated by Barthes' colleague, Claude Lévi-Strauss. Yet viewed from the perspective of the synchronic now of current events and everyday life, the myth assures both forerunners and destiny a coherence of communal aspirations and the comprehensibility of discrete events.

As its title suggests, "Myth Today," the essay from which the above citation derives, explores the uniquely contemporary functions and uses of the myth.[1] The myth is a species of metalanguage, of messages that not only have their own content but also indicate the structures and forces at play in language itself. Barthes draws on linguistics and other social sciences in treating the myth as a linguistic artifact, but writing in 1957, he also applies a Marxian analysis of the socioeconomic uses of the myth and examines the manner in which these uses either confirm or disrupt a preexisting ideological order. Though identified with Marx and certain national states that acknowledged the influence of Marx's works, such an analysis is indispensable to an understanding of the internal and external structures and functions of artifacts.

As notable instances of "myth today," Barthes offers us a photograph from *Paris Match* of a saluting black African soldier in a French uniform[2] and "the new Citroën,"[3] an automobile whose body signifies an impenetrable internal perfection. The image of the Senegalese soldier asserts the necessity and internal harmony of the

French sphere of influence. In part owing to Barthes' receptiveness
to such thinkers of the Frankfurt School as Benjamin and Adorno,
whose analyses encompassed philosophical, literary, and sociolog-
ical domains, he anticipates, before the electronic media are almost
universally disseminated, the harmony elicited, depicted, and even
demanded by the mythic image. He is scrupulous in distributing the
utility of the image denuded of tension to both ends of the political
spectrum, to any agency enriched or extended through public confidence.

Barthes' myth is an instrument of resolution. Its blunt tools are
capital to any organization wishing to avail itself of mythic power.
They include a foreshortening of history and absorption in the fictive present and the personalization (or personification) of events
represented by characters with which the spectator or target can
identify (both methods that have been stocks-in-trade throughout the
history of television). Barthes devises the term "ninism" ("neither-
norism") to describe the act in which the mythic image nullifies any
internal conflict it may harbor. Neither-norism is a "mythological
figure that consists in opposing two contrary [views] and then re-
jecting them both by playing [balancer] them off against each other."[4]
Mythic representation asserts by means of circular reasoning (tau-
tology); it reduces qualitative issues and judgments to quantitative
demonstrations (e.g., polls); and it lends itself to slogans catchy in
their brevity but excessive in their simplification.

Early on, then, in an intellectual era whose developments have
proceeded so frenetically that it can scarcely still be called our own,
it became evident that critical disinterest would necessarily have to
address the totalization and reductiveness of mass culture. The manipulative power of the resolving function, whether called the myth
or some other name, increased as the media for its dissemination
became more ubiquitous. At a moment in this era considerably closer
to the one in which I write, Milan Kundera characterizes this as-
surance and enforcer of harmony, particularly as it pertains to a
different sociopolitical configuration, as totalitarian kitsch.[5] In the
passage from *The Unbearable Lightness of Being* cited at the beginning of this chapter, kitsch is hardly alien to the Barthesian myth.[6]
In the interest of a humanizing sentimentality, kitsch squelches
questions, camouflages conflicts, and evaporates doubt. It attacks
individualism, which here may be regarded as a rubric for what

Jacques Derrida would call local difference. Kundera, like Barthes, specifies that the resolving function is not the sole property of any form of government or nationality. "Since opinions vary, there are various kitsches: Catholic, Protestant, Jewish, Communist, Fascist, democratic, feminist, European, American, national, international" (*ULB,* 257).

"All her life" Sabina, an expatriate artist who departs from her native Czechoslovakia following the Russian invasion of 1968, "had proclaimed kitsch her enemy" (*ULB,* 255). "Living for Sabina meant seeing. Seeing is limited by two borders: strong light, which blinds, and total darkness. Perhaps that was what motivated Sabina's distaste for all extremism" (*ULB,* 94). Sabina is capable of practicing a precise and rigorous discretion in her love life, for "only by doing so could she live in truth" (*ULB,* 133). Her life may be described as a sequence of betrayals of the fathers, natural, political, and surrogate, who attempt to squelch her interests and energies. She finds as much kitsch in the distended index fingers and the artificially wavy hair of her fellow Czech émigrés as in the official pronouncements of the regime.

In another of his major works, Kundera characterizes the state-sanctioned aura of tranquility as a forced amnesia that produces in adults a childlike lack of concentration and awareness of the past. *The Book of Laughter and Forgetting* begins with the Czech government's obliteration of one Clementis, who fell into disfavor, from virtually all public records and hence from history; his sole surviving trace is the image of his hat in a picture out of which he has been otherwise edited.[7] The volume ends with an allegorical picture of the public as a mass of unruly children who have internalized and obeyed the state's directive to forget. The Czech émigrée Tamina is received into a frightful child-utopia after her last effort to assemble from Prague the material traces of her life with her now deceased husband founders. Surrounded by children, she loses first her sanity and then her life when her efforts to remember in a significant way are definitively thwarted.

Kundera observes a correlation between a culture's memory, the status of its language, and the quality of its music:

> "The first step in liquidating a people," said Hubl, "is to erase its memory. Destroy its books, its culture, its history. Then have somebody

write new books, manufacture a new culture, invent a new history. Be-
fore long the nation will begin to forget what it is and what it was. The
world around it will forget even faster."
   "What about language?"
   "Why would anyone bother to take it from us? It will soon be a matter
of folklore and die a natural death."
   Was that hyperbole dictated by utter despair?
   Or is it true that a nation cannot cross a desert of organized forgetting?
None of us knows what will be. (*BLF*, 159)

If the agencies of resolution, East and West, propound and encourage a certain forgetting, if memory in part functions as a repository of discrepancy, Kundera finds in pop music a particularly
virulent instrument of kitsch.[8] This music literally cuts across ideological and territorial borders, leaving a wide swath of undifferen-
tiated sound and cognitive distraction in its wake.

   If it is true that the history of music has come to an end, what is left
of music? Silence?
   Not in the least. There is more and more of it, many times more than
in its most glorious days. It pours out of outdoor speakers, out of miser-
able sound systems in apartments and restaurants, out of the transistor
radios people carry around the streets.
   Schönberg is dead, Ellington is dead, but the guitar is eternal. Ste-
reotyped harmonies, hackneyed melodies, and a beat that gets stronger
as it gets duller—that is what's left of music, the eternity of music.
Everyone can come together on the basis of those simple combinations
of notes. They are life itself proclaiming its jubilant "Here I am!" No
sense of communication is more resonant, more unanimous, than the
simple sense of communion with life. It can bring Arab and Jew together, Czech and Russian. Bodies pulsing to a common beat, drunk
with the consciousness that they exist. No work of Beethoven's has ever
elicited greater collective passion than the constant repetitive throb of
the guitar. (*BLF*, 179–180)

Kundera's critique is as descriptive of the general function of kitsch
and Barthesian mythology as it is of one type of music. The music
that he describes, however, is at the heart of sanctioned state-culture
in Eastern and Western television.
   For example, a recent advertisement campaign for McDonald's
hamburger restaurants televised in the United States consists of a

series of vignettes in which people from various ethnic, racial, age, and cultural interest groups are all shown improvising a rhythmic accompaniment (with spoons, straws, etc.) to a jaunty rendition of the McDonald's song. The nation is thus united, if not under God then under this music. The advertisements depict a well-lubricated, utopian America (as Louis Marin has defined the term in his discussion of Disneyland)[9] from which the divisive forces exerted by different interests and needs have been eliminated. The promise of happiness (familial, marital, social, ethnic) unmarred by divisions and uncertainties is not merely a merchandising tactic used to promote various goods and services. The resolution of conflicts and ambiguities in the interest of ideological and social tranquility may be regarded as the basic principle and mission of the high-resolution screen known as television. Across the gamut of subgenres that it has developed, television sets into play and dramatizes the (political, social, criminal, ethnic) forces that could instigate upheaval or raise imponderable questions, but it then resolves potentially major dysfunctions, at least on the thematic level, before the final set of advertisements. The ideological as well as dramatic drift of series such as *Love Boat* and *Fantasy Island* is the ability for disparate elements of narrative and theme to be, in the end, neatly wrapped up and packaged. Television sports, on the other hand, enable the tensions camouflaged and masked in other forms of programming to be released—but in an arena largely devoid of ideological resonance. Sports hysteria is conflict staged precisely within a conceptual and policy vacuum. International or Olympic competition reinstates an ideological dimension within sports but as an occasional supplement in which aggression is exported *away* from the home front.

The scope of representation in television addressing the mass audience is encyclopedic, but the development and ultimate elimination of conflict is formulaic. The argument of Todd Gitlin's recent book, *Inside Prime Time,* "hangs on the problem of uncertainty and the [television] industry's attempts to overcome it."[10] In specific detail, this book portrays the inability of American television as an institution to depart from outmoded approaches to programming and to tolerate ambiguity within its productions or individuality on the part of its producers. The tradition of American television demands "clear plot resolutions" (*IPT,* 274). Although with good reason Git-

lin celebrates the recent emergence of series such as *Hill Street Blues*
and *St. Elsewhere,* whose "messiness" of sequence and setting underscores the persistence of the social questions they raise, even
such innovative attempts are engulfed within a medium whose
overarching interest is the assertion, representation, and implementation of harmony.

Television is surely the most powerful instrument of kitsch in the
United States. Its sphere of influence and conventions widen as other
nations elect to import rather than duplicate its productions. Mass-
audience television has not only transformed the way its viewers
spend their time; it has also exerted a tangible impact on their habits
of thought and their relation to language. And yet the specific conventions and forms that television has evolved are far less important
than the resolving function it has served, which may just as well
be designated "myth" or "kitsch."

From the outset of the current intellectual moment after the Second World War to the very recent past, from Barthes in the West
to Kundera in the East, the role of the critic has actively confronted
the reductionism and totalization to which the instruments of cohesion have resorted. Concurrent with the dissemination of the electronic media and the ideological simplifications they often implement has been an investigation, unprecedented in the breadth of its
scope, into the nature and complexity of language. The intricacy of
language, the rhythmic alternation between the positing and withdrawal of its associations, is itself the undoing of the simplicity that
kitsch, the contemporary myth, or television assert. If a tranquilized
passivity is the ideal designated and served by kitsch, literacy is a
hyperawareness of the ambiguities, distinctions, and unresolved
questions set into play by language, even as it orders human affairs.
Let it be clear that certain interests are at stake in this and the following chapters. If we define literacy not merely as a decoding and
encoding of words but as a wider set of interpretative skills incorporating the disjunctive effects of language, then where literacy is
disseminated, the simplifications of kitsch will lose their credibility
and possibly their tranquilizing effect. Conversely, where the *general* level of literacy declines and where its skills are restricted to
a *smaller* segment of the population, the marginalization of academic and artistic activities will increase and long-standing suspicions toward intellectuals will flourish.

An Age of Language

The period linking Barthes to Kundera—roughly the past thirty years—has witnessed a succession of approaches to literature, art, philosophy, and the social sciences as breathlessly accelerated as the technologies that have advanced over the same time. Within a single generation, the experiential probings of phenomenology underwent at least two major revisions (phenomenological readings of literature and a deconstructive exposé of the biases of phenomenology). The thrust of the political and moral admonitions made by postwar existentialism was redirected into the minute attention accorded the structures of language and social institutions by the human sciences, whose formalistic tendencies were then challenged. New Criticism, which attempted to endow the literary object with an integrity and rigor at least in part derived from logical analysis, was initially eclipsed by a set of social, psychological, and linguistic models of reading. Interestingly, its approach was remarkably consonant with the careful explication of philosophical and literary texts that would gain prominence in the 1970s. Historical studies of literature and art shifted away from the genealogies of the artworks and artists toward an examination of their perception and reception in time. In the study of psychoanalysis, areas that were marginal at the outset of this period, such as object-relations, borderline states, and the imaginary, blossomed into central areas of study. In the course of this generation and particularly since the late 1960s, feminist studies have had a pronounced methodological as well as thematic impact on virtually every discipline and significant issue in the arts and humanities.

It seems entirely likely that an intense inquiry into the role of language as a decisive factor in human thought, behavior, and social organization will emerge as one of this century's prominent contributions. The major innovations of the past thirty years in the studies of literature, art, philosophy, and human behavior and organization have witnessed a shift away from the empirical phenomena and data comprising the traditional objects of science and toward the linguistic infrastructures that make possible both the artifacts and behaviors observed and the disciplines that observe them. There is in fact a peculiar symmetry to the century: It ends somewhat as it began. Writers including Kafka, Freud, Proust, and Joyce inaugurated the century by submerging themselves in their linguistic medium and exposing its deep structures, intricacies, and anomalies. In a sense, the emergent field known as critical theory has for the past thirty years repeated this movement, but it has redirected the earlier emphasis on the production of aesthetic objects into a pursuit and dramatization of the structuring role that language has played throughout the history of systematic thought. Not only have writers such as Roland Barthes, Michel Foucault, Claude Lévi-Strauss, and Jacques Derrida acknowledged the decisiveness of language in shaping the possibilities and findings of human thought; they have also initiated an exhaustive inquiry into the occasionally marginal texts of philosophy, science, and the social sciences in order to demonstrate the continuity of this structuring role. In addition, critical theory has allowed the rhetorical qualities of language to penetrate and influence its own findings and productions. This explains how the writings of Barthes and Derrida stylistically have more in common with the texts of Kafka, Joyce, and Walter Benjamin than with many of the philosophers and social scientists who comprise the subjects and occasions for their essays.

In different ways, Barthes, Foucault, Lévi-Strauss, and Derrida mark a transition away from the study of objects ostensibly existent in the external world and toward the study of the language in which the various disciplines "think" and are articulated. Midway through the century occurs a structuralist moment, when its fascinations with language are translated into the terminologies of its ongoing rhetorical and scientific traditions. This structuralist event bears particular affinities to the productions of high modernism. The alignments that it both crystallizes and elaborates, however, become a critical point of departure for the skewed tendencies known as the post-modern. Our century's structuralist experiment thus coincides with and stands between its modernist and post-modern phases. One artifact among many that could be selected as an instance of this redirection of attention toward the role of language at the beginning of the current intellectual moment is Albert Camus' 1947 novel, *The Plague*.[11] Superficially, no novel could more successfully assimilate and summarize for its readers an actual and major world event, the recently terminated Second World War. The plague that breaks out in the colonial city of Oran, Algeria, holds the entire population of the city under its sway until the epidemic ends; the plague is a metaphor eliciting a full range of responses from heroism to cowardice on the part of its characters. The novel registers a sequence of mass-psychological responses to the catastrophe that may well parallel the public moods historically initiated by the war. Camus infuses into his description of a dying boy a sense of tragedy and poignancy indicative of events broader in their scope than a fictive epidemic.

No novel could be more historical in its orientation, more outward in its direction, and more existential in its vision. And yet each of the five major characters in the novel is a writer, and the style and uses of each one's writing bear heavily on his part in the drama. We learn in the end, of course, that Bernard Rieux has not only tested his personal and medical skills to the limit in combating the plague; he has also written the narrative. The one character in the novel with whom Rieux achieves what Camus elsewhere calls solidarity is Tarrou, a slightly disreputable sort who frequents Spanish dancers and nurtures aesthetic pretensions. Tarrou writes private observations of the everyday scenes around him with the precision and detachment of the best feuilleton writing. Aesthetically as well as personally, he is Rieux's closest counterpart in the novel. His written irony combines both the involvement and the detachment necessary for confronting plagues, whether bacteriological or human in their nature. Tarrou's style therefore merges with Rieux's language at its most powerful moments. Father Paneloux writes sermons, and in the interval between the two samples of his work incorporated into the novel, his world view undergoes considerable tempering: As a result of the events narrated, both his moralism and his distance from his congregation are reduced. Interestingly, Rambert, the only character who, by attempting to violate the medical quarantine of the city, acts on his horror, cynicism, and personal needs, is a journalist. Rambert allows the realism of his discourse to infect his interpretation of the unfolding events and his reaction to them. The minor functionary Grand furnishes an instance of an unfulfilled artist, a writer whose hesitations and limited verbal powers imprison him within the first sentence of the creative writing project of his lifetime. But even a character stymied in his writing can figure within the novel's overall play of characters and events. Rieux's writing encompasses certain of the discursive attributes of each of the other main characters.

Camus' *The Plague,* then, even while it gropes for images and fictive events capable of assimilating historical catastrophe, is seldom far from an allegorical exploration of various modes and possibilities for writing. It may therefore serve as one instance of the manner in which throughout the twentieth century, and in an introspective fashion since the Second World War, language has become an event at least as decisive as the happenings that it might seem to record or embellish.

We thus arrive at a paradox evident at the outset of this study that will, in all likelihood, be impossible to overcome. A generation that has experienced a massive diffusion and consolidation of kitsch and television, and the sedative resolution they perform, has also spawned a linguistic investigation unparalleled in its breadth and detail. These two phenomena are skewed. Indeed, since literacy is the limit of kitsch, and kitsch camouflages and shunts aside the ambiguities unearthed by literacy, these tendencies coexist at oblique angles and cross-purposes. Kitsch, whether of the totalitarian or parliamentary variety, consolidates itself while the study of letters refines itself only in a space characterized by pronounced indifference or repressive tolerance. The unabated proliferation of kitsch coupled with the confinement of an increasingly sophisticated literacy to a miniscule population could lead to dire political consequences.

The primary and secondary school systems and the universities are invested with the formidable task of mediating between kitsch and literacy. They are the battleground on which the appeals for good citizenship, moderation, and professional responsibility meet with the doubts and discriminations tantamount to basic literate training. One would assume that reasonably efficient schools and universities would effect for most of the population the same type of compromise between the thrusts of kitsch and extreme linguistic play as that produced by other humanizing institutions. And yet, the current disjunctive state in which kitsch and literacy develop in almost total indifference to each other suggests that schools and universities have vacated the strategic but also uncomfortable ground between language neutered of its invective and language hyperaware of its complexity.

Speeds and Cities: The Division of Labor

Even a thumbnail sketch of the intellectual milestones of the past generation cannot avoid confronting the breakneck pace with which these developments have occurred. The very speed with which approaches and models supplant each other is now a prominent feature of the intellectual landscape. This informational and speculative acceleration, which of course coincides with several technological revolutions, is not without its tangible impact on the nature and constitution of the literate community.

In a variety of contexts, contemporary philosophy and literary criticism have questioned the Romantic and mythic scenario that always depicts the present moment as the aftermath of a loss or as the shattered remnants of some prior unity or totality. Indeed, it would be both facile and inaccurate to state that a unified intellectual community once existed and that its cohesion has since been destroyed by the pace or multiplicity of recent inquiries. At the same time, however, the current speed of fresh approaches and refinements does seem to have engendered a certain fragmentation among academic, intellectual, and artistic enterprises sharing a common commitment to the exploration and dissemination of literacy. On the one hand, the multiplicity of artistic productions, publications, and academic approaches is indicative of the extraordinary intellectual fecundity of our times. On the other hand, to the extent that parallel enterprises compete and work at cross-purposes, an obfuscation of the very tangible political and social stakes of literacy has taken place.

Our particular intellectual climate owes much of its distinction to the fragmentation spawned by the exceptional intellectual vitality of our era and by the professionalization of knowledge. A remarkably broad range of scientific, social scientific, and humanistic disciplines exacts high discursive tariffs from its readers in the form of specialized nomenclature. While intellectual improvisation necessitates some degree of unfamiliarity, the overall picture is one in which the "common" literate reader is increasingly remote from the "state of the art" and in which the independent critic and the institutions of higher learning have taken separate paths.

An aggravated specialization within the intellectual division of labor not only increases the difficulty of disseminating research and its salient questions to a broad public; it also submerges the interests and politics of literacy itself. Arriving at an informed definition of literacy is a major undertaking in its own right. However this notion is defined, and there are several possible approaches, a veritable panoply of cultural and educational institutions is devoted in some way to its advancement. Yet where disciplinary protectionism prevails within the current intellectual landscape, where improvisation fails to account for its own synthesis, the *interest* of literacy drops out of sight in the fissures between competing enterprises. Some degree of synthesis is necessary to remind literate institutions what they share with each other and with Kundera's Sabina: a fundamental divergence from kitsch.

Some of the indifference or hostility with which various literate institutions regard each other is simply ideological in nature, reflecting prior ideological, moral, metaphysical, and even theological choices. Other seemingly insurmountable obstacles among enterprises sharing a literate mission may be described as functional in nature. A journalist with a staff position, a university professor, and an autonomous intellectual such as a freelance translator may share an interest in a particular field, be it the nineteenth-century French novel or African politics. Yet the individuals in each of these three categories are subject to markedly different expectations and demands.

The journalist, the professor, and the autonomous intellectual work under strikingly varied conditions, are paid differently, in manner if not in scale, and are accorded different forms of recognition. In a sense, any fundamental divergences in their perspectives derive from the differentiation at the very heart of literate articulation. The prevailing conditions for intellectual work are, at the same time, highly successful in obscuring any productive consensus that might prevail among diverse segments of the intellectual field. Such a consensus, while it must be tested every step of the way, is a potentially decisive resource, with important sociopolitical consequences. Current conditions are not particularly conducive to its discernment or its realization, however. The hypothetical intellectuals to whom I refer above may substantially agree on the importance of Balzac or the future alignment of Senegal, but given the remoteness of the environments they inhabit, is it any wonder that they cross each other's paths like ships in the fog at night? While such functional issues as job security, the steadiness and degree of remuneration, freedom of schedule and intellectual pursuit, and the magnitude of support (e.g., administrative) responsibilities surely play a role in this fragmentation, it and its numerous consequences should hardly be accepted as givens. The moment at which the commonality of literate concern does not betray the differentiating function of language is a decisive realization whose pursuit should be ongoing.

Indeed, the current state of cooperation among the various institutions devoted to the promulgation of literacy is questionable at best, prompting Gore Vidal, in a memorial article on Italo Calvino, to write, "The circuits between the English departments, where our tablets of literary reputation are now kept, and the world of journalism are more than ever fragile and the reception is always bad."[12] At a good many American universities, for example, the school of education functions as an autonomous and largely professional entity. University organization thus encourages a separation between educational studies, which has at its disposal the results of hands-on research conducted in the classroom, and the academic departments of philosophy, linguistics, English, modern languages, and mathematics, where fundamental inquiry into such intimately related topics as writing, semiotics, and cognition takes place. A separation between the more practical and more philosophical approaches toward literacy cannot bode well for educational policy and service in the future. The budgetary and service constraints under which universities have organized themselves are no doubt responsible for such anomalies.

The genres and modes of writing itself have been overtaken, in recent years, by a pronounced specialization. "Creative writing," "academic research," "intellectual journalism," and "trade" publications are terms treated quite distinctly, with specific connotations regarding their respective styles, purposes, and audiences. "Creative" writers affiliated with academic departments at universities often worry that according to institutional values their enterprise is secondary.[13] Such constraints as sales and marketing, on the other hand, often drive scholars away from "trade" publishing houses and toward the specialized audiences served by university presses.

I have thus far employed a temporal metaphor, the acceleration of intellectual developments, as a means of representing the current, and in all likelihood, ongoing fragmentation of the literate community. But this dispersion may be also visualized geographically, on the map of its development.

An extraordinary sequence of interdisciplinary contributions to the humanities, sciences, and social sciences took place in Paris in the mid-to-late 1950s. France is not a country that suffers any serious discrepancy among its political, economic, intellectual, and artistic capitals. If anything, the need in that country is and has been for decentralization, for a better distribution of the Parisian treasures. Major developments over the past thirty years in the areas of structuralism, semiotics, and post-structuralism have, in spite of their initial unfamiliarity, occurred in Paris along with innovations in other, not always adjacent fields such as drama, film, and painting. In a country such as France, important developments radiate outward from the intellectual and artistic capital to the rest of the country.

Whether intentionally or not, the problem of centralization has been, in a sense, preempted in the United States. The groundbreaking products of the French capital have entered the United States through such backwater ports as Baltimore, Maryland, and Binghamton, New York. Despite recent signs of recognition (I think of the February 9, 1986, article on criticism at Yale in *The New York Times Magazine*),[14] the established intellectual capitals of the United States, such as New York and Boston, have remained curiously indifferent to the likes of Derrida, Jacques Lacan, and Jean-François Lyotard.[15] The emphasis at both ends of the ideological spectrum in such centers, if popular publications are to be taken into account, tends to curl back on the preservation of the American humanistic tradition and its comparative advantages. While this is at times a laudable purpose (depending on the specific historical case at hand), it is not necessarily conducive to the most efficient and timely reportage of major intellectual trends.

The tradition of higher American education is to be commended for the window on all known universes it has opened across a vast land. And yet it is no longer acceptable that a scattered sampling of college towns—among them Norman, Oklahoma, Tucson, Arizona, and their counterparts in the East—should be the principal and in many regions the only ports of entry for a breathtaking sequence of intellectual developments. The time has perhaps arrived for an improved coordination of activities and information that operates more in the interest of cultural diffusion than canonization.

There are at least two major preconditions for such a coordination. On the one hand, academic writers in the sciences, social sciences, and humanities will need to make a more concerted effort than ever before to consolidate a well-informed readership beyond the confines of the campus.[16] The implications of this adjustment will be methodological and terminological. Although a translation of neologisms in accordance with the conceptual repository maintained by various readerships is possible and overdue, gestures of professorial simplification alone will not suffice. In effect, academic writers need badly to devise a new type of discourse if they are to reach more than a purely academic readership. Kundera's highly effective amalgam of fictional narrative, philosophical speculation, and political commentary serves as one particularly attractive model. We may well find that certain other contemporary works of fiction, such as Calvino's *t zero*[17] and *If on a winter's night a traveler,*[18] are better at dramatizing some scientific and philosophical problems than the standard scholarship. If academic critics are to assist in the extension of a readership for theoretical work, we will need to learn better from the "objects" of our scrutiny. Our discourse, taking a cue from Jacques Derrida, will perhaps more openly acknowledge its own fictionality.

If we are to trespass beyond the self-perpetuating limits of the campus and focus on professional scholarly training, academic writers will also need to learn more from intellectual journalism and assimilate some of its methods. Up until now, the burden of maintaining an informed general readership has been borne almost exclusively by independent and staff journalists who have received little encouragement and recognition from the academy. And yet it is these individuals who, in every journalistic piece they write, address the problem of translating context-specific concepts and terms for a variety of readerships. The literary styles of Walter Benjamin and Roland Barthes have profoundly influenced several generations of students of literature. Any sharp separation between journalistic and academic enterprises is, in the context of the importance of these writers, both ironic and dysfunctional.

There can be no radical reassessment of the traditional usages and expectations of language without some conceptual violence and rhetorical disfiguration. The litany of reproaches in response to the improvisations of contemporary critical theory is now familiar. It disregards the etiquette of standard scholarship. Its findings are too fragmentary, concentrating on one small segment of a work or concept. It ignores the principles of compositional proportion and entertains outrageous word plays beyond the intentions of the "primary" authors under discussion. Its neologisms are highly obscure and idiosyncratic. It has often focused on the secondary works or marginalia of the authors and periods to which it has interpretatively addressed itself.

And yet no area of inquiry has assumed greater responsibility for the contemporary conditions of language and its own status as linguistic process and artifact than contemporary critical theory. The linguistic and terminological excesses for which it is often alone taken to task run across the gamut of contemporary academic research, as any uninitiated reader of cognitive science or particle physics has discovered.

It is the contention of this study that the current technology's confirmation of the totalizing function, whether called myth, kitsch, or television, constitutes one of the pressing sociopolitical issues of our day and that contemporary critical theory can confront it as productively as any other field. The politics of literacy are by their very nature submerged. The demands of schooling, "basic skills," and cultural transmission are implicitly quieter—in Marshall McLuhan's terms, "cooler"—than the needs for weaponry and medical research. Yet enormous political, social, environmental, and cultural consequences ride on the politics of literacy and its short- and long-term resolutions. Will literacy, in its broader sense, be extended so that a sharing of intellectual and cultural wealth takes place irrespective of economic and technological modifications to the workplace and the division of labor? Or will, as several current treatments of the subject suggest, the broad linguistic discriminations of literacy remain, as they traditionally have, in the hands of a small and limited technocracy? As the answers to these and related questions emerge, their impact will be awesome on the most concrete as well as abstract levels.

As the study that combines the literary, philosophical, and social scientific inquiry into the dimensions of language, the paradigmatic medium of transmission, critical theory maintains a deep, implicit concern for pedagogy and the broader skills of literacy.[19] The writings of Barthes, Foucault, Lévi-Strauss, and particularly Derrida are of decisive importance in the definition of literacy and the demonstration of the cross-purposes at which its apprehensions and the agencies of ideology, the instruments of kitsch, work.[20] Because it is situated at the interstice between philosophy, linguistics, literary studies, and the social sciences, critical theory has managed to demonstrate the applicability of formal philosophical operations to situations and artifacts far afield. The notion of mediation, for example, is crucial to an understanding of what the mass media disseminate and repress. Scenarios of authority, usurpation, and supplementation explored in some detail by contemporary critical theory can substantially illuminate the submersion phenomenon that clouds current politics and that both obfuscates the significant choices and actions of political agencies and submerges their present and future implications. By the same token, for the public to appreciate the full impact of nuclear and cybernetic technologies, the longstanding intellectual traditions—of the sublime and the material—must also be articulated.[21]

Were any emblematic image to preside over this volume, it would derive from a climactic moment in William Carlos Williams's American epic, *Paterson*.[22] A library burns. The culture in which it is situated allows this to happen. The event, laced with metaphors from the field of physics, dramatizes the flow and transfer of energy within and between books. It also indicates the distance, the measured indifference, that prevails between the library and its sociopolitical home.

The library, the time-honored bastion of learning, remains, despite all the technological innovations of our day, a crucial weapon in literacy's arsenal. The present volume explores the issue of literacy from a variety of perspectives: as a sociopolitical question, a theoretical construct, and as a topic that has, to a surprising degree, shaped and colored the literary works in which it has emerged as an urgent concern. The burning library may dramatically unleash vast stores of energy, but it is at the same time propelled toward oblivion. Although no informed treatment of the issue of literacy could claim or even hope to be exhaustive, the image of the conflagration nevertheless casts its shadow from those angles that we do provisionally explore.

Function and Articulation

Like any large concept, literacy means different things to different people. For many, it means the technical skills necessary to write one's name, to decode nonspecialized language, to express every-day needs and thoughts. On a practical level, this type of competence enables people to perform several functions autonomously. They can complete a job application, vote, provide and use various types of insurance, and write letters to individuals and agencies with which they are engaged in fundamental personal and social relations.

In an age so thoroughly marked by the speed of its developments and its business, we tend to forget how pervasive the need is for even this basic and technical type of literacy throughout the industrial and nonindustrial worlds, how its effective teaching and learning could improve the quality of life of vast populations. Even at the university level, a large and some would say increasing share of energy and resources is being devoted to the transmission of "basic" verbal skills and their quantitative equivalents.

The absolutely quintessential skills of technical literacy involve a fundamental and minimal exposure to sign-systems or semiological codes. While the extension of these competences ultimately leads to the production and comprehension of the most complex artistic and scientific achievements, there is a whole range of tasks and functions for which stripped-down, functional literacy will not account.

What is termed "functional literacy" falls within the sphere of associative reasoning, equation, and positing identity. While it may harbor the seeds of complex semiological operations, it stops at the *association* or the equation between words and things, between signs and essences. It is possible to sign a document and even decode its language without being able to interpret its significance or discern its inconsistencies or hidden "catches." The repossession of a mobile home and its furnishings in Werner Herzog's 1979 film, *Stroszeck,* is not merely another episode in an adventure of rootlessness and civil cruelty. It is an allegory of the contemporary collision between functional and articulate literacy, between preliteracy and its schooled extension. The unfortunate Bruno can sign a loan contract with the Wisconsin bank. He is not, however, prepared verbally or emotionally for its impact on his life. The drama of signed but not understood documents, contracts, and commitments is an emblem of the confrontation between widely divergent levels of literacy in our age.

Functional literacy stops before reaching a general facility with codes. It may account for the inscription of a signature, the use of the telephone directory, alphabetical sorting or filing, or even legal commitments of vast sums of money. Among the competences and acts for which it does not necessarily provide are the following: discerning the relative merits and disadvantages of opposed political positions; gaining a perspective on the historical position and interests of one's socioeconomic group or groups; and interpreting and appreciating the significance and placement of heavily coded artifacts from such areas as architecture, music, the plastic arts, cinema, and literature. Functional literacy demarcates a domain of concrete language acts crucial to the conduct of personal life and the formation and exercise of personal identity.

Articulate or broader literacy, on the other hand, implicates a set of competences that may not, on the surface, seem essential and that are predicated on superfluous money, time (leisure), and personal energy. Broader literacy or "cultivation" is traditionally associated with material excess and its temperamental counterpart— whim, fancy, or imagination. Yet from a communal perspective, in terms of the sociopolitical and cultural options available to various groups and their members, the critical and interpretative skills of articulate literacy play a far more decisive role than their functional counterpart.

It is my assumption that some historical awareness of precedents and the ability to discriminate critically between socioeconomic alternatives can only assist a community in sorting out its options. It is also my assumption that the critical skills of broader literacy and the cultural experience they facilitate can enhance the quality of life even when they are not automatically linked to an individual's vocational activity or economic resources. Educational institutions in the West are under increasing pressure to place all nonessential (or "humanistic") study at the "service" of vocational training (while in the East schools are compelled to package the humanities with ideologically useful subjects). Still, the major events of twentieth-century history suggest that broader critical skills can substantially improve the quality of life for the traditional underclasses of many societies even before the material rewards that might accompany the acquisition of these skills are actually forthcoming.

This book therefore concerns itself not with the minimalist model of associative or functional literacy but with the broader sense of literacy as semiological preparation and the ability to discern the semantic and logical differences, discrepancies, and anomalies activated by various forms of language. It treats literacy not as a number of tasks that are either mastered or not but as a set of competences that are themselves in a constant state of transition. Indeed, the growth and enhancement of these powers are possibilities that members of advanced societies should expect and positive values that sociopolitical agencies should, wherever possible, promote. Such agencies should support public education and cultural enterprises and, by nontotalitarian means, encourage literate standards in mass communications.

Contemporary critical theory has stressed that "reading" and "writing" are not reducible to "functional" skills or acts. These activities, in their philosophical implications, extend to the very constructs that human beings have devised to account for their existence, knowledge, and experience. As the processes bearing most heavily on the quality of thought itself, reading and writing play a decisive role in the imaginary life of individuals and groups. The expectations surrounding reading and writing can therefore enrich— or impoverish—the relations that individuals have with their fellow human beings and their work, the economic and social aspirations that they maintain for themselves and their families, their role in the political and social events around them, and even their access to "unconscious" life, whether in the form of artifacts or dreams.

One of the underlying motifs of the recent literature on this topic seems to be that, in an electronic age, the broader facility with language necessary for articulate literacy has become a goal that is somehow untenable. It we accept the proviso that value has both tangible and intangible forms, the following observation will suffice for now: The quality of literacy that a community attains will be roughly equivalent to what the community pays for it.

Literacy and Difference

Tomas, who had spent the last ten years of his medical practice working exclusively with the human brain, knew that there was nothing more difficult to capture than the human "I." There are many more resemblances between Hitler and Einstein or Brezhnev and Solzhenitsyn than there are differences. Using numbers, we might say that there is one-millionth part dissimilarity to nine hundred ninety-nine thousand nine hundred ninety-nine millionths parts similarity.

Tomas was obsessed by the desire to discover and appropriate that one-millionth part; he saw it as the core of his obsession. He was not obsessed with women; he was obsessed with what in each of them is unimaginable, obsessed, in other words, with the one-millionth part that makes a woman dissimilar to others of her sex. . . .

To be sure, the millionth part dissimilarity is present in all areas of human existence, but in all areas other than sex it is exposed and needs no one to discover it, needs no scalpel. One woman prefers cheese at the end of the meal, another loathes cauliflower, and although each may demonstrate her originality thereby, it is an originality that demonstrates its own irrelevance and warns us to pay it no heed, to expect nothing of value to come of it.

Only in sexuality does the millionth part dissimilarity become precious, because, not accessible in public, it must be conquered. . . .

So it was a desire not for pleasure (the pleasure came as an extra, a bonus) but for possession of the world (slitting open the outstretched body of the world with his scalpel) that sent him in pursuit of women.

— Milan Kundera, *The Unbearable Lightness of Being*

The (pure) trace is differance. It does not depend on any sensible plentitude, audible or visible, phonic or graphic. It is, on the contrary, the condition of such a plenitude. Although it *does not exist,* although it is never a *being-present* outside of all plenitude, its possibility is by rights anterior to all that one calls sign (signified/signifier, content/expression, etc.), concept or operation, motor or sensory. This differance is therefore not more sensible than intelligible and it permits the articulation of signs among themselves within the same abstract order—a phonic or graphic text for example—or between two orders of expression. It permits the articulation of speech and writing—in the colloquial sense—as it founds the metaphysical opposition between the sensible and the intelligible, then between signifier and signified, expression and content, etc. If language were not already, in that sense, a writing, no derived "notation" would be possible; and the classical problem of relationships between speech and writing could not arise. Of course, the positive *sciences* of signification can only describe the *work* and the *fact* of differance, the determined differences and the determined presences that they make possible. There cannot be a science of differance itself in its operation, as it is impossible to have a science of the origin of presence itself, that is to say of a certain nonorigin.

— Jacques Derrida, *Of Grammatology*

If, as I assert, twentieth-century art and literature have been heavily colored by their concern for the structuring role of language, the coincidence between this fascination and one particular philosophical theme throughout the century is nothing less than astonishing. The construct to which I refer is that of difference. As twentieth-century thought has explored the dimensions and qualities of language in artistic productions and through conceptual elaborations, the notion of difference has cropped up in a bewildering array of contexts, from Saussure's linguistics and its adaptations by Barthes and Lévi-Strauss, to Ludwig Wittgenstein's compulsive distinction-making, to Martin Heidegger's articulation of Being, to Derrida's *différance*. It may well be that no era giving credence to the complex play of language could *avoid* the problem of difference.

As we have seen, a mature literacy is differential as well as associative; it demands competence in the discernment of distinctions and incongruities as well as in the positing of equivalencies. Twentieth-century artists, philosophers, and linguists, in their near-ubiquitous grapplings with difference, demonstrate concern for the linguistic status of their productions and for their literate reception by their audience. Twentieth-century literature and philosophy are therefore obsessed by the notion of literacy. Their inquiries into difference are illustrative of the fact.

The passage from *The Unbearable Lightness of Being* cited at the head of this section is a pivotal one in Kundera's evolving body of fiction. It reveals the conceptual underpinning beneath the pervasive motif of sexual variety in Kundera's novels. Though not exclusively the property of Kundera's narrators, described by Philip Roth as cocksmen, the cultivation of new partners not only provides thematic entertainment and vicarious enjoyment; it is also a freedom by which Kundera's fictive surrogates define themselves and their capacity for growth. And yet the above passage suggests that cocksmanship is as much in the interest of difference as any tangible experience. As important as the particular traits of the women that Kundera's sexually active males add to their repertory may be, the need and desire for difference in its own right are what primarily drive the mens' quest. Although he is not the first to do so, Kundera places the theme of eroticism, which has preoccupied such a large portion of the history of the novel, on the verge of the theoretical problems of coherence and classification embedded in the use of language.

Kundera makes this explicit. Tomas, the male protagonist of *The Unbearable Lightness of Being,* "was not obsessed with women; he was obsessed with . . . the one-millionth part that makes a woman dissimilar to others of her sex" (*ULB,* 200). This minute but decisive difference emerges along a linear sequence of women, yet it derives from the more fundamental one that prevails between two different economies. "Making love with a woman and sleeping with a woman are two separate passions," specifies Tomas early in the novel (*ULB,* 15), and he repeatedly asserts the distinction between erotic encounters and the longer-term commitments of love and the housekeeping arrangements that love may engender. The relation between love and eroticism would be described by Jacques Derrida as supplementary. The supplemental relation between extended love and erotic difference receives its most comprehensive philosophical treatment in the works of Søren Kierkegaard.[23]

Derrida's writing is carefully calibrated to the idiosyncrasies of the topic at hand or the "local" context, so that its dissection and extraction usually involve some violence. The above citation from *Of Grammatology*[24] is no exception to this rule of thumb. It suggests why difference is such a central concern. Like Kundera's eroticism, Derridean *différance* is capable of endless particular manifestations but is also situated at the border of two wider economies. It encompasses both the generalized linguistic difference that for Saussure defined the relation among signs and the more conceptually abstract interplay between countereconomies that appear in *Of Grammatology* under the rubrics of phoneticism and writing.

In the modest class lectures that would later be compiled and edited by his students, the Swiss linguist Ferdinand de Saussure initiated our century with a number of capital formulations on language that have influenced philosophy, the social sciences, art, and literature to the present day. Among several of the achievements of the 1915 *Course in General Linguistics* that may be counted as revolutionary was a putting to rest of essentialist notions of naming that had, since Plato, asserted some inherent relation between the nature of objects and the names they were accorded in their respective languages.[25] Saussure decisively asserted that the relationship between objects and their names is arbitrary, a chance function of historical usage. In another gesture that was to prove crucial for twentieth-century philosophy and social science, Saussure divided the sign, which is the constitutive unit of language, into its signifier

and its signified, its written, spoken, or pictorial form and its meaning, its semiotic and semantic functions. He debunked essentialist
theories of naming and the evolution of languages by asserting the
arbitrary connection between the signifier and the signified of
the sign. "The bond between the signifier and the signified is arbitrary. Since I mean by sign the whole that results from the associating of the signifier with the signified, I can simply say: *the
linguistic sign is arbitrary*. The idea of 'sister' is not linked by any
relationship to the succession of sounds . . . which serves as its
signifier in French" (*CGL*, 67). If naming proceeds in an arbitrary
fashion, how does the lexicon of a language evolve? It is here that
Saussure assured the decisiveness of difference at the outset of the
century. A sign acquires its meaning not from any essential relation
between the signified and the signifier but in relation to the *other*
signs in the lexicon whose signification it does *not* share. Signs are
distributed not integrally but differentially. In English, a horse is a
horse not owing to any "horseness" inherent in the word but because the signifier "horse" refers *not* to a pig, an orange, a type-
writer, or love. Saussure states this far more elegantly:

> Everything that has been said up to this point boils down to this: in
> language there are only differences. Even more important: a difference
> generally implies positive terms between which the difference is set up;
> but in language there are only differences *without positive terms*. Whether
> we take the signified or the signifier, language has neither ideas nor
> sounds that existed before the linguistic system, but only conceptual and
> phonic differences that have issued from the system. The idea or phonic
> substance that a sign contains is of less importance than the other signs
> that surround it. Proof of this is that the value of a term may be modified
> without either its meaning or its sound being affected, solely because
> a neighboring term has been modified. (*CGL*, 120)

This passage both elaborates the differential distribution and evolution of the signs in language and extrapolates some of the logical
and temporal implications of this difference. Language's discriminations are in relation to one another and not to some transcendental
("positive") value. There are no values, entities, or essences *prior*
to language. There is no *prior*. Signs are related, precisely, by relativity. Relatedness takes precedence over intrinsic essence or value.
Signs change not *in themselves* but in relation to one another, in
compensation for changes in the network of signs.

Saussure thus formulates a principle of general differentiation that characterizes the linguistic field and the manner of its articulation. In *Of Grammatology,* Derrida detects an oral bias in Saussure's work that he finds inconsistent with a purely differential distribution of signs. He nonetheless relies heavily on the notion of a linguistic field articulated by its implicit difference. And yet this comprehensive differentiation, which pervades the microscopic transactions of language, does not exhaust the construct of *différance*. *Différance* is a functional and a relational term; it characterizes both the internal operation of language and its interface with the philosophical concepts that are made possible by language and that apply a number of logical, metaphysical, and ontological constraints to it. There is an ideological component, or torque, to the construct of *différance*. Although Derrida invariably calibrates his analyses to the local particularities of the texts at hand and the specific traditions they invoke, he pursues, through an astonishingly broad array of contexts, the complex interplay between the process of logical, moral, and aesthetic *containment* imposed on language and the fundamentally linguistic anomalies and uncertainties that will simply not submit to the conceptual instruments. The discourses of theology, politics, history, science, and even philosophy and linguistics all occasion this tension.

Différance is thus a comprehensive rubric for language's relational aspect. It differs from the concepts and beliefs that attempt to abbreviate or circumvent the full range of its suggestions; for Derrida, it also differs, radically and interestingly, from itself. It begs to differ even with the figures of speech that it devises in order to domesticate itself. In the passage from *Of Grammatology* at the beginning of this section, *différance* is systematically embedded in our communications and even in our thought, yet it admits of no science to explain or regulate it.

In its vast effort to account for the linguistic nature of its output, our century has moved a considerable distance from the differential parameters of Saussure's flattened (synchronic) linguistic field to a Derridean *différance* whose subversive influence can be traced at various points in the history of philosophy. The exploration of difference coincides with an implicit concern for the conditions of literacy and the reception of discursive and artistic productions. We say that language, in the hands of a master, is an instrument capable of articulating the finest distinctions, and yet it is more accurate to presuppose that the nuances are already implanted in the medium. The twentieth-century inquiry into difference is nothing other than an attempt to apply philosophical rigor to an aesthetic sensibility that emerges from Romanticism with sublime pretensions and some value attached to merging, a narcissistic withdrawal of difference between the subject and the individuals or images to which he is attached. The precisions that result from this line of questioning coincide with the principles of a literacy whose resources only *begin* with the association between the signifier and the signified. Some of the way stations between Saussure and contemporary critical theory are perhaps not entirely without interest.

The Viennese philosopher Ludwig Wittgenstein is justly remembered for bringing a mathematical rigor to bear on the deployment of language. A famous qualification from *The Blue Book* enjoins philosophy "to say no more than we know."[26] Even the structure and the sequence of the propositions in the 1921 *Tractatus Logico-Philosophicus*[27] are calibrated to a language that stays within the limits of its certainty, a language whose form duplicates the boundaries of knowledge. Wittgenstein's world is coterminous with its language. *"The limits of my language* mean the limits of my world,"* specifies Proposition 5.6 of the *Tractatus Logico-Philosophicus*. Wittgenstein surveys these limits both positively and negatively, from the perspective of their extent and their containment. Proposition 4.463 specifies:

> The truth-conditions of a proposition determine the range that it leaves open to the facts.
>
> (A proposition, a picture, or a model is, in the negative sense, like a solid body that restricts the freedom of movement of others, and, in the positive sense, like a space bounded by a solid substance in which there is room for a body.) (*TLP*, 69)

The image of a perfect container, neither too small nor too large for its contents, defines the program of Wittgenstein's early philosophy. Philosophical propositions are "picture[s] of reality" and "model[s] of reality as we imagine it" (Proposition 4.01). The aggregate of these propositions is to correspond to the structure and limits of the world, as it can be rigorously formulated. "Without philosophy thoughts are, as it were, cloudy and indistinct: its task is to make them clear and to give them sharp boundaries" (Proposition 4.112). Philosophy's mission is, then, austere and demanding. Before it reverts to the complications of subjectivity and the phantoms of metaphysics in explaining incongruous states of affairs, its duty is to acknowledge the impossible. In keeping with the modesty of its scale and claims, the *Tractatus Logico-Philosophicus* is capable of this admission. It closes, "What we cannot speak about we must pass over in silence."

We remember Wittgenstein for this poignant and brave profession of faith in philosophical and linguistic rigor, and yet for almost a decade, his faith departs him. On the other side of the silent watershed that divides his career, Wittgenstein's pictures and models of reality have become metaphors rather than mathematically coordinated (and subordinated) propositions. The structuring metaphors admitted into the textual fabric of *The Blue and Brown Books* intersect with, while denying any logical priority to, the fears and experiences of the psyche: the eye, the hand, the color red, a fire in Kings's College. It is essential to recall that linguistic explorations of sensation and synergy in *The Blue Book* and the language games of *The Brown Book* maintain Wittgenstein's commitment to philosophical and linguistic rigor. They continue to treat misconceptions of reality as failures of articulation and to approach with extreme caution constructs harboring subjective and psychological nuances. But the distance afforded by the metaphors and language games of Wittgenstein's later work is conducive to an ongoing qualification, a positing and abandonment of distinctions, that cannot "fit" into the mathematical precision and ordering of postulates in the *Tractatus Logico-Philosophicus*.

No activity has higher precedence in *The Blue and Brown Books* than the formulation of the *differences* among propositions that would otherwise appear similar or identical. The discourse of *The Blue and Brown Books* is nothing less than obsessed with the articulation of the differences among various linguistic models. It is this obsession that joins Wittgenstein's investigations to the rereading of phenomenology that culminates in deconstruction. Deconstruction and logical analysis, although in some respects inimical, are both moments in a twentieth-century immersion in the conditions of language that revolves around its logical anomalies and its articulation of difference. Wittgenstein's discourse, particularly in the early works, is oriented to a point of total hypothetical contraction, while deconstruction proceeds by an expansive release of the formulations and possibilities held in check by extrinsic ideological constraints. In their thrust and orientation, these movements are thus at odds, yet in their qualification and elaboration of difference, logical analysis and deconstruction join a common twentieth-century exposition of the conditions of literacy.

Although *The Blue Book* opens in a world still linguistically determined, the acid test that it repeatedly applies to language concerns the iterability or transferability of personal experience. Still loyal to his credo that philosophy clarifies and sharpens thought, Wittgenstein questions the exact manner in which and the degree to which someone's language is capable of conveying his or her experience. While stopping short of asserting that such experiences as feeling pain and seeing colors cannot be conveyed, he nonetheless qualifies considerably what might be otherwise regarded as straightforward and unproblematical acts of communication. Early in the *The Blue Book* he takes "our craving for generality" (*BBB*, 17, 18), which he also calls "the contemptuous attitude towards the particular case" (*BBB*, 18), to task for dissimulating the conceptual violence involved even in our most prosaic descriptions. There are even several types of generality responsible for the illusion that one person can hear and interpret what another intends. One is akin to the likenesses that unite certain members of a family or is "comparable to the idea that *properties* are *ingredients* of the things which have the properties; e.g., that beauty is an ingredient of all beautiful things as alcohol is of beer and wine, and that we could therefore have pure beauty, unadulterated by anything that is beautiful" (*BBB*, 17). This is a linguistic generality that relates to the particular instance as Hegel's thing is the manifold of its individual traits; Hegelian perception envisages the trait's detachment from the manifold in a way similar to Wittgenstein's abstract ingredient, but it also sees the detachment as occurring at the cost of the manifold's dissolution. Wittgenstein also provides an archetypal model for the abstraction necessitated by successful communication: "the man who has learnt to understand a general term, say, the term 'leaf', has thereby come to possess a kind of general picture of a leaf, as opposed to pictures of particular leaves" (*BBB*, 18). Whether the generality involved in communication is structural, metaphysical, or scientific in nature, its pervasiveness is such that Wittgenstein releases a barrage of instances—including symptoms, pains, catastrophes (the King's College fire), and synthetic constructs (the centaur)—to challenge and delimit it.

This ethical as well as intellectual and methodological repugnance of generalization furnishes a backdrop for a sequence of qualifications and precisions throughout *The Blue and Brown Books* that would otherwise appear obsessive and myopic. On one level, the fine shades of distinction that would presume to correct conceptual distortions by means of linguistic precision convey an impression of precious armchair philosophizing conducted at some distance from the world's substantial problems. To be sure, Wittgenstein's distinction-making proceeds by virtue of its own inherent pleasure. And yet on a far more profound level, both language and philosophy have no more decisive and vital a function than to delineate differences, even when the stakes—and the distinctions—are minute.

It is in the context of the *tuning* of a linguistic instrument whose possible utility—and conceptual value—increase only in the *range* of its distinctions that *The Blue and Brown Books* abound in differences. In pursuing the difficulites attending even the seemingly simplest acts of indication, Wittgenstein observes the different possible meanings that accrue to the substance of the message, its performance, and even to the identity of its speaker:

> The difficulty which we express by saying "I can't know what he sees when he (truthfully) says that he sees a blue patch" arises from the idea that "knowing what he sees" means: "seeing that which he also sees"; not, however, in the sense in which we do so when we both have the same object before our eyes: but in the sense in which the object seen would be an object, say, in his head, or in *him*. The idea is that the same object may be before his eyes and mine, but that I can't stick my head into his (or my mind into his, which comes to the same) so that the *real* and *immediate* object of his vision becomes the real and immediate object of my vision too. By "I don't know what he sees" we really mean "I don't know what he looks at," where 'what he looks at' is hidden and he can't show it to me; it is *before his mind's eye*. Therefore, in order to get rid of this puzzle, examine the grammatical difference between the statements "I don't know what he sees" and "I don't know what he looks at," as they are actually used in our language. . . . This leads us to consider the criteria for the identity of a person. Under what circumstances do we say: "This is the same person whom

I saw an hour ago?" Our actual use of the phrase "the same person" and of the name of a person is based on the fact that many characteristics which we use as the criteria for identity coincide in the vast majority of cases. I am as a rule recognized by the appearance of my body. My body changes its appearance only gradually and comparatively little, and likewise my voice, characteristic habits, etc. only change slowly and within a narrow range. We are inclined to use personal names in the way we do, only as a consequence of these facts. This can best be seen by imagining unreal cases which show us what different 'geometries' we would be inclined to use if facts were different. Imagine, e.g., that all human bodies which exist looked alike, that on the other hand, different sets of characteristics seemed, as it were, to change their habitation among these bodies. Such a set of characteristics might be, say, mildness, together with a high pitched voice, and slow movements, or a choleric temperament, a deep voice, and jerky movements, and such like. . . . If a man tries to obey the order "Point to your eye," he may do many different things, and there are many different criteria which he will accept for having pointed to his eye. If these criteria, as they usually do, coincide, I may use them alternately and in different combinations to show me that I have touched my eye. If they don't coincide, I shall have to distinguish between different senses of the phrase "I touch my eye" or "I move my finger towards my eye." If, e.g., my eyes are shut, I can still have the characteristic kinaesthetic experience in my arm which I should call the kinaesthetic experience of raising my hand to my eye. (*BBB*, 61–63)

Emerging out of the great void that surrounds knowing what another person means, this sequence of passages from *The Blue Book* is struck at every angle by differences: between one's own and another's consciousness as models, among different "geometries" that may be evoked as hypothetical bases for personal identity, and in the meaning of particular phrases as they pass to and from the stations of the communicative chain. Acts are different when viewed from different angles, words are different according to different speakers and speech functions, and personal identity, to the extent that it bears upon language, is different from itself. By virtue of the homonymic byplay that Wittgenstein admits into his discourse, the "I" that turns out not to be "L. W.," at least not exactly, becomes the eye that is, in the final segment of the above citation, both the message and the organ perceiving the basic act of indication. Even the differences that proliferate from the above passage are different: the intersubjective divide between "individuals" is not the same as the conceptual difference between models, which is in turn of a different order than the semantic particularities of phrasing. It is in this sense that Wittgenstein can explore the gradations of meaning in the words "lighter" and "darker" with an intensity equal to that of his pursuit of the distinction between "bounded" and "unbounded" games (*BBB*, 91, 138–39).

The above passage provides ample indication that, when pressed, both the philosophizing and the hypothetical subjects—and the experience that they ostensibly undergo—dissolve amid the incongruity among the assumptions called into play by their very operation, while the etymological and syntactical difference between words, a very precondititon of the discourse, continues unabated. Difference, then, is not merely an interest or theme of Wittgenstein's discourse; it predicates the very possibility of its formulations. Although capable of allowing certain incommensurable phenomena within his view to pass by in silence, Wittgenstein articulates the specifications and expectations for a rigorous philosophical language. The effects of his investigations have been profound; they have influenced both the practice of formal philosophy culminating in the current speech-act theory[28] and the New Criticism, which has shaped an approach to literature that has been adapted by generations of professors and students. The concern for difference implanted in these outgrowths of Wittgenstein's thought may partly account for the receptivity with which deconstruction has been greeted in the Anglo-American sphere.

Although with different emphases and approaches, Claude Lévi-Strauss and Roland Barthes both undertake their explorations into the operation and social function of signs in wonder at the linguistic course that Saussure set for the twentieth century. While Barthes studies the ideological and rhetorical motivation of various codes in his own culture,[29] Lévi-Strauss reads the sometimes asymmetrical structures of conceptual systems, social organizations, and artifacts deriving from cultures unsurpassed in their remoteness. Saussurian insights and discriminations—regarding the differential distribution of signs, their arbitrariness and motivation, and the slow evolution in language by which the local usages of the *parole* first disfigure and then join the normative lexicon of the *langue*—seldom slip below the horizon of Barthes' and Lévi-Strauss's purview. Lévi-Strauss's treatment of myth as an artifact with a *relational* content, sharing language's analogical and distinction-making functions, is an example of the twentieth-century shift of attention away from phenomena and toward their linguistic infrastructure. And yet where he effects this redirection, in his 1957 "The Structural Study of Myth," Lévi-Strauss observes the Saussurian *langue* and *parole* at work in the mythological creation of the "Savage Mind."[30]

The remarkable survey of "primitive" societies that Lévi-Strauss completes over his career enables him to remark "that so many common elements and systematic relations continue to exist in different local organizations. This suggests a rigor, a tenacity and fidelity to distinctions and differences on a theoretical plane."[31] The parallelism of social structures in widely divergent settings is a problem of logical classification that preoccupies Lévi-Strauss at several points in his work. But the intellectual efforts on the part of the tribes he observes, in such areas as classification, naming, and mythology, are possessed of a seriousness that becomes a fundament of his approach. "This thirst for objective knowledge is one of the neglected aspects of the thought of people we call 'primitive'. Even if it is rarely directed towards facts of the same level as those with which modern science is concerned, it implies comparable intellectual application and methods of observation. In both cases the universe is an object of thought as much as it is a means of satisfying needs" (*SM*, 3).

In analyzing the intellectual practices of the peoples he studies "in the field," Lévi-Strauss thus opens a window on the possibilities for reading and interpretation in the mid-twentieth century.

"Primitive" classification and naming are at the heart of Lévi-Strauss's interest, because, situated at the juncture between conceptualization and linguistic usage, they reveal the possibilities for localized abstraction. Both in his efforts to represent and interpret the habits of people beyond the sphere of influence of Western thought and in "primitive" practices, the notion of difference plays a pivotal role:

> In fact, the delimitation of concepts is different in every language, and, as the author of the article "nom" in the *Encyclopédie* correctly observed in the eighteenth century, the use of more or less abstract terms is a function not of greater or lesser intellectual capacity, but of differences in the interests—in their intensity and attention to detail—of

particular social groups within the national society: "In an observatory a star is not simply a star but B of Capricorn or ζ of Centaur or of the Great Bear, etc. In stables every *horse* has a proper *name—Diamond, Sprite, Fiery,* etc." Further, even if the observation about so-called primitive languages referred to at the beginning of the chapter could be accepted as it stands, one would not be able to conclude from this that such languages are deficient in general ideas. Words like "oak," "beech," "birch," etc., are no less entitled to be considered as abstract words than the word "tree"; and a language possessing only the word "tree" would be, from this point of view, less rich in concepts than one which lacked this term but contained dozens or hundreds for the individual species and varieties. (*SM,* 2)

This citation illustrates what Lévi-Strauss will elsewhere call "the concern with differentiating features which pervades the practical as well as the theoretical activities of the people we call primitive" (*SM,* 73). It demonstrates that the activity of classification is not contingent on the level of abstraction that the category wields over the particular instance. "Primitive" classification takes place in the absence of a systematic hierarchy of genuses and species. It is therefore particularly bound to the differential distribution of signs that Saussure observes in language.

Lévi-Strauss reads "primitive" organizations, social and intellectual, by systematizing the differences generated by the cultures that he observes. In the case of the myth, he registers the relations that the various segments illustrate, and he arranges the various episodes according to whether they repeat, reverse, or rearrange this relation. "The time constituent units of a myth are not the isolated relations but *bundles of such relations,* and it is only as bundles that these relations can be put to use and combined so as to produce a meaning" (*SA,* 211). Lévi-Strauss gathers singular relations into bundles, which he deals out like a deck of cards (*SA,* 213–15, 218–19). He then reads the "meaning" of the myth from the tabulated "hands." Similarly, in the case of primitive societies,

the existence of differentiating features is of much greater importance than their content. Once in evidence, they form a system which can be employed as a grid is used to decipher a text, whose original unintelligibility gives it the appearance of an uninterrupted flow. The grid makes it possible to introduce divisions and contrasts, in other words the formal conditions necessary for a significant message to be conveyed. *(SM,* 75)

Whether he calls the resultant instrument a grid or a bundle of relations, Lévi-Strauss engages in his own classification when he organizes his data. The superimposition of relations and differences produces a text in its own right that can be interpreted or "read out" in terms of several programs. Lévi-Strauss describes the multiple critical approaches sustained by the tabulated compendium of data as a transposition or translation of codes: "the systems of naming and classifying . . . are codes suitable for conveying messages which can be transposed into other codes, and for expressing messages received by means of different codes in terms of their own system" *(SM,* 75–76). It is at the moment when Lévi-Strauss interposes the composite organization of the grid or the bundle that he deviates from a commitment to difference on its own terms. The interpretation of data by tabulation is inimical to the discipline by which Wittgenstein restricts his claims to what measured philosophical language will allow, and it is inimical to *différance,* Derrida's term incorporating the micro- and macroscopic manifestations of incongruity in language. But Lévi-Strauss's tabulation affirms and is predicated by the time-honored practices of the social sciences, whose corpus his work intends to join and enhance. His readings of seemingly alien and impenetrable habits and artifacts are informed to a remarkable degree by the discernment and pursuit of difference.

If Martin Heidegger and Jacques Derrida are more consistent than Lévi-Strauss in the elaboration of differential notions according to their internal logic, this is in part because such formal consistency is closer to the program of their enterprise. Even though Martin Heidegger entitles one of his essays "Identity and Difference," he is far from being the first major thinker of the century to observe the growing decisiveness of a concept of difference as it proliferates throughout literature and the work of other philosophers. Nor is he the first to impart, in a chain of crystallizations beginning with Saussure and Peirce, the parallel crises in which the concept of identity and the attempts to invoke its authority increasingly find themselves. Already in the *Tractatus Logico-Philosophicus,* Wittgenstein specifies, "It is impossible to *assert* the identity of meaning of two expressions" (Proposition 6.2322). In light of the mission that Wittgenstein ascribes to philosophy, to clarify and sharpen the boundaries of thought, the assertion of the identity of two different linguistic formulations is problematical at the very least. In *The Blue and Brown Books,* Wittgenstein begins to establish a comprehensive overview of all factors, agents, and activities involved in an act of communication. In the context of this overview, the identities of the communicator and the recipient of a message are every bit as difficult as the "identity" between two different usages of language. In the midst of the passage from *The Blue Book* that we cited on page 33, one in which the role of difference within the inquiry becomes explicit, Wittgenstein explores the nuances of meaning attaching to the subject involved in the communicative act. In that passage, Wittgenstein considers the circumstances and "criteria for the identity of a person" *(BBB,* 61). Two possible bases for this identity are the continuity in time of certain physical and temperamental traits attributed to the person, which, as Wittgenstein points out, nonetheless change in time, and the definition of a person "by means of his memories" *(BBB,* 62), a manifold whose composition is every bit as fraught with difficulties.

Martin Heidegger's overall philosophical project may be described as the repetition of the classical project of Western ontology—with a crucial difference. Instead of regarding Being and its corollaries as a pure and neutral essence invested with the ideality of the Platonic forms, Heidegger would recommence the history of ontology by treating Being as a linguistic entity whose qualities are akin to those of densely written poetry, that is, of language programmed to acknowledge and compensate for its own anomalies, including its multiple meanings, its syntactical impenetrability, and its alogic. Heidegger claims that this linguistic constitution is in fact closer to the Greek conception of Being than the purely formal post-Platonic notion, implying that the main part of the history of ontology has arisen from and reinforced a misconception. It is important to note that several of Heidegger's most powerful demonstrations, in his effort to reinstate the linguistic constitution of Being, assume the form of pedagogical interpretations of linguistic artifacts at what he considers an ultimate level of density. Such important essays as "What Are Poets For?," "Language," and ". . . Poetically Man Dwells . . ." revolve, respectively, around important poems:[32] Rilke's *Sonnets to Orpheus* and "The Force of Gravity,"

Georg Trakl's "A Winter Evening," and Hölderlin's "In lovely blueness blooms the steeple with metal roof. . . ." The genre of philosophical essay that Heidegger devises not only shifts the prevailing current in the history of ontology, but it also redirects philosophical inquiry toward the *reading* of key texts, toward a literate understanding of the linguistic interplay within artifacts underlining and comprising major developments in the histories of writing and thought.

Saussure, in his functional account of the synchronic features of a language, set himself on a collision course with a notion of difference, as did Wittgenstein in rigorously weighing the conceptual nuances of various formulations. Heidegger confronts difference as he stages a scenario in which linguistic involution reinstates itself as the origin, and conditioning agent, of subsequent conceptual crystallizations. In one of his essays, "Language," Heidegger's notion of difference arises from Trakl's poem "A Winter Evening." Heidegger separates his conception of difference "from its usual and customary usage. What it names now is not a generic concept for various kinds of differences. It exists only as this single difference."[33] This encompassing difference characterizes the relationship between the work of art and the linguistic, cultural, and historical contexts in which it arises. In Heidegger's terms, it transpires between world and thing:

> The speaking of the first two stanzas speaks by bidding things to come to world, and world to things. The two modes of bidding are different but not separated. But neither are they merely coupled together. For world and things do not subsist alongside one another. They penetrate each other. Thus the two traverse a middle. In it, they are at one. Thus at one they are intimate. The middle of the two is intimacy— in Latin, *inter*. The corresponding German word is *unter*, the English *inter-*. The intimacy of world and thing is not a fusion. Intimacy obtains only where the intimate—world and thing— divides itself cleanly and remains separated. In the midst of the two, in the between of world and thing, in their *inter*, division prevails: a *dif-ference*.
>
> The intimacy of world and thing is present in the separation of the between; it is present in the dif-ference. . . .
>
> The word consequently no longer means a distinction established between objects only by our representations. Nor is it merely a relation

obtaining between world and thing, so that a representation coming upon it can establish it. The dif-ference is not abstracted from world and thing as their relationship after the fact. The dif-ference for the world and thing *disclosingly appropriates* things into bearing a world; it *disclosingly appropriates* world into the granting of things.

The dif-ference is neither distinction nor relation. The dif-ference is, at most, dimension for world and thing. (*PLT,* 202–3)

In Trakl's poem, Heidegger finds an occasion for characterizing the complex interaction between the work of art—the labored thing—and its various contexts—the world—a subject he also pursues in his essay "The Origin of the Work of Art." The difference fulfills a synthetic function *between* the artwork and its world. In Heidegger's scenario, the historical, linguistic, and material conditions of the world find a consummation, a flowering, and an illumination in the work of art, which in turn joins and modifies its world. In his essays Heidegger stresses the drama between the long-term precedents and implications of the artwork and its more circumscribed production and impact. Qualified and modified by its immediate world, the artwork arises out of a timeless linguistic "earth," whose repository it will ultimately join.[34] The artwork is thus the main character surrounded by a high drama in which the longer and shorter dimensions of time and language play themselves out. The mutual interpenetration and qualification by the labored thing of art and its world derive much of their dynamics from the interplay between the Saussurian *parole* and its *langue.*[35]

Heidegger's difference is then, quite literally, the *setting* of the linguistic artifact, what sets it off from the otherwise tyrannical conditions of its world. The conditions of this setting are not tranquil and harmonious. The artwork appropriates, or steals, its linguistic resources. It distorts and displaces any "original" meaning that may be ascribed to these resources for its own purposes. It appropriates and exhausts what it needs, thus joining a modernistic preoccupation with waste and its treatment (which will be more fully explored in Chapter 4 of this book.) If the artwork *discloses* the ambiguities that have been camouflaged by conceptual pretensions to thoroughness, it does so only by virtue of a linguistically sanctioned, unavoidable theft and violence.

Following Wittgenstein's lead, then, and in a refrain that Derrida, with important qualifications, will repeat, Heidegger exposes the weakness of positing identity:

> What the principle of identity, heard in its fundamental key, states is exactly what the whole of Western European thinking has in mind— and that is: the unity of identity forms a basic characteristic in the Being of beings. Everywhere, wherever and however we are related to beings of every kind, we find identity making its claim on us. If this claim were not made, beings could never appear in their Being. Accordingly, there would then also not be any science. For if science could not be sure in advance of the identity of its object in each case, it could not be what it is. By this assurance, research makes certain that its work is possible.[36]

The principle of identity is strident and all-pervasive. It is indispensable to thought-systems and scientific procedures that rely on equations and equivalencies. Its rather loud claim is, however, of limited validity. In "Identity and Difference," a planned obsolescence has been built into this principle, which founders when language enters the picture.

> Thus we think of Being rigorously only when we think of it in its difference with beings, and of beings in their difference with Being. The difference thus comes specifically into view. If we try to form a representational idea of it, we will at once be misled into conceiving of difference as a relation which our representing has added to Being and to beings. Thus the difference is reduced to a distinction, something made up by our understanding (*Verstand*).
>
> But if we assume that the difference is a contribution made by our representational thinking, the question arises: a contribution to what? One answers: to beings. Good. But what does that mean: "beings"? What else could it mean than: something that *is*? Thus we give to the supposed contribution, the representational idea of difference, a place within Being. But "Being" itself says: Being which is *beings*. Whenever we come to the place to which we were supposedly first bringing difference along as an alleged contribution, we always find that Being and beings in their difference are already there. It is as in Grimm's fairytale *The Hedgehog and the Hare*: "I'm here already." . . .
>
> this thing that is called difference, we encounter it everywhere and always in the matter of thinking, in beings as such—encounter it so unquestioningly that we do not even notice this encounter itself. Nor

does anything compel us to notice it. Our thinking is free either to pass over the difference without a thought or to think of it specifically as such. But this freedom does not apply in every case. (*I and D*, 62–63)

Difference emerges only when the representational function of language becomes explicit, only when language underlines and compensates for the discrepancy between words and things. The place of Heideggerian difference is the *between* that intervenes, in representation, between the signifier and its signified. In the above citation not only the difference itself but two of its crucial qualities explode with the suddenness of revelation: Difference is ubiquitous but submerged, i.e., marginal, and it has *always* subsisted, and has asserted its influence. It is therefore equiprimordial to Being. We are free to notice or not notice difference and its subtle undermining of identity and its corollaries, but our awareness will not, of its own right, deprive it of its locus or activity. Like Saussure's lexicon, the ontological ground of Being is, then, *differential* in nature.

Listening carefully to Heidegger, Derrida *hears* the need to adapt philosophical discourse to the linguistic complexity of its medium. He hears the marginal, ubiquitous, and subliminal accompaniment that the poetic range of language *plays,* in Heidegger's work, to its systematic deployment in philosophy and science. Derrida listens to Heidegger and learns from him. But he also hears the subtle tonalities resonating from Heidegger's self-imposed confinement to a single plane of inquiry. Heidegger can never quite abandon the hope that the poetry he privileges will replace the essential status and sanctity with which *Being* is invested in classical philosophy. Heidegger never departs from the ontological field. He never relinquishes the expectation that he is the thinker who will, through the reinstatement of language to its primordial status, furnish a final solution for classical ontology. In his meticulous readings of Heidegger's work, Derrida is thus able to discern *through* the importance that his predecessor attaches to linguistic complexity the summons and demand for presence: the desire that language nonetheless harbor, despite its representational absences and dislocations, some vestige of an essence. Because of the residues of an ancient philosophical wish in Heidegger's work, his notion of difference never encompasses the multifaceted linguistic discrepancy with which Derrida invests *différance*.[37]

In light of the preceding discussion, any attempt to articulate Jacques Derrida's *identity* must appear not only constitutionally problematical but also perverse. Yet Derrida has himself acknowledged the issue and has confronted it in his work, through the construct of the signature, among others.[38] Is Derrida simply equatable with the sum of his texts? This is an antiseptic approach to the problem. But who, then, is that individual who travels around the world giving lectures and whose face now begins to peer at us from the pages of mass publications? Is he an approach to reading and interpretation known as deconstruction? But this identification flies in the face of Derrida's insistence that each text and critical arena generates its own terms for its singular deconstructive activity. "Derrida," like his writings, is an intangible quality. His work, his methodological models, and his activities as a major intellectual figure of our day deprive each other of their defining clarity and stand in what he would call a supplemental relation to one another.

Yet this writer, were he to undertake such a problematical and in all likelihood outrageous task, would define Derrida, after one of his book titles, as a *position,* the position from which any artifact of language dismantles itself by revealing its *biases* in whatever form they apply.[39] These may assume the form of conceptual closure, logical determination, thematic unity, formal repetitiveness, ideological orientation, or any of the *centrisms* that enforce or instrument ideas: generic (sexual), ethnic, racial, cultural, and even anthropomorphic.

The position from which Derrida has chosen to formulate his writing is difficult, for him as well as for his readers. It is, first of all, no small task to *gain* the marginal perspective from which texts, documents, and artifacts retract both their not always simple messages and the concepts that seem to inform their meaning. And yet as difficult as it is to achieve the overview from which language *begins* to account for its own complications, it is even more strenuous to *maintain* this position amid a panoply of possible approaches and to do so when addressing a philosophical tradition whose internal differences—of context, form, and idiom—are vast. Still, were I to characterize Derrida's contribution to date and to engage in a reduction that the rabbis scorned as reading the Torah while standing on one foot, it would be as a consummately difficult struggle to maintain an equally difficult position, the position that Derrida has variously described as that of the margin, the supplement, the *pharmakon,* and of writing itself. Derrida's position is that of a radical *imbalance* that sustains itself from text to text and context to context. Its paradigm may well be the tightrope walker in Nietzsche's *Also Sprach Zarathustra,* whose feat is tantamount to staying on the verge of falling.[40]

To treat Derrida as a position is undoubtedly reductive, but it may spare us a number of misprisions of even greater violence. Associating him with deconstruction inevitably presses this *set* of interpretative practices, whose preeminent characteristics include improvisation, toward formalization and a repetition uninformed by the specificities of context. Formalizing deconstruction would be akin to the literalizing of a poetic metaphor, taking it at its word, but irreversibly emptying it at the same time. "Derrida" could be the texts he has written, and has written about, a kind of canon. But we would then face the problem of identifying which essay, book, or figure of speech designed to embroider a particular situation represents the "true" Derrida.

Regarding Derrida as a difficult but very fruitful position spares us this onerous and unsatisfying task. It also removes a certain historical and existential burden from Derrida the person. A position is somewhat independent of a man and may even exist before him. Associating Derrida with a position enables us to say not that Derrida *invented* his position, or articulated "language's eye-view of the world" for the first time, but that he elected to *inhabit* this position and operate according to its terms, in all likelihood with greater comprehensiveness, rigor, inventiveness, and *range* of application than probably anyone else, in the philosophical domain, since Nietzsche and in literature since Kafka. Jorge Luis Borges's story "Tlön, Uqbar, Orbis Tertius" also provides for a position, a counterdomain to the standard practices of Western thought, maintained by a "secret society" of marginal thinkers that endures in time. The position of a counterdomain absolves Derrida of both responsibility and originality with respect to the acknowledgment of—and adaptation of discursive procedures to—linguistic structuration. Although he has done much to clarify and consolidate it, the position preceded Derrida, and although perhaps with less originality and flair, others in his line of work have undoubtedly *shared* it with him. The nature of the Derridean position, and the rigor with which it has been maintained, also explain why Derrida has consistently refused to place his work at the service of any national, political, or ethnic agency, however sympathetic or unsympathetic he may personally be to its views.

With respect to the exploration of difference that in twentieth-century art and thought has coincided with the acknowledgment and dramatization of the structuring role of language, it is crucial to recall that for Derrida, each artifact or text spells out the terms according to which it both configures and dismantles its meaning. He shares with Wittgenstein a profound distrust of the "craving for generality" and the "contemptuous attitude towards the particular case" that occasion and accompany abstractions. As early in his work as *Of Grammatology,* Derrida articulates the analogy between global metaphors and general laws, between the suppression of local idioms and differences and the suspicion toward writing that has existed throughout the history of Western philosophy. Particular texts as well as geographical regions assert their local differences, which rigorous and nonauthoritarian reading is obliged to respect. *Différance,* in *Of Grammatology,* illustrates not only language's relation to its own elements and to the concepts which it makes possible. It also characterizes the singularity of each text and the specifications for reading that avoids reducing or dissolving those particular traits. Derrida thus adopts the perspective of the local difference at two decisive moments in *Of Grammatology:* first, when he discerns Claude Lévi-Strauss's implicit biases in his studies of native peoples—biases that appear "between the lines" of the casual, almost optional "human interest" anecdotes incorporated into *Tristes Tropiques*—and second, when he observes the predetermined role of local differentiation in Rousseau's evolutionary account of *The Essay on the Origin of Languages.*

Différance is, then, a figure demarcating a marginal zone where the particular, the unique, and the incommensurate may reside in autonomy from the broader systems that threaten to assimilate, absorb, or reduce them. At the moment in *Of Grammatology* when he challenges the cynical complicity with which Lévi-Strauss deprives the Nambikwara children of their individuality by inciting them further to reveal each others' names, Derrida carefully formulates the conceptual and political violence that centralized systems can impose on the particular case, on what differs from itself as well as from its defining system:

There was in fact a first violence to be named. To name, to give names that it will on occasion be forbidden to pronounce, such is the originary violence of language which consists in inscribing within a difference, in classifying, in suspending the vocative absolute. To think the unique *within* the system, to inscribe it there, such is the gesture of the arche-writing: arche-violence, loss of the proper, of absolute proximity, of self-presence, in truth the loss of what has never taken place, of a self-presence which has never been given but only dreamed of and always already split, repeated, incapable of appearing to itself except in its own disappearance. Out of this arche-violence, forbidden and therefore confirmed by a second violence that is reparatory, protective, instituting the "moral," prescribing the concealment of writing and the effacement and obliteration of the so-called proper name which was already dividing the proper, a third violence can *possibly* emerge or not (an empirical possibility) within what is commonly called evil, war, indiscretion, rape; which consists of revealing by effraction the so-called proper name, the originary violence which has severed the proper from its property and its self-sameness [*propriété*]. We could name a third violence of reflection which denudes the native nonidentity, classification as denaturation of the proper, and identity as the abstract moment of the concept. It is on this tertiary level, that of the empirical consciousness, that the common concept of violence (the system of the moral law and of transgression) whose possibility remains yet unthought, should no doubt be situated. The scene of proper names is written on this level; as will be later the writing lesson. (*OG*, 112)

While the incommensurability of the local, the singular, the "special case" may be characterized by a certain "originary" violence, which is really more of a strangeness, the efforts directed at domesticating and institutionalizing such anomalies are far more brutal. "To think the unique within the system" is a strain; it is unsatisfying from the perspective of the comprehensiveness of whatever system applies and also because this exercise will, in the end, restrict the total freedom and mystifying satisfaction of the unique. Thinking the unique within the system is one of many possible ways of articulating the tension that Derrida, if we regard him as a certain position, is willing to sustain. And yet in the above passage Derrida witnesses the destruction of this tenuous way station in the wake of a far more general, rigid, and moralistic invasion and control.

By the same token, Derrida questions the geographical and metaphysical schemes by which Rousseau accounts for the evolution of languages in *The Essay on the Origin of Languages* and other writings. Rousseau's assertion that language was first articulated in the North to compensate for the lack of felicitous cooperation that prevailed between mankind and nature in the South furnishes an occasion for Derrida to elaborate and sharpen two of his key notions: the supplementary status accorded to writing and certain aspects of all language over the course of Western thought; and the stresses and fissures that inevitably surface in the firm foundations that human beings provide for their species, their religions, and their conceptual systems. For Derrida as for Nietzsche, a suspicious repression goes hand in hand with fabulations of ascertainable, decisive, and harmonious origins.

And yet the schemes that Rousseau crystallizes as skeletal supports for his fictive narrative of linguistic evolution bring mystifying notions of pure originality and linguistic subservience and unreliability into play. They also illustrate vital linguistic features. Rousseau divides the compass, for example, into a linguistic North and South. Writing gains ascendency in a geographical North characterized by need, cold, separation from nature, and cold reason. The South is, by contrast, a domain of passion, desire, and directness of expression. The music and accent of language come from the South as well. Derrida not only questions the order and presuppositions of this scenario; he also regards it as an illustration of Rousseau's awareness that the systems of language are *constructed around* the incommensurate and indelibly local. Rousseau's geographical chapters in *The Essay on the Origin of Languages* "describe . . . that before local difference, there is nothing that one may call language. . . . local differences between the two poles of language always amount to an articulatory play" (*OG,* 251). "Language, passion, society, are neither of the North nor the South. They are the movement of supplementarity by which the poles substitute each other *by turn.* . . . Local difference is nothing but the *différance* between desire and pleasure. It does not, then, concern only the diversity of languages, it is not only a criterion of linguistic classification. It is the origin of languages. . . . From here on, I shall constantly confirm that writing is the name of this *différance*" (*OG,* 268). As was suggested at the outset of this discussion, then, Derridean *différance* is both *within* language and *between* it and concepts. It thus becomes an index of language's multifaceted relational function on a far more comprehensive level than either Wittgenstein's careful phrasing or Heidegger's *dif-ference.*

Derrida's insistence on the local accents and idiosyncrasies of language provides for a curious affinity between his philosophical enterprise and the work of modern American poets, such as Ezra Pound and William Carlos Williams, who spoke in the "American grain" and treasured local and regional idioms and nuances. Pound preserves cultural remains deriving from many points of the compass not only for posterity but also in the name of their specificity: their local phrasing and color. Williams's fragmentary aphorism in Book Five of *Paterson,* "Anywhere is everywhere," is on the one hand a synecdoche enabling us, in Blake's words, "to see the world in a grain of sand."[41] On the other hand, it is also a remark on classification that Derrida can well understand: The local and the unique *are* the universal, to the extent that the universal exists.

More that an affinity, a sympathy, or a conceptual pivot, local difference is a perspective that Derrida incorporates into his method of approaching texts. He devotes as much energy to "assembling" the concepts and formal and logical devices necessary to make a major document in the history of Western thought as he does to "deconstructing" it or revealing its various points and types of fixity. Both in assembling and dismantling a particular piece of ideological machinery or economics, he pays careful attention to the particularities of phrasing: In large measure, the text under discussion furnishes the terms both for its reading and for the disclosure of its blind spots. The interpretative devices that Derrida deploys vary from text to text. By contrast, the same piece of writing may justify the application of methods incongruous to each other. During the exposé of Lévi-Strauss's ethnocentric biases and affinities to logocentrism, as well as to the tradition of suspicion toward writing and its implications in Western thought, Derrida resorts to a large assortment of logical devices, some quite recognizable from traditional philosophy. At the same time that he engages in a broad ideological critique of a deluded ethnocentrism that defines itself as its opposite, Derrida extrapolates or reads in suppressed meanings "between" Lévi-Strauss's lines (*OG,* 121, 130), exposes Lévi-Strauss's blindness to his own insights (*OG,* 123), assembles and marshals some of Lévi-Strauss's passages against others (*OG,* 125, 132), uncovers suppressed biases or prejudices (*OG,* 127, 128, 129), reveals violence in the form of arbitrariness (*OG,* 129, 130), demonstrates Lévi-Strauss's lack of rigor (*OG,* 130), and applies simple logic, in this case, deductive reasoning, to Lévi-Strauss's exposition (*OG,*

134). It is precisely the variety of approaches that Derrida is willing to improvise that enables his elucidations of literary, philosophical, and social scientific texts to fulfill the polemical thrust of *différance*. The open-endedness and local flavoring of Derrida's interpretative method extend to the complex figures that he has improvised in his major readings: I think here of such figures as the *pharmakon,* the hymen, the heliotrope, and the tympany.[42] Emerging specifically from the language of the texts in which they figure, these complex tropes function both as emblems somehow compressing and focusing the issues at stake and as shifters easing the translation between the exegetical, theoretical, polemical, and performative levels of the interpretation. Such comprehensive yet specific figures deriving from the language of the text under discussion constitute the highest level of generalization that Derrida willingly entertains.

Controversial as it has been, then, the set of textual approaches known as deconstruction incorporates devices both singular and familiar. Deconstruction is the most recent major recrystallization in a history of difference initiated by Saussure and Peirce and preoccupying a major segment of twentieth-century critical theory. While deconstruction may draw heavily on this line of inquiry, it does not claim either to exhaust or consummate it.

Kundera demonstrates convincingly that the narcotizing banter of *kitsch* spans *both* the empires and spheres of influence labeled as "Communist" and "Western," and that *kitsch* is prodigiously successful in adapting to the demands of its particular context. We live at a historical moment when the various political parties of the West encounter increasing difficulty in demonstrating and even articulating their *differences* from each other, when economic conglomerates or megaorganizations threaten to absorb the much more specialized goods and services furnished by small businesses, and when the electronic media determine public knowledge to an unprecedented degree. One of the effects of automation and wholesale marketing in the West, radiating from the United States to Western Europe, seems to be a built-in unemployment spanning most levels of social stratification. We thus face the following anomaly: unemployment consolidates its position, while an entire array of specialized crafts and skills disappears. On the one hand, mechanization and large-scale commerce *dispense* with a certain number of functions and positions and marginalize the people who fill them. At the same time, they render numerous small enterprises unprofitable for those who operate them. Structurally implicit unemployment in the United States is evident in every direction, and yet one often travels a good distance to buy a man-made loaf of bread.

This paradox, while still only emerging in the advanced industrial societies of Europe, will follow as a result of the same economic principles that produced it in North America. In the United States, the political process offers itself as the arena in which to address these and related issues of public policy. But in that country, the two prevailing political parties resist the ideological articulation of their positions to such an extent that candidates for elective national and local office often avoid, in political announcements, identifying their party affiliation. Party politics in the United States is thus situational rather than long-term, practical rather than theoretical, obfuscatory rather than explicit. The avoidance of ideological articulation provides political parties and leaders with a certain freedom to act spontaneously. By not committing themselves to a preconceived spectrum of options extending from "right" to "left," Republicans are free to implement "leftist" policies (such as Richard Nixon's *rapprochement* with the People's Republic of China), and Democrats are able to be fiscally and socially conservative when the political climate demands. And yet the persistent avoidance of political articulation and differentiation in the United States submerges historical interests, alliances, and commitments and renders long-range planning difficult, if not impossible.

What we have learned about language in the twentieth century applies significantly to a number of fields and decisive, current questions. The way we conduct business, economics, and politics and the hopes and expectations we have for science and technology are a few of the general areas in need of greater elucidation by notions of difference and articulation. The role and value of such "applications" have not yet been adequately established within the academic sphere, partially owing to a division of labor still queasy about interdisciplinary studies and partially because of insular criteria of academic distinction and reward.

The findings of contemporary critical theory, as the field that has dedicated itself to the study of conceptual and ideological arbitrariness, are thus indispensable to many overused academic and practical concerns. If Jacques Derrida, in remaining consistent with a quite specific marginal position (which would productively question the opposition between theory and praxis), has thus far avoided such applications, this does not imply that their need has been preempted or eliminated. At the same time, no fruitful analysis of any text, artifact, event, or phenomenon will take place without the meticulous attention to language that Derrida's work has exemplified.

Only through the dissemination of a *differential* literacy are individuals prepared to read the particularities of their cultural heritage, their political and social interests, and the future eventualities that they are free either to accept or resist. Differential literacy is the primary means available to a society for the diffusion of its cultural wealth and future economic opportunity. The *cost* of differential literacy, in comparision with its functional counterpart, is high indeed, but then so are the expenses exacted by its restriction: costs measured in social disaffection, nonproductivity, and the waste of human talent and resources. The skills of a differential literacy also come at a high cost, in terms of commitment and energy, on the part of those who seek them. A redefinition of these skills and a retooling of schools and universities to disseminate them more effectively are major social undertakings that cannot be accomplished until literacy becomes an articulate public value.

With all the technological advances of the past generation, the classroom remains the basic setting for the dissemination of literate skills, whose primary *medium* is still the careful reading of books and other documents and artifacts. A recent critical literature that has arisen in response to the question of literacy gives ample indication both of the importance of the issue and the commitment of its authors. Yet for a variety of reasons, this literature, which will be reviewed in Chapter 5 of this book, often despairs at the difficulty of transmitting literate skills to a major segment of the population. My own approach isolates the definition, problem, and historical and ideological contexts of differential literacy in a sequence of texts that have proven decisive to modern and contemporary attitudes toward language and culture. Only through a careful reading of such works can we locate both the impasses and possible solutions to the debilitating effects of a certain illiteracy.

High-Resolution Screen

We return, at the end of this introductory chapter, for a better look at the image of television, the most prevalent medium and instrument of kitsch in the Western world. For some, the above prescription for a return to the classroom and its basic skills may convey an austere mood and punitive tone. Lest this be so, a brief survey of television's internal world, of the utopia that this appliance both projects and seems to contain, may prove useful in characterizing the classroom's *alternative*. I speak from the perspective of one raised and socialized, so to speak, among the particularities of American prime-time television, but in their *Reading Television,* John Fiske and John Hartley assure us that those television conventions proceeding from the medium itself are international in character.[43]

Television is a synaesthetic linguistic medium, with visual and auditory components, and at least on one level must be treated as such. Fiske and Hartley provide an invaluable prolegomenon to this type of analysis. Their approach is semiotic; they pay particular attention to the signs that television transmits, the codes that relate them, and the various social and communicative functions that television fills. Their book, in justice to the medium itself, demonstrates that the television message is no more exhaustible than any other linguistic artifact. Although the linguistic play that a careful reading can underscore in the visual and oral languages of television is as rich as its counterparts in novels and poems, such exegeses are beyond the scope of the present discussion.

Todd Gitlin and others have pointed out the heavy technical, substantial, economic, and political constraints under which television programming is produced.[44] There are as well serious cognitive limits to the experience of watching and listening to a medium whose messages (in the United States) are interrupted by commercial announcements for nine out of every thirty minutes. The commercials themselves present tantalizing objects for sophisticated exegesis. In light of these multifaceted checks, television appears as a form of language restricted and controlled by itself and convoluted by this internal tension. Strategically located within the large complex of activities and individuals necessitated by television production is a certain self-surveillance that defines the medium's ideological function. This internal surveillance goes on regardless of the origin of the programming or its politico-ideological setting. It is precisely as an ideological instrument that television works at cross-purposes with the dissemination of literacy.

In the course of its nearly forty-year history, television has evolved a set of genres and conventions designed to attract and entertain different segments of the public and to promote a variety of goods, services, and public opinions. Nothing could appear more diverse, say, than the broadcasting of the Indianapolis 500 automobile race and the domestic melodramas aimed at entertaining a daytime audience of retirees and largely female homemakers. And yet, I would argue that television, as opposed to literary texts, is unified and integrated in one respect: its ideological dimension. Its dual purpose is to resolve and to reconcile: to resolve conflicts and differences and to reconcile its audience with prevailing socioeconomic and political conditions. What unifies the most distinct subgenres lies beneath the surface of the *subject* of the representation and its historical and technical *conventions*—but it is all the more powerful for this camouflage and submersion.

If the ideological offerings of television seem more diverse than they are, this is no doubt due to the gradations in the realism of its representations. Television news, rarely acknowledging any possible biases on the part of its producers and reporters, is presented as a completely objective account of events taking place domestically and abroad. The picture, if not the commentary, of a sports event is the most graphic video representation possible of physical acts transpiring on a field or court. A televised sports event is an instance of ultrarealism and intense conflict and action deprived of ideological significance. A team may "represent" Philadelphia or even "the Iron Curtain," but the furious energy of the game does not translate into any articulate ideological position. The appeal of game shows and soap operas also depends on the maintenance of at least one level of ultrarealism. The game show depicts dreamlike rewards (or at least possibilities) bestowed on individuals selected for the "normality" with which they represent their social classes, regions, and emotions, while the soap opera incorporates the pace of nontheatrical (everyday) time into its representations of everyday acted-out desire. The dramaturgy of soap opera is a scaled-down, minimalist theatrics. The actors are extraordinary only in one respect: by virtue of their presence on the screen. They are otherwise to behave as individuals living the ebb and flow of life rather than as dramatic characters. The genre of the soap opera, which has for some seasons migrated from its original daytime setting to the so-called "prime time," demonstrates the cooperation between television's cathartic options and the realism of video photography. The attraction of the soap opera is precisely its fidelity to the dimensions and pace of lived experience while it offers the vicarious satisfactions of domestic infidelity and crime.

The literality of television representation is thus not antithetical to or mutually exclusive of the fantastic domain of satisfied desire that it also entertains. These factors, however, are at play in every form that the medium crystallizes. Every subgenre of advertising as well as programming emerges from a particular calculus involving the literal and cathartic representational impulses of the medium. A common matrix of possibilities thus accounts for both a football victory bringing glory to the city of Philadelphia and a detective program reasserting the vigilance of the authorities and the error of crime while it *entertains* with images of sex and violence; The same matrix gives birth to both a sequence of recent "dream" advertisements (e.g., Chanel perfume), with surrealist imagery, and the concrete litany of the "Veggie-matic": "It slices, it dices! . . . " Depending on its outcome, a televised sports event may satisfy (or frustrate) a viewer's identification with a team, a city, or certain players; the news may confirm or shock one's expectations concerning the world situation; and a prime-time drama may reward certain dramatic and sexual curiosities, but these forms, despite their very different conventions, arise from a common set of representational possibilities.

It is within these representational parameters that the subgenres of programming *act on* the audience in their respective ways. It may be said, regarding the performative level of television, that criminal dramas *warn us away,* above all from theft and murder, that situation comedies *reaffirm* the values of domestic stability (even when they accommodate the changing forms of the family), that televised sports *elicit and purge* interest in conflict devoid of ideological content, that musical extravaganzas *satisfy* aesthetic and sexual curiosity, that theme-oriented television films *domesticate* and *reduce the scale* of current social concerns, and that miniseries *totalize* and present scale-models of an integrated and thoroughly coordinated society no segment of which has been lost from view. By the same token, a large share of American advertisements contains vignettes of *consumer ecstasy* in which characters not only enjoy the merchandise being marketed but also transcend the limits imposed by age, occupation, and familial and marital status. An advertisement for Löwenbräu beer depicts a son's completion of a college education not as a potentially divisive moment in the life of a family but as its apotheosis. Mass-consumed items—beer, soft drinks, fast food, cereals—are often framed within an epic setting in which as many representatives from the various social, racial, ethnic, and age categories of society as can be credibly crammed into the picture simultaneously revel in the commodity being advertised. Advertisements of this type including the McDonald's campaign mentioned earlier and the Kellogg's Corn Flakes message in which a large family achieves vocal as well as social unanimity in a midwestern field, sell the utopian bliss of harmony, akin to psychological states of merging, as much as they promote *the product*.

It would of course be difficult, for a variety of reasons, to present, in a field, a mass of assorted Polygrip Denture Adhesive users plying their dentures at the same time. Products used in private settings are often sold by sex or science, depending on the degree of discretion violated. Like the utopian festival of consumer joy, the scientific advertisement, in which the product and its use are objectified, neutralized, and sanitized of any possible embarrassment to the viewer by the testimony of an "expert," is a uniquely American creation, now advancing to foreign shores. (Indigenously European advertisements, deriving from a tradition of mnemotechnics, elaborate on an initially striking image or metaphor.) The drudgery of housework and the delicacy of minor physical infirmities can be "laundered" by scientific demonstrations and rhetoric. The aura of the female (and, increasingly, male) body is the vehicle powering the sale of cosmetic and private commodities: bath soaps, shampoo, lingerie, perfume. The automobile, which in American culture functions as the shifter of linguistics, a vehicle superimposed at once on the territorial limits of the nation, the house, and the bedroom, commands and deserves an advertising form *sui generis*. Automobile advertisements on television pass from travelogue and scientific demonstration to scenes of family bliss and sexual triumph, often under insignias furnished by totemic animals with the smoothness of the newly assembled products.

According to the collective imaginary that may be extrapolated from most American television programming and advertisements, the exemplary American, to be sharply distinguished from antiheros such as J. R. Ewing of *Dallas,* is an egalitarian, immune to ethnic, racial, and class bigotry, a loyal child, faithful partner, and responsible parent, not to mention a sexual virtuoso, whose fair share of the national wealth and destiny is pending if not already in hand. This dream may, in the classical Freudian sense, reconcile us to the harsher realities of our lives, but it also vanishes when the television screen darkens.

The elimination of difference not only defines the social conditions of the family comedy and the panorama of Coke drinkers that repeats itself, like the backdrop of Renaissance paintings, to the horizon. The dissolution of difference is at once the condition of the utopia and the ideological claim, the operating principle, and the experiential effect of the medium. And if the endless pollyannaish *announcement* of unity on the thematic level does not deliver a serious enough blow to the articulate skills of habitual television viewers, the cognitive havoc wreaked by the systematic commercial interruption of the *leitmotif* goes a long way toward ensuring a certain intellectual damage. For several generations now, American instructors of college English, in whose hands rests the final chance to correct the linguistic deficiencies of students, have witnessed a decline in written fluency and mental concentration, a decline for which television is at least in part responsible. Although greater attention to the dissemination of the broader literacy and to the literate level of mass communications will surely come at a cost to government, educational institutions, the television industry, and perhaps to business in general, the restriction of articulate skills surely poses serious threats to the maintenance of democratic traditions based on self-reliance.

The development of sports programming in our era provides a graphic example of both television's limits and its challenge. Baseball, a game whose roots extend deep into the nineteenth century, represents a mythic struggle of individualism. During the main part of the game, primary offensive and defensive responsibilities are *delegated,* respectively, to the batter and pitcher. "Teamwork" primarily involves defensive cooperation, although in a number of specialized (and rare) plays (e.g., "hit and run") there is offensive collusion. Football, on the other hand, dramatizes a bureaucratic organization not dissimilar to the one prevailing in the workplace of many of its observers. All play, offensive and defensive, is collaborative in nature. Functions are specialized and not easily interchangeable. The quarterback and backfield provide the impetus and direction of management. Football, like all major American team sports other than baseball, is time-manipulative: It transpires under constant anxiety about the clock.

Since the early 1960s, football has gradually replaced baseball as the sport most preferred by the American public, for reasons implicit in the above paragraph. Yet baseball, with its heroic confrontations and its more "natural" time framework, has continued to thrive, producing a fine counterpoint to the sport metaphors with which Americans play out the conflicts of their lives. Over the same period, sports programming on television has worked hard to wean viewers from purely local identifications and interests, so that the drama of the competition extends to all cities and sports. The mythic calendar of sports has replaced the ritual calendar of religion, which for Walter Benjamin declined during the age of mechanical reproduction.[45] The interplay between baseball and football (and the latter's temporal variants) thus presents, in a microcosm, the representational possibilities available to sports: to embroider and fabulate, in the mythic struggle of baseball, or to reproduce and exercise the stress of corporate life in football. Baseball is the far happier vestige of a more carefree, "natural" time, but it manufactures its own brand of dramatic tension. As suggested above, both sports transpire in an ideological vacuum.

With access to more and more homes in the Western world, the medium of television has a democratizing potential, an ability, perhaps unprecedented in history, to transmit and share the cultural resources of the world.[46] And yet the medium's time-honored principles stress that it avoid controversial conficts, deflect attention away from substantial issues and toward entertaining characterization, and submit to, rather than attempt to raise, the "common denominator" of audience articulate skills. In *Inside Prime Time,* Todd Gitlin has admirably chronicled the development and maintenance of these principles by the managers of the television industry.[47] The "television-industrial complex" is for him above all an economic apparatus driven by the profit motive and catering to the at times fickle tastes of a mass audience. Sophisticated social scientific testing and survey techniques are deployed in order to determine the tastes and habits of this audience, but in the end the decisions that establish the nature, literate level, and sequence of television offerings are in the hands of the executives of the television industry. By their own account, these executives form a remarkably small, closed, and incestuous cadre whose instinct is, given the risks they take, to repeat or recombine past successes rather than to readjust modes, programming goals, or intellectual content. According to Gitlin, these executives are the Kafkaesque gatekeepers who assure the conceptual as well as aesthetic blandness of the commercial medium. The bureaucratic enterprises they manage, with offices carrying such names as "Standards and Practices," are primed for the preemptive detection and elimination of controversy. Gitlin quotes one such executive from an American television network as saying, "I'm not interested in culture. I'm not interested in pro-social values. I have only one interest. That's whether people watch the program. That's my definition of good, that's my definition of bad" (*IPT,* 31).

For us to ascribe all the problems of a vast enterprise to a small set of individuals in executive positions would be to repeat the television delusion that makes "the single most important factor in series success . . . the appeal of its major characters" (*IPT,* 67). Indeed, on a practical level, whether by virtue of past conventions, present personnel, or ideological bent, the TV industry limits the conceptual horizon of its offerings by engaging in a self-censorship that coincides with the industry's laudable intention to advance the rights of individuals and groups. Gitlin chronicles some of the most striking instances of this censorship over the past fifteen or so years. A 1971 episode of *The Young Lawyers,* which revolved around a black female attorney, was rewritten calling for a white substitute, while a 1979 series, *Today's F.B.I.,* granted that agency veto power on any aspect of programming. Another series, *American Dream,* which frontally addressed the problem of racial tension and related issues in the United States, initially underwent considerable cosmetic surgery and was then prematurely terminated. "People of color aren't the only ethnic minorities to run afoul of network and advertiser timidity," writes Gitlin. "Given the large number of Jews who hold top positions in the networks and production companies, it seems surprising that Jewish characters are scarce on the screen. But television is still a site for the great American drama of assimilation, and the ethnicity of executives and suppliers doesn't necessarily determine characters. In the end, the networks fall back on their sense of market-place predilections" (*IPT*, 184).

Again and again, commercial television reiterates, conceptually, technically, and thematically this drama of assimilation. The drama may celebrate multiethnic diversity, but it also empties the screen of the organizational, conceptual, and social complexities that the viewers confront on a daily basis. Structurally and thematically, the plots of dramatic programs are supposed to *resolve*. "There's no way you can resolve the Nazis marching down the street," muses a producer cited by Gitlin about a projected episode of *American Dream*, (*IPT*, 106). *Hill Street Blues* and *St. Elsewhere*, two recent series that have begun to demonstrate what a differential yet entertaining American television could be, claim distinction, in part, from their refusal to adhere to this norm of resolution. "To thicken the plot" of *Hill Street Blues* "further, most of the episodes were written in four-show blocks, with at least four major stories running concurrently, each starting in a different moment and not resolving at all" (*IPT*, 274).

Resolution is at once the promise, technique, message, and result of all kitsch, including its particular manifestations in television. Ongoing and substantial tensions and issues are bypassed, while artificial ones are created to embellish particular occasions with dramatic interest.

> The fundamentalist crusade to "clean up television" was founded on a recognition that television entertainment amounts to politics conducted by other means. For if the networks muffle controversy, they also delight in the semblance of it. Again and again television acknowledges social and cultural conflicts, if only to tamp them down in the process of "resolving" them. But no matter how it muffles and oversimplifies controversy to go with what it sees as the tidal flows of public taste, television cannot help but generate conflict of its own. (*IPT*, 248)

At its ultimate reaches, the controversy to which television gives rise extends to a debate on the uses and nature of language. The balancing act necessitated by the divergent imperatives to maintain autonomy from state control, to spare minorities from the generalizations of some hypothetical "prevalent view," and to educate, edify, and entertain represents a difficult and challenging task. At the same time, even the *articulation*—and the debate in public forum—of the issues emanating from the intellectual, literate, and cognitive impact of the electronic mass media would constitute a significant advance beyond the self-perpetuating simplification that currently prevails. Gitlin's account *chronicles* the intense self-surveillance and smoothing over of the questions that might illuminate the public's positions and options, but the reduction of pressing issues and the resistance to change are evident from the "products" themselves. Television provokes conflict, as Gitlin asserts, not only because of its questionable operating principles and management, but also because of its vast, and largely untapped, potential to educate its audience and improve the literate, if not material, conditions of its environment.

Program

Writing productively and constructively about the problem of literacy necessarily involves a careful reading of specific texts—in the same sense that the proverbial omelette cannot be cooked without eggs. In the age of computers, fast food, and television, close reading does not come easily. It is slow, tedious, and, as Marshall McLuhan saw in his pioneering media analyses, "cool" in comparison to electronic media richer in sensible feedback.

Chapters 2, 3, and 4 in this volume all present detailed readings of literary works—by Hawthorne, Melville, and such modern American poets as Ezra Pound, Wallace Stevens, and William Carlos Williams. What these texts have in common is an awareness of the problems surrounding their comprehension by their readership, an articulation of the conditions for their own literacy, and a concern for their future status as written artifacts. Several of the works, especially Hawthorne's *The Marble Faun* and Pound's *Cantos,* coincide with crucial historical moments in the determination of the literate options available to the culture in which they arose. All of these works define, and to some extent create, their own readership. There is a pedagogical element in their design and an underlying awareness of the politics of literacy: the threat that literary "undecidabilities" pose to the climate of consensus (in Melville's terms, confidence) often demanded by political agencies. The coherence of such writers as Italo Calvino and Milan Kundera, in addition to those named above, may appear to be utterly tenuous, worthy only of Borges's Chinese encyclopedia. But each of these authors demonstrates a profound concern for literacy and in so doing makes a substantial contribution to its theory.

It is perhaps presumptuous to suppose that a series of close literary readings could have any tangible impact on a problem as "real" as illiteracy or on the world which seems to perpetuate rather than combat it, and that they could assist in an upgrading of cultural resources or facilitate a consensus among institutions and individuals who disseminate literacy. What is, after all, a literary work, and what could its workings be? The artifact of writing, as Jacques Derrida has assembled its attributes, is superfluous, ornamental, useless, wasteful, and conducive to all sorts of mischief.

This volume begins under the assumption that there remains unfinished business in the classroom of language, a setting that appears, from the perspective of "hotter" media and our accustomed ambiance of speed, increasingly spare and forbidding. But like all of the holdover agenda from childhood, personal and collective, an unconsummated immersion in the broader skills of language grows rather than declines in its dysfunctional impediments until it is decisively confronted. The readings in this book attempt to confront those impediments head on.

The book ends by returning to the notion of literacy as a public issue whose decision is still in process. It reviews the current literature on this subject, and it questions the despair that seems to cloud the considerably different approaches to this decisive issue of our day.

Ultimately, literacy is much more powerfully dramatized than defined or advocated. If the following essays can productively join this demonstration, they will have succeeded in their purpose.

2

The Marble Faun *and the*
Space of American Letters

Nathaniel Hawthorne's romance, *The Marble Faun: Or, The Romance of Monte Beni,* can hardly be taken to task for the meanness of its aspirations.[1] This novel sets out to perform for all subsequent American letters no less than the function that graduate school fills for the preprofessional. It proposes to acclimate, adapt, and socialize American letters within the institutional framework of European culture. Once this task is completed, there will be no tension or discrepancy between American writing, which issues from a geographical as well as conceptual margin, and a mainstream of European thought that emanates from far more venerable origins. There will be a coincidence between the sources of European and American culture: Any fundamental difference or otherness will have been rooted out of the origins. The margins in the intertextual confrontation between Eastern and Western hemispheres will be resolved. American letters will have in effect studied in Europe on an exchange program so that they may someday join the faculty of a university of a universal Western culture. In this manner they will have attained literacy.

The splicing of American letters upon the trunk line of Western civilization is a major undertaking, and in order to bring it to fruition, Hawthorne mounts a multifaceted campaign. Hawthorne's urgency in cultivating American letters and bringing them to a state of moratorium[2] is so intense that it marshals a wide range of fictive resources and levels of conceptual complexity. Even the plot of the

novel is an instrument fitted out for this construction job. Hawthorne literally sends his two American innocents, a painter named
Hilda and a sculptor named Kenyon, to school in Rome. The novel
begins in a Roman gallery as the Americans survey the artistic roots
of their heritage like two criminals drawn back to the scene of some
indeterminate crime. So powerful is the setting of the European repository that Henry James will return to it at the outset of his first
novel with an international theme, *The Americans,* where Christo-
pher Newman gawks at the treasures and copyists of the Louvre.
As befits a novel in which so much material is devoted to an internal
system of characters, qualities, and symbols, Hawthorne's Americans, Hilda and Kenyon, have already encountered a pair of counterparts, Miriam and Donatello, when the novel begins. In the first
scene, Donatello is the conversation piece, for his companions have
noted an uncanny resemblance between him and a marble faun by
Praxiteles. The resemblance plays between Donatello and the statue,
yet both sides of the resemblance themselves hover in figural suspension. Both Donatello and the faun are grab bags of between-
states. The faun is an amalgam of opposites. It is "marvellously
graceful, but has a fuller and more rounded outline, more flesh . . .
than the old sculptors were wont to assign" (8–9). "The nose is
almost straight but very slightly curves inward" (9). Although stone,
"it is impossible to gaze long at this stone image without conceiving
a kindly sentiment toward it" (9). Just as Praxiteles's statue, a venerable and very substantial point of departure for the Americans and
American art in their quest for culture, fuses grace with fleshiness,
geometry with organic form, and lapidary death with living affec-
tion, Donatello, the statue's human counterpart, is himself a synthetic manifold of opposites. "In some long-past age, he must really
have existed. Nature needed, and still needs, this beautiful creature,
standing betwixt man and animal, sympathizing with each, comprehending the speech of either race, and interpreting the whole
existence of one to the other" (13). Native to two time warps, the
ancient and the modern, this beautiful Italian is also a hybrid linking
the diverse families of the human and natural world, as articulated
in terms of nineteenth-century anthropology and anthropocentrism.
Yet while Donatello plays the role of synthesizer, of translator among
the races, ages, and tongues, he himself is marked by "an indefin-
able characteristic . . . that set him outside of rules" (14). Dona-

tello, the living marble faun, set in the age contemporary to the fictive time of the novel, sounds the keynote of ambiguity and uncertainty that pervades all of the novel's characters (save Kenyon, the straight man) and virtually all of its important actions. The marble faun provides the occasion for, and is occasioned by, a resemblance. Both sides of the resemblance themselves turn out to be divided and uncertain. Even the resemblance that might seem to combine the incongruous parties is ambiguous, taken half earnestly and half jokingly by its perceivers. The ambiguity that the novel introduces in its title character and its ur-scene seems to make it a veritable program of contemporary theoretical interests and themes: Its basis is a relation, a figure of speech. The novel seems to declare the priority of these linguistic facts over any more abstract reality. But this is a founding novel. The question is not *whether* such ambiguities, as intimated by the above citations, are brought into play, but how they figure in the overall game plan. *The Marble Faun* is a novel that, while *acknowledging* certain concerns that are extremely *au courant,* entertains *higher* aspirations for its productions.

The other character to whom the Americans correspond in the novel's symmetrical coupling of transoceanic pen pals is Miriam, who in her own unique ways is as enigmatic as Donatello. Of uncertain ancestry and race, she is a sort of pan-European mongrel: She may be a German princess, "offspring of a southern American planter" (23), or even part Jewish. She is also characteristically vivacious, but it is in one of her rare moments of serenity that her description is couched in the Romantic conventions surrounding the image, a point that will figure in any historical assessment of the novel. Miriam hovers as much as her cohort. "She resembled one of those images of light, which conjurers evoke and cause to shine before us, in apparent tangibility, only an arm's length beyond our grasp; we make a step in advance, expecting to seize the illusion, but find it still precisely so far out of our reach" (21).

For all her sprightly vivacity, which makes her an embodiment of the Romantic Appearance, or *Erscheinung,*[3] Miriam is nevertheless plagued from the outset of the novel by dark memories and ominous threats. Her torments, the dark side of her uncertain origins, soon appear on stage in the person of a swarthy and unkempt persecutor, who, like Donatello, is divided between ancient and modern emanations. This figure is known to the other characters as the

Model, an appellation associating him with a certain evil, within a Manichean scheme, as indispensable to the work of art as its edifying qualities. When the Model, by pursuing and harassing Miriam, pushes her and Donatello to the brink, Donatello responds in kind by throwing him over the precipice of the Capitoline Hill. This murder is the focal and climactic event of the novel.

Through this murder, the naive American Artists are exposed to a timeless, congenital, and ineffaceable corruption that haunts the European bedrock of American culture. It is for this reason that Hawthorne repeatedly describes Rome as a heap of concentrated and somewhat excremental junk, anticipating the fundamental concern with garbage that preoccupied such twentieth-century writers as T. S. Eliot, Ezra Pound, and Wallace Stevens:[4]

> Rome, as it now exists, has grown up under the Popes, and seems like nothing but a heap of broken rubbish, thrown into the great chasm between our own days and the Empire, merely to fill it up. . . . If we consider the present city as at all connected with the famous one of old, it is only because we find it built over its grave. A depth of thirty feet of soil has covered up the Rome of ancient days; so that it lies like the dead corpse of a giant, decaying for centuries, with no survivor mighty enough even to bury it. (110)

Having removed his American innocents to a culture-Mecca set upon a quagmire of putrescence and morbidity, a scenario not unlike the quaking that Faust discovers in the Grecian foundation of civilization in *Faust II*,[5] Hawthorne makes Hilda and Kenyon accessories to the murder by forcing them into the position of voyeurs or witnesses to Miriam and Donatello's activities. A scene in Chapter 12, in which the American's unnoticed, observe Miriam as she is pursued by her tormentor, rehearses the Americans' role as implicit accomplices in the crime. This collusion in the crime of two Europeans, who are as enigmatic as their ancestries are timeless, goes to the heart of the novel's program. Hawthorne exposes his exemplary Americans to the congenital disease within the European past so that *we* may live. By Texan standards, Rome is only a few steps away from the Venice of Thomas Mann and venereal disease.[6] Hilda and Kenyon contract the venereal disease inherent within European history so that the American public—contemporary to the novel's writing and future—will be shielded, vaccinated, against the infection. If the Americans Hilda and Kenyon get a bit soiled in the course of their odyssey, their fall is nonetheless fortunate, for it ensures the moral and physical health of future generations. Hawthorne fuses the timeworn motif of the fortunate fall with the advances of nineteenth-century immunology in synthesizing a recuperative historical framework for American letters. Just as Hilda and Kenyon will return home sadder but wider, American letters will recuperate and make the most of the degeneracy to which they are exposed when grafted upon the tree trunk of European cultural history.

In the wake of the murder, the quartet of paired characters splits up. Donatello retires to his ancestral Tuscan home, Monte Beni, where he later receives Kenyon for an extended visit. Monte Beni is the setting of the deepest penetration made by an American into European culture and its past. Here Kenyon imbibes the Sunshine wine that is a quintessence of presence and locality, and he also hears about the legend that identifies Donatello as a living bridge to the most primordial stratum of myth.[7] The two friends go on a walking tour of Italy devoted to the philosophical and perceptual activity of observation. Their trip is described as a sequence of absorptions into self-sustaining scenes that are invested with iconic sacredness. The tour terminates when, by prior arrangement with Kenyon, Miriam appears on the scene. The European lovers reunite both to consummate their knowing love and to prepare for their inevitable punishment. During this time Hilda has withdrawn in order to expiate her rather tenuous guilt. Failing to restore her sense of moral uprightness through a solitary appreciation of artworks, she turns to a priest of St. Peter's. Although she resists her urge to convert to Catholicism, her confession to the priest reconciles her both with the fallen ways of the world and with the historical tradition consummated by the church, whose otherness she previously experienced as rejection and loss. Hilda's confession is her equivalent to Kenyon's sojourn at Monte Beni. If Kenyon effects the aesthetic and historical facets of the American-European graft, she accomplishes the same on the theological front.

The ending of the novel is a sequence of reminiscences in preparation for a predetermined close. Kenyon discovers Miriam and Donatello in the Roman campagna, where they set him on the track of the absent Hilda. He finds her amid the anarchy of the Roman

carnival, having caught one final glimpse there of his European co-
horts.[8] Particularly telling of Hawthorne's cultural program is the
fact that, in the aftermath of their European experience and discov-
eries, Hilda and Kenyon renounce their art or drastically revise their
artistic activities. Hilda rejects the amorality of art (338–39), whereas
Kenyon dissociates himself from the burden and contagion of the
European past (409, 412). The *culmination* of Hawthorne's histor-
ical-cultural program thus includes a *retreat* from its aesthetic
concerns and activities. In his master plan for American culture,
Hawthorne is ultimately content with an illiterate audience, one incapable of reading the moral indeterminacies that he playfully sets
before it.

I have provided a thumbnail sketch of the manner in which the
plot serves as a vehicle for the novel's cultural and institutional program. One basic paradox that certain of the details I have cited
suggest is that, in concretizing a recuperative and synthetic program, Hawthorne takes frequent, almost obsessive recourse to *negative* qualities and operations. The narrative freely admits the limits
of its knowledge about the characters and its inability to establish
clarity and coherence. In a description that could only please contemporary fashion, the novel describes itself as an embroidered text
"into which are woven some airy and insubstantial threads, inter-
mixed with others, twisted out of the commonest stuff of human
existence" (6). Such a scenario is tantalizing, as are the novel's
repeated allusions to hovering, ambiguity, and mystery, and its fascination with figures and relations such as the status of the *resemblance* between Praxiteles's statue and Donatello. Such concerns
might suggest that Hawthorne cast the future of American letters on
a foundation of "post-structuralist" apprehension, that the American
Renaissance was simultaneous with "the end of the book and the
beginning of writing."[9]

Homer Brown has often surmised that all American literature may
be regarded as a construct of European Romanticism.[10] Another in-
terpretion of the novel's negative capabilities, one perhaps more
fruitful than that which simply appropriates nineteenth-century
American literature in line with current concerns, is that the uncertainties proclaimed by *The Marble Faun* are part of a positive system: the speculations about understanding, reflection, and intuition
formulated by such Romantic writers as Schlegel and Hegel. The

ambiguities in the novel, the mysteries that Hawthorne introduces when the facts will not tally, and the farce in which the novel ends comprise not so much the violation of a systematic thought as a specific system in its own right. Contemporary critics such as Jean-Luc Nancy, Philippe Lacoue-Labarthe,[11] and Rodolphe Gasché[12] have performed the inestimable service of formulating the limits that condition constructs which would otherwise seem to hypostatize infinity and unrecuperable negativity. Hawthorne may allow a certain amount of ambiguity to play in his novel, but when necessary, when historical and institutional destiny calls, he rewinds the slack in his narrative line in the interest of the cross-cultural graft outlined above. *The Marble Faun* may thus serve as a case of repressive fictive tolerance in nineteenth-century American literature.

To this point we have examined the wider outlines of Hawthorne's project primarily in relation to the story line. Yet in addition to the story, Hawthorne provided two other primary dimensions of the novel as implements of the grafting process. In its literary allusions and historical references, the novel constructs a *historical framework* whose operation is analogous to the problems involved in its cultural aspirations. If a historical system may be discerned in the work, in which mythological, theological, art historical, and Romantic sources are appropriated as sequential yet overlapping contexts for the novel's inscription, a system of characterization also functions in which figures and events become legible in terms of a comprehensive semiological code. By endowing all the major characters with the same attributes, including an artistic medium and a color, Hawthorne constructs a lexicon for decoding the novel's actions and assertions. Hawthorne's cultural and institutional program, both for the novel and American letters, receives its positive assertion in the form of these systems of history and characterization. On a thematic level, the novel's ambiguities and mysteries, such as the question whether Donatello's ears really resemble those of Praxiteles's faun, or the matter of Hilda's disappearance before Kenyon reclaims her at the carnival, collide with these systems. The narrative *professes* a whimsy, playfulness, and impenetrability that seem to belie its attempt to construct a historical platform for American letters and a characterological system for itself. But the work of Nancy, Lacoue-Labarthe, and Gasché enables us to discern the collaboration of the novel's subsystems with the imponderables that apparently undermine them. The novel's professed and dramatized hovering, its narrative gaps, and its closing farce collude with its restricted system and belong to the nineteenth-century traditions of reflection, imagination, and irony. At stake in the conflicts of *The Marble Faun* are not merely the novel and the American literature adjacent to it but the aesthetic and philosophical traditions to which it annexes itself.

Before even venturing to determine whether the novel's ambiguities overthrow its systematic arrangements or collude with them, some more basic observations may be useful, specifically regarding the text's historical and characterological systems.

The Theoretical Framework

Like a hyperanxious parent, Hawthorne pursues his ambitions for his novel by trying to secure for it the best possible *connections*. When in Chapter 27, "Myths," he traces Donatello's ancestry back to a point when mortals freely disported with nymphs and other supernatural creatures, Hawthorne "connects" American literature to the Pelasgian creation myth, as far back, in Western terms, as one can go. The novel's historical program proceeds by establishing connections. *The Marble Faun* is Hawthorne's D-Day for American letters, securing four successive yet simultaneous bridgeheads on the European coast. By means of allusion, Hawthorne summons ancient myth, early church history, the Renaissance, and British Romanticism to different contexts and in relation to different characters. We have already observed the mythological dimension of Donatello. The malevolent Model derives from the early church by virtue of his association with the legend of Memmius, an early proselytizer sent by St. Peter into Gaul. This particular moment captivates Hawthorne because it precedes the Protestant-Catholic schism. In light of Hawthorne's ambition to couple American culture to a *unified* mainstream of the Western tradition, the Protestant-Catholic break is an inconsistency that must be circumscribed. Hawthorne repairs this tear by appealing to the legends of the early church and by staging Hilda's confession to the priest, even though neither the narrator nor Kenyon can resist ventilating their anti-Catholic prejudices.[13] Miriam is a character surrounded in the high drama of the Renaissance, and that is why she is repeatedly linked to the Medicis and Cencis, whereas Hilda, a sisterly figure from the pages of Wordsworth, is a woman endowed with a certain ambiguity but deprived of action.

It is important to emphasize that the novel's four primary allusive areas serve Hawthorne both in sequence and in a randomly scrambled arrangement. Just as Donatello and the Model are divided between eternal and contemporary emanations, the novel's temporal framework encompasses both diachronic and synchronic configurations. In this fashion Hawthorne achieves an effect similar to that of the *mise en scène* of D. W. Griffith's film epic, *Intolerance,* in which alternating scenes of Babylonian barbarism, Christ's crucifixion, and the St. Bartholomew's Day massacre form a backdrop to the contemporary American world. Making *his* four historical contexts for the novel simultaneous or synchronous enables Hawthorne to ground any character or event in a European connection. Donatello's forebears were protohumans who conversed with the demigods; Miriam steps, as it were, off the canvas of Guido's *Beatrice Cenci,* and so on. Hawthorne can and does flit back and forth between mythology and Romanticism as the occasion demands or suggests. But a sequential sense of the epochs also has a place within the novel's strategy. Both Hawthorne's novel and Griffith's film operate as historical syllogisms. In order, the historical frames function as the premises of an argument whose conclusion consists of the artwork and the world of its setting. The historical precedents of these artworks retrospectively endow them with the force of inference or necessity. The latest historical moment of these works, whether the American labor unrest in Griffith's film or the nineteenth-century émigré art world in the novel, becomes the inevitable conclusion of the preceding historical events.

In his historical design for the novel, Hawthorne wants things both ways. He coordinates his buttressing of the events in the historical past at every point with a more encompassing sequential movement of historical and logical dimensions. This split or doubled historical configuration and imperative explains why so many characters and artifacts in the novel, notably fountains, marble basins, cemeteries, and Rome itself, require both a continuous and sequential existence.

The intricate coordination that grafts the living present of nine-teenth-century America and the fictive world of the novel upon the predetermined and hopelessly corrupt past informs virtually every significant character, object, and event in the book. So pervasive is the influence of this temporal juggling act that one could argue that the novel's motifs of hovering and indeterminacy are a function of its synthetic temporal framework. The gesture of superimposing the contemporary time of the novel on the continuum of history be-comes the novel's exemplary act in founding American culture and in fulfilling its genealogical and cultural imperatives. This act is repeated with a ritualistic urgency throughout the novel's settings and with regard to its privileged symbols. Donatello is described often as an evolutionary primitive who somehow preserves the an-imalistic, autochthonous, and Dionysian qualities of his forebears. Yet if the instinctive Donatello hovers at the border of statuary rep-resentation in the form of Praxiteles's faun, Roman marble, which Hawthorne describes in terms of female genitals, moves in just the opposite direction, toward the organic and the slightly seedy. In the fountain in Miriam's courtyard, "the patches of moss, the tufts of grass, the trailing maiden-hair, and all sorts of verdant weed that thrive in the cracks and crevices of moist marble, tell us that Nature takes the fountain back into her great heart" (38).

The paradox of the hard but sexually soft and fecund fountain extends throughout the novel's system of indeterminacies, itself a paradoxical formulation. Ephemeral persons or experiences such as the drinking of the "Sunshine wine" from Donatello's estate, a wine so rooted in its local point of origin that it spoils if moved, can evoke the remote past. Under the influence of Donatello's primitive and Dionysian revelry (of the kind that Keats projected onto his urn, to which the narrative makes sure to allude), "here, as it seemed, the Golden Age came back again, within the precincts of the sunny glade; thawing mankind out of their cold formalities; releasing them from irksome restraint; mingling them together in . . . gaiety" (88). Conversely, statues and artifacts of marble, while receptive to gra-dations of movement and emotion, sublimate the eternal out of the ferment of the ephemeral. The repose that Kenyon, who as a sculp-tor or shaper is godlike and Hawthorne's strongest lobbyist in the novel, extracts from Cleopatra is an example of the novel's temporal oxymoron from eternity's eye-view. "A marvellous repose . . . was diffused throughout the figure. The spectator felt that Cleopatra had sunk down out of the fever and turmoil of her life, and, for one instant—as it were between two pulse-throbs—had relinquished all activity" (126). "Soon apotheosized in an indestructible material, she would be one of the images that men keep forever, finding a heat in them that does not go down, throughout the centuries" (127).

But Hawthorne is not content merely to *initimate* the aesthetic idealism that prevails in the novel and that serves as a prolegomenon to any future American art. When Kenyon, on the eve of Miriam and Donatello's final judgment, discovers an ancient statue in the Roman campagna, its description is couched in terms of the Hegelian classicism in which the artwork and the ideal merge:[14] "The beautiful Idea at once asserted its immortality, and converted that heap of forlorn fragments into a whole, as perfect to the mind, if not to the eye, as when the new marble gleamed with snowy lustre; nor was the impression marred by the earth that still hung upon the exquisitely graceful limbs, and even filled the lovely crevice of the lips" (423–24). So sublime and ethereal is this artwork, an inspiration for American as well as European art, that the narrator exhorts us to ignore the dirty space between its labia. Organic as well as classical, this artifact is an exemplary inspiration to a Romantic aesthetics.[15]

The countertemporalities of the ephemeral-eternal and the eternal-ephemeral bonded by the artworks in the novel also imply a sexual division of labor, a subject to which we will return. The feminine is, so to speak, the workhorse behind these historical and cultural programs, acknowledged as an energy source but kept well under harness. For the moment, in line with the novel's temporal order, it is worth noting that the masculine art of sculpture with its aspirations to permanence is sharply contrasted to the painting practiced by Miriam and Hilda, which is evidently a feminine medium. Miriam describes her own art as "too nervous, too passionate, too full of agitation," that is, too hysterical and rooted in the present, for the repose of sculpture (116). The cause of Miriam's suffering is apparently the fact that, instead of assuming Hilda's submissive role as a copyist, she has pretensions of being a productive artist in her own right. From the evidence supplied by the text, Miriam's sin is not some mysterious deed shared by herself and the Model but her artistic hubris, compounded by the fact that her studio is littered

with her portraits of other haughty and castrating women: Jael, Ju-
dith, and Salome.

The Systems of Characterization and Symbolism

The novel's systems of characterization and symbolism are every
bit as determined and coordinated as its temporal scheme. This conclusion becomes particularly unavoidable in light of the observation
that each of its five major characters is identified at least by means
of a double, an artistic medium, a color, a natural element, a metaphysical realm, and a judgment. Not only do the main characters
comprise arche- or prototypes, but certain of their qualities or activities are associated with objects that acquire symbolic consistency
or equivalence. The functioning of a closed symbolic system within
the novel is reinforced by the fact that some of its symbols, notably
sunshine, snowflakes, stains, the color red, and shadows, are repeated in similar contexts in Hawthorne's other novels and tales.[16]
In addition to his historical project, then, Hawthorne undertook a
lexicographical one; that is, he attempted to found an American lexicon of symbols and moods. As has been superbly documented in
John Irwin's book on the American hieroglyph, Champollion's decoding of the Rosetta stone and its American impact could well
comprise the historical context for such an enterprise.[17] Hawthorne's lexicon, of course, begins with the letter A, specifically,
the sinfully ornate scarlet letter that survives within an American
cultural repository, the Salem customs house: "a certain affair of
fine red cloth, much worn and faded. There were traces about it
of gold embroidery, which, however, was greatly frayed and de-
faced. It had been wrought, as was easy to perceive, with wonderful
skill of needlework; and the stitch (as I am assured by ladies con-
versant with such mysteries) gives evidence of a now forgotten act."[18]
The narrator's disclaimer regarding his intimacy with such effem-
inate activities as embroidery notwithstanding, the impetus for *The
Scarlet Letter*'s narration consists of a partially eradicated but nonetheless radical trace of writing, whose marginality is linked to a
"certain affair" in the novel. The origin of Hawthorne's moral
melodrama in a love affair and a piece of tracery parallels *The Mar-*

ble Faun's setting off from the *omphalos* of a riddle, concerning Donatello's ears. Yet as uncontainable as the original mark may be, Hawthorne devotes enormous resources to civilizing it. He even goes so far as to build a native American dictionary around the A. This dictionary, with its built-in *grammar* of customs and usages, extends as far as his last novel, *The Marble Faun,* where it confines the characters to rather tight-fitting costumes.

The term that Hawthorne applies to his program of containing his characters in an iterable symbolic system is allegory. And he announces his allegorical design on at least two occasions: when describing the frescoes of the saloon at Monte Beni in Chapter 25, and more importantly, when describing the bracelet that Kenyon gives Hilda as a wedding present, which is the last act of the novel. Because the bracelet had once belonged to Miriam, it symbolizes the passing of the mantle of the European past into American hands. Its own rigorous order intimates that of the novel's characterological and symbolic systems: It "became the connecting bond of a series of seven wondrous tales, all of which, as they were dug out of seven sepulchres, were characterized by a sevenfold sepulchral gloom" (462). As the proof and contract of Hilda's forthcoming marriage to Kenyon, the bracelet weds the system of the novel's characterization to the equally closed and teleologically oriented metaphysics of marriage.

The typecasting of *The Marble Faun,* then, is not merely accidental or even lazily obsessive; it is also a strategic weapon within an arsenal devoted to the grounding of American culture from the bottom up, from the letter A. Within this system, Donatello serves as an ancient-modern, animal-human shifter who opens the space for the novel's coordinative movements. His medium is dance; his natural element is sunshine, hence his own vintage of Sunshine wine; his colors are green and gold; and his origin is the earth, the rustic Tuscan countryside from which he stems. He has two doubles, an inanimate one in the form of Praxiteles's statue and a mythological one in Pan (90). His consort Miriam, on the other hand, has as her double a witch who would be as at home in Salem as in Rome or Munich; among her artistic productions is the painting of a "woman with long dark hair who threw up her arms with a wild gesture of tragic despair, and appeared to beckon him into the darkness along with her" (41). Miriam's medium is original painting; her natural element is shadow; her origins are indeterminate both in nationality and in time, making her a figure for European historicity; she communicates with the supernatural. She bears the burden of an original sin introduced into the narrative as a literal metaphor. "Men have said that this white hand once held a crimson stain," her tormentor reminds her the only time they converse in the novel (97). In the novel's color code, Miriam is associated with red, a color that for Hawthorne combines the allure of sensuality and the perdition of hell.

As an American Lucy Gray or paragon of the Romantic Woman, Hilda will only truck with pure white. She often provides the occasion for the novel's ample supply of allusions to the English Romantics, particularly to Wordsworth, including the narrator's assertion that "all of us, after a long abode in cities," have a need of "rural air" (75). Whereas Miriam is "subject to fits of passionate ill-temper" (35), Hilda is "even like a flower" (55). In a metaphoric sense, Hilda dwells "beside the Dove," for her double consists precisely of the doves whose caretaking comes with her apartment.[19] If Miriam communicates with the underworld, Hilda's residence above the city and its mortality affords her an immediate access to heaven. It is by virtue of her innocence and almost excessive spirituality that "since her arrival in the pictorial land, Hilda seemed to have entirely lost the impulse of original design" (56). A total woman, her relentless and formless empathy qualifies her to be a copyist. "She was endowed with a deep and sensitive faculty of appreciation. . . . She saw, no, not saw, but felt—through and through a picture; she bestowed upon it all the warmth and richness of a woman's sympathy; not by any intellectual effort, but by this strength of heart, and this guiding light of sympathy, she went straight to the central point" (56–57). Although going directly to the central point may get her in more trouble than she has in mind, Hilda does not waste any intellectual energy in the effort. In fact, she does not have any intellect to waste, having been relieved of hers by the narrator's system of stereotypes. If Donatello is a living image, Hilda is the ideal antenna or receiver of images (58–59).

One of the few variations allowed by this rigid machinery of pairs and common denominators consists of the possibilities opened up by a fifth party. If Donatello and Miriam are lovemates united in Manichean opposition, Miriam's true soulmate, with whom she shares elective affinities, is the Model. Like Miriam, the Model belongs to a realm of shadows and communicates with the underworld. His art form is precisely modeling, that is, serving as a representational source rather than being a producer of painted images. As a source of images, the Model usurps the place of God in art: He interposes himself between the artist and the sanctioned nothingness known as divine inspiration or absolute knowledge. His color is black; his mode of existence is persistence; as a usurper, his double is Satan, and he is the only one of the characters condemned to anything more substantial than moral death.

In sharp contradistinction to the Model, Kenyon is an original art producer in the full sense of the term. His "grand, calm head of Milton" was not copied from any one bust or picture and yet is "more authentic than any of them" because of his omniscience re- garding "all-known representations of the poet" (117–18). If not an exact double of God within the novel in the sense that no character could be one, Kenyon is at least a high priest: Marble, according to the narrator, "ensures immortality to whatever is wrought in it. . . . Under this aspect, marble assumes a sacred character; and no man should dare to teach it unless he feels within himself a certain consecration and a priesthood, the only evidence of which, for the public eye, will be the high treatment of heroic subjects, or the delicate evolution of spiritual, though material beauty" (135–36). As a sculptor, Kenyon is thus the pope or at least the American archbishop in an idealistic religion of art. His feet are so much on the ground from which emanates stone, his personality is so marble that he even elicits the narrator's occasional irony, the only char- acter to do so. The only one whose origins, however murky, are not specified, he is a truly self-made American man.

This heavily coded system of characterization comprises a grid for the decoding of actions and symbols. The dramatic characters in the story become symbolic ciphers in a language proper to the novel. Because the novel's facts are organized on a grid, the dra- matic characters are able to fill in missing information about them- selves and each other. Thus the natural antipathy that a character as healthy as Donatello has for the Model telegraphs how loathsome the latter is before we know exactly why. Given Hilda's fully doc- umented profile as a paragon of spirituality and chastity, we are to infer that during her absences nothing in her propriety goes amiss, even though she eventually turns up at carnival time suspiciously dressed in white domino.

Such a schematic deployment of dramatic characters drastically reduces the distance between two senses of the word "characters": as human surrogates and as ideograms or talismans. The novel's great images are as dramatic as its characters; conversely, these symbols are every bit as typecast and encoded. Our previous discussion of the novel's historical framework suggests what the co-ordinates of the internal symbolistic index might be. Virtually all of the novel's memorable images are described in terms of their temporal conditions, the state of hovering, or both. There are many passages in the novel of striking poetic power and complexity, yet even the most forceful descriptions, whether of Rome or the Cap-uchin burial ground, demand decipherment in terms of these codes. If sunshine and snowflakes exist at an extreme of immanence and temporal immediacy in the novel, the permanent sublimation ef-fected by statuary and marble is its diametrical opposite. Virtually all of the novel's other recurrent images are to be situated between these extremes. Gardens, whether the Borghese or Medici, and the fountains they contain, regard the temporal synthesis between pro-cess and permanence from the perspective of change. Rome, as a decaying labyrinth and historical palimpsest, and the figures of sar-cophagi and graves, while tolerating a measure of activity, are closer to the repose achieved by marble. The artifacts at both ends of the continuum belong to the infinite cycle of nature and art, in which nature ultimately recuperates the artifice extracted from it. The in-finity that Hawthorne ascribes to these stately cycles is a stock-in-trade of Hegelian dialectics, where the diametrical opposites, when they can no longer stimulate linear growth from each other, begin to revolve around each other in infinite cycles.[20] "The shifting, in-destructible, ever new, yet unchanging, up-gush and downfall of water" (143) in a Roman fountain are thus merely the *liquid* version of a temporal paradox that assumes both more solid and more ethe-real forms. And of all the examples of change that we might se-lect—whether of the "frail, yet enduring and fadeless pictures" cast by stained-glass windows (304) or of the Roman cathedral to which Hilda, in the wake of the murder, retires, where worshipers "in the hottest fever-fit of life . . . can always find, ready for their need, a cool, quiet, beautiful place of worship" (355)—of all the novel's many temporal oxymorons, none is as shining as the Capuchin burial ground: "But, as the cemetery is small, and it is a precious privilege to sleep in holy ground, the brotherhood are immemorially accustomed . . . to take the longest-buried skeleton out of the oldest grave, and lay the new slumberer there instead. Thus, each of the good friars, in his turn, enjoys the luxury of a consecrated bed, attended with the slight drawback of being forced to get up long before day-break, as it were, and make room for another lodger" (192–93). Despite the passage's image of mortuary substitution and a funereal residue or palimpsest, it belongs to a controlled economy in which the temporalities of randomness and evolution are coordinated.

Riddles, Mysteries, Secrets, the Farce

Our appreciation of the overdetermination and coordination in the novel's historical framework and its systems of characterization and symbolism now places us in a position to return to our initial, possibly central question: For all its rhetorics of indeterminacy and epistemological limit, is the novel a post-structuralist classic whose historical home base in the nineteenth century is merely a fictive illusion, an indiscretion to be glossed over? Or is it possible that the novel's blatant cloudy spots do not *oppose* the highly manipulated temporal and semiological systems we have explored but rather *belong* to these almost clumsily managed economies? If so, we would have to *untrack* the novel *elsewhere* than in its publicly announced blind spots. In other words, the novel's blind alleys, appearing on the literal level in the labyrinthine Rome that anticipates Jorge Luis Borges's landscapes,[21] are detours that act as a *screen*[22] to divert our reading from touchier points. To deconstruct the novel we would have to *resist* following the leads that it provides and find an entrance less to its liking.

The Marble Faun is thus a text that attempts to mislead its readers by opening the *wrong* facade to critical penetration. While undertaking a historical program that could only be regarded as irreproachable by its audience, the novel nonetheless resists the honorable task that it proclaims and so laboriously fulfills. The playful gestures by which Hawthorne *retracts* the arrangements that he organizes place the contemporary reader in a double bind that may well be the ultimate extension of the question concerning Donatello's ears. We can, on the one hand, point to evidence that the novel's assertions of indeterminacy belong to Romantic conventions of irony, reflection, and infinity—and argue that the novel conforms to its generic and historical specifications: It is a Romantic text that, because of transoceanic time lag, was composed in 1860 instead of 1810. Our contemporary ability to reconstruct an epoch in terms of its epistemological and metaphysical limits would thus open the door to a revised notion of literary history, one in which even violent textual manifestations can be placed, if not dated.

Yet in addition to this historical response, the novel's double signals afford us at least one other out. If the novel's *stated* indeterminacies do not finally unhinge it, there may be other indiscretions that do, of the sort that beg to be glossed over. The novel's misogyny, the structurally superfluous but persistent allure of a feminine sexuality *everywhere* in Rome and the narrative, would be one instance of a given that it takes for granted but upon which it founders. In addition to the traces of a persistent femininity that the novel cannot assimilate and that it greets only in a confusion of embarrassment and revulsion, it makes mistakes in terms of its own characterological system; it breaks its own codes. Of many such instances, a striking one is when Miriam, in shadowing Kenyon and Donatello in their travels, steps into the shoes of her tormentor. Also in this vein, certain key symbols entertain variant meanings. Joyous sunshine appears once as deception (152), and at the end of the novel the previously pristine marble becomes a medium of death (377, 390–91). Yet even the novel's exceptions marshal an appeal to the system that initiated the symbolic division of labor. If there is something to the novel's riddles, to the sleight of hand that the narrative underscores as it disclaims any knowledge of Donatello's ears or Hilda's whereabouts, this something consists of the schizophrenic bind in which the text still places the reader. *The Marble Faun* is a novel that is Romantic for all the reasons it would presume to be modern; yet it lends itself to our contemporary critical practices precisely where it is Romantic. It is this anomaly that makes the novel compelling today, for all the positivity of its program and the tedium of its execution.

The remaining goal in this survey of the novel, then, is to suggest some of the book's fake transgressions and their sources and to indicate what some of the camouflaged entries into its systems might be. It could well be argued that the novel's most aggressive profession of its radicality consists of the secrets to which it is privy but which it withholds from the readership. From the novel's ur-scene in the museum to its retrospectively annexed conclusion, the narrative transpires between riddles. The novel opens and closes with the tantalizing ambiguity concerning Donatello's ears. This riddle, which conceals something in the act of indication and innuendo, is the model for the novel's other acts of striptease. Why does Hilda have to deliver a package for Miriam to one Luca Barboni at the Palazzo Cenci? Where does Hilda disappear to? The novel's secrets impose a double loyalty on the characters. Sometimes they are in the know and collaborate with the narrator, as when in the conclusion Hilda dangles before the reader an answer as to her whereabouts. Donatello's ears connote a matter of knowledge the narrator withholds from all, except Donatello, of course. In the novel's professed and dramatized secrecy, it enters the split epistemological field of Romantic irony that extends from Hegel's multiple perspectives of *in itself, for itself,* and *for us,* to Kierkegaard's fictive surrogates.[23]

But secrets assert far more than ambiguity and imponderability. As Neil Hertz observed in his illuminating analysis of Freud's *Case of Hysteria* (1907),[24] secrets, on both sides of their striptease, their provocation, and their masking, act out a hysterical assertion of authority on the part of the bearer of knowledge. And indeed, it is precisely in some of the novel's most congenial passages, those bestowing their fullest blessing on current critical conventions, that narrative control most blankly asserts its authority:

> In weaving these mystic utterances into a continuous scene, we undertake a task resembling, in its perplexity, that of gathering up and piecing together the fragments of a letter, which has been torn and scattered to the winds. Many words of deep significance—many entire sentences, and those possibly the most important ones—have flown too far, on the winged breeze, to be recovered. If we insert our own conjectural

amendments, we perhaps give a purport utterly at variance with the true
one. Yet, unless we attempt something in this way, there must remain
an unsightly gap, and a lack of continuousness and dependence in our
narrative. (92–93)

This is merely one of several interjections by the narrator that present the highest level of diacritical awareness encompassed by the
text. The concerns with textuality, fragmentariness, and absence introduced thematically in this passage make it and the novel irreproachable. The passage returns to the frayed letter, which is the
archetrace of yet another founding novel; it describes the narrative
as woven; it acknowledges losses in its continuity that imply the
impossibility of any totalization in representation. Yet this passage,
which is so straightforward, almost noble, in its acknowledgment
of representational limits, also betrays the dependence that it fos-
ters. And this betrayal takes the form of a disclaimer: In *eschewing*
gaps, lacks, and narrative dependence, the text intimates the pattern
of manipulation that it establishes. Ostensibly undermining the forms
of narrative authority that it disavows, the text demands the reader's
dependence and asserts its own authority—its power to disseminate,
withhold, and doctor evidence. Rather than deny the structure of
authority, this passage disqualifies competitive and ostensibly other
varieties of authority in reserving its own. Behind this ironic, wink-
ing voice, then, are the assertions of its own indispensability, inviting the reader into complicity with its authority. For the reader
to laugh with this narrative voice at its jokes of impenetrability is
for him or her to participate in a masochistic punishment. It is for
this reason that the novel labors so tediously and unsuccessfully in
the direction of good jokes.

Closely related to such disclaimers of coherence and totality, which
emanate from the voice of the narrator, are the novel's settings of
farce, frivolity, and abandon. To Søren Kierkegaard, the farce, whose
ancient ancestor was Aristophanes's *Clouds,* was the privileged vehicle for irony.[25] The farce unveiled in Kierkegaard's brief tract
Repetition demolishes the orders into which it collides. It robs the
proscenium arch of its effectiveness as a theatrical and epistemological divider; it briefly revolutionizes the social order by teles-
coping the classes together; it incorporates both stupidity and randomness into theatrical design, disqualifying the generic profiles of

aesthetics.[26] So too did Hawthorne hope, in composing romances, confections neither too frivolous nor nihilistic, to synthesize an aesthetic hybrid, if you will, a generic New World. But whereas the farce at the center of *Repetition* detonates tensions within a paradoxical, double inquiry into the structures of displacement, desire, and objectivity, the farce of *The Marble Faun* acts out a violence that the novel's temporal and symbolic systems never entertain. Whereas Kierkegaard's farce is the aesthetic correlative to an aphoristic utterance that resonates in discontinuity, that abandons any argumentative line or ulterior design in building a cloud chamber of incongruous assertions, the pandemonium of *The Marble Faun* is ultimately held in check for illustrative purposes. The "riotous interchange" of the carnival where Kenyon goes to find Hilda is described in terms that associate the scene with the apocalyptic paintings of Brueghel and Bosch. "A biped, with an ass's snout, brayed close to his ear, ending his discordant uproar with a peal of human laughter. Five strapping damsels (so, at least, their petticoats bespoke them, in spite of an awful freedom in the flourish of their legs) joined hands, and danced around him, inviting him, by their gestures, to perform a horn-pipe in the midst. Released from these gay persecutors, a clown in motley rapped him on the back with a blown bladder" (445). It is this world of anomie, transvestitism, and excess, replete with Flemish hybrids and bladders, that the exemplary American must negotiate before he can claim his mistress; it is a scene reminiscent of the horrifying *rite de passage* depicted in the film *Zulu*. Yet just as Brueghel's and Bosch's apocalyptic panels depend on the evolutionary and teleological schemes that they violate with such a flourish, the revelry in this novel does not go to waste; it serves a higher purpose. Even during the novel's pandemonium, its violence is allegorical in a naive sense, belonging to well-established patterns of representation. The Titaness who makes an untoward display of sexual aggression to Kenyon in this scene, shooting a popgun at him in revenge for his indifference, is like Miriam a foil to Hilda's acceptable submission (445–46). The mock coroner's inquest that Kenyon observes after this assault suggests an anxious, even morbid uncertainty on his part just at the moment when his private portion of the eternal-feminine[27] is to be revealed and his separation ended. The historical utility of the novel's slapstick and farce is only confirmed by the ease with which Kenyon can repress such disturbing manifestations: "Fortunately, the hu-mours of the Carnival pass from one absurdity to another. . . . In a few moments, they vanished from him, as dreams and spectres do, leaving him at liberty to pursue his quest" (446–47). This spec-ulative quest for a woman who is a revelation, a fate, and a destiny is undertaken to appeal to the American public as much as to satisfy Kenyon's drives. The allegorical uses of the carnival violence root this historical, metaphysical, and sexual *Wanderlust* in a closed rep-resentational system.

If the novel's secrets and farce ultimately succumb to its ge-nealogical imperatives, so too does its elaborately dramatized fas-cination with the image. We have already observed how both Hilda and Miriam share the imagistic qualities attributed to women by Romantic writers as diverse as Hegel, Goethe, and Wordsworth. Yet the narrative's imagistic concern extends to an entire rhetoric of observation, indication, and setting. Hawthorne invests both the frames around aesthetic objects and the sites of scenes with consid-erable reverence. Whether paintings, statues, or scenes, the images in Hawthorne's text increase in sacredness when they are arranged in sequence in the halls of a museum or by a roadside. The primary rite in Hawthorne's art-religion for an emerging American *cultus* consists of pilgrimages, several of which take place in the novel, through stages or stations of the image. In his program for American letters, Hawthorne would convert the European museum into a sec-ular cathedral. It is in accordance with this quasitheological ima-gistic reverence that Hawthorne begins the novel in a museum, that he applies the formulation "Scenes by the Way" as a rubric for Kenyon and Donatello's peregrinations, and that concurrent with these wanderings Hilda experiences "The Emptiness of Picture Gal-leries." It is under the influence of the aesthetics of the image that moments such as Donatello's dance and the ramble of the aesthetic émigrés are set in such tightly constructed and closed scenes. In his reverence for images, Hawthorne accords them enormous power. The eloquence of the narrative's key descriptions, such as of Roman ruins or the Capuchin cemetery, constitutes Hawthorne's effort to harness this divine, yet somewhat uncanny power. The hope that the narrative founds in scenes and images is no less than messianic. The title of Chapter 33, "Pictured Windows," describes both the glasswork of the Gothic cathedral and Hawthorne's fictive program, in which the image is the source of energy and illumination. Not only does the statue that Kenyon unearths in the campagna mediate and represent the ideal, it is a talisman for the magic hopes that the novel invests in the Romantic tradition of the image: "How happened it to be lying there, beside its grave of twenty centuries? Why were not tidings of its discovery already noised abroad? The world was richer than yesterday, by something far more precious than gold. Forgotten beauty had come back, as beautiful as ever; a goddess had risen from her long slumber, and was a goddess still" (424).

The only apotheosis that Miriam and Donatello are permitted as they prepare to repay society for their crimes is their transformation into an image. "He still held Miriam's hand; and there they stood, the beautiful man, the beautiful woman, united forever, as they felt, in the presence of these and eye-witnesses, who gazed so curiously at the unintelligible scene" (323). Thus images both inhabit the privileged space of a mandala and constitute the possibility of redemption and salvation.

But for all the sacredness in which the novel's images are sheathed, it remains an open question whether they ever gather the energy to break the centripetal force exerted by the novel's representational system. The images of this narrative share the fate of its pandemonium. Their potential autonomy and self-referentiality is proferred and then retracted by an allegorical system that simply will not relax in its assimilative compulsion. Hawthorne's images are toilet-trained spots of time, engendered by the same speculative system but abortive in the pursuit of their own fragmentation. Thus the mock autopsy at the carnival must immediately be applied to Kenyon's interpretative quandary, and the "figure in a white robe" is not allowed to walk alone. "Such odd, questionable shapes are often seen gliding through the streets of Italian cities" (392). Yet no sooner is this apparition mentioned than its glide comes to a halt, for while the narrator concludes that the figure is a mystery, he fills in its possible significations, all related to the expiation of guilt.

In its appeals to secret knowledge, image, farce, and narrative unreliability, the novel lifts the curtain on a theoretical New World, but like Dr. Strangelove, it cannot restrain its gestures of a far more questionable loyalty to its native land of Romantic conventions. The novel *claims* a certain indigenous American radicality, but it *betrays* its subservience to and replication of fixed systems of sexual identification, historical determinism, and symbolic equivalence, all varieties of the metaphysics of representation. This work thus opens the space for, initiates, a tradition which continues today and under which we all still labor. On the one hand, there is a freedom of expression in American culture that encourages the shock values of yesterday and today, from Gothic horror to the very literal representations of violence and sexual activity in television and film. On the other hand, coinciding with, perhaps underlying, this literal freedom is a suspicion toward language that corresponds to the closed economies, the enforcers of restraint, in the novel. The marginal placement of the university and the cartoon vision of intellectuals throughout the history of the American cinema and electronic media are manifestations of this suspicion. A recent American cinematic fad, a series of films in which a violence of unprecedented literality is acted out against liberated or sexually aggressive women, is illustrative of *The Marble Faun*'s double bind. These films achieve new heights of shock and explicitness, yet underlying them are very old, even classical fears and inhibitions. Miriam is an ancestor of the horny housewife in *Dressed to Kill* and the teacher in *Looking for Mr. Goodbar*. Even more fundamental than the fear of the aggressive woman is the suspicion of the linguistic capabilities that she contains. When Kenyon and Hilda trivialize and revise their aesthetic commitments, they consummate a program in which Hawthorne's fiction will permanently wean the American public from its interest in aesthetic and linguistic ambiguity.

In writing of the closure and obsolescence of a Romantic text, I myself have violated certain conventions. The basic values of entertainment and critical showmanship compel me to write alluringly of an ambiguous text to the triple credit of the text, the theoretical attitudes I bring to bear on it, and myself. Yet my own previous attempts to analyze this novel vacillated in the interstice between the text's counterimperatives: to regard it either as uncannily contemporary or as deceptively radical. The "radical" casting of this work convinced me that I was merely paraphrasing or updating Romantic conventions in textual terms, that I was creating, in effect, a "new, improved" *Marble Faun*. So unsatisfactory was this alternative that I acquiesced to another that was not without its own limits. In writing of a Romantic work from the perspective of its closed subsystems, I was opening the door for a literary-historical division of labor in terms of ages, sequences, and developments. I hoped that it would be possible to distinguish placing the work in its conceptual and metaphysical age from merely *dating* it in any simplistic sense. For these reasons I wrote about *The Marble Faun* as a Romantic text in the light of its Romantic conventions. The experience has certainly been romantic.

3

The Deconstructor and the Politician: Melville's The Confidence-Man

1.

Given the intensity with which signs, pronouncements, and arguments are questioned in *The Confidence-Man*,[1] the titles of its chapters are to be commended for honesty in advertising. The title of the first chapter, for example, describes exactly what takes place within it, "A mute goes aboard a boat." Wearing the cream-colors of neutrality, a man, whose fleecy hat suggests the fleecing activity of skulduggery, steps aboard a Mississippi riverboat on an unspecified April Fools' day. This character, whose voicelessness makes him a writer by necessity, instigates a crisis in interpretation that will preoccupy the entire novel: He merely inscribes one line on a blackboard. At first glance this pronouncement is of "an aspect so singularly innocent" (7) as his own. It possesses the form of an equation, the certainty of a truism, and the stability of an eternal truth: "Charity thinketh no evil." In the random inscription of this pronouncement—and in the ensuing public controversy that compels the mute to list further predications regarding charity—the text provides us with the germ of a scenario that will, like the word "charity," remain constant despite whatever revisions it undergoes. And in this scenario pronouncements—often as unimpeachable as the mute's—are made before a public that must interpret them. *Must* interpret them because these statements, despite the negative form in which the novel's first example is disguised, implicitly harbor an imperative, a call to action. As a legion of later fraud-episodes will attest, the pronouncement, "Charity thinketh no evil," implies, "contribute to the charities that approach you for a donation." It is fitting that the mute's first inscription alone should be able to trigger a minor public disturbance because the wider issue at stake, one continuing throughout the novel, is the status of public or political language. Pronouncements of the same formulaic and moralistic sort will emanate from a variety of characters who exhort their auditors to consummate actions, usually on philanthropic or humanitarian grounds. The auditors who are the targets of the words may be convinced, or as the complexity of the confrontations increases, they may offer resistance. Even in the novel's first pages, the sides of the conflict ensuing from public pronouncements are delineated. There is the exhortation to action, which is often disguised in the most neutral predications, and there is the refusal to act. There is the appeal for belief, the naive reading, the taking of the word at its word, and there is the cynical repudiation of the claims at the basis of the appeal. The continuous sequence of operators in the novel will be accompanied by a less populous but no less adamant string of cynics. However the novel embellishes its dramatic situations and allows its thematic interests to wander, underlying the involutions are always an attempt to persuade and a testing of the interstice between language and action.

In the first and paradigmatic situation of the mute, public resistance induces him to make a series of amendments to the initial pronouncement. Charity "suffereth long and is kind," "endureth all things," "believeth all things," and "never faileth" (7). Paradoxically, as emended or changed, charity is always all-encompassing and enduring. An ideal, charity manifests the universality and eternity of the ideal. Paradoxically again, the invoker of the ideal is the one who relativizes it, who fills in new substitutions on the blackboard of substitution, and who is aware of the fluctuations on the stock exchange of language. Indeed, all of the operators who follow in the mute's path occupy a similarly anomalous position. Deploying the duplicitous and fictive potentials of language, they are the most authoritarian enforcers of the ideals orienting the social and intellectual orders of society. The characters who possess fictive or critical competence disclaim it and in fact proclaim it in others to constitute a public menace. The most dogmatic promoters of order and authority are those who exercise critical skills yet who publicly renounce them. *The Confidence-Man* is an extended meditation on the relationship between the language of politics, which culminates in action and is therefore fundamentally reductive, and the language of criticism, whose alternation between the perspectives of idealization and penetration is endless.

The Confidence-Man is systematic in the way the encyclopedic novels most indebted to Hegel's *Phenomenology* are. Not only is it oriented to the ideal—to its emptiness as well as its imperatives— but the operators who emerge and vanish in the wake of the mute represent the vital subsystems making up the social order: commerce, medicine, philanthropy, theology, and higher education. Not only does the novel incorporate a social microcosm, but it dramatizes the functioning of a philosophical system. When the numerous discrete encounters of the first half of the novel give way, in the second half, to the less successful but far more speculative fraud-attempts of a character known as the "cosmopolitan," the universal man, the novel in effect sublates itself to a higher level of generality. Yet this novel, which is so striking in its capacity to encompass both referentially and conceptually, is punctuated throughout by wild misusages and a language play that points to the insubstantiality of systems, to the groundlessness in reaction to which systems are a cosmetic effort at containment.

The internal organization of the boat that is the setting for the novel's attempts at persuasion is that of a writing desk: "Fine promenades, domed saloons, long galleries, sunny balconies, confidential passages, bridal chambers, staterooms plenty as pigeon-holes, and out-of-the-way retreats like secret drawers in an escritoire. . . ." A floating writing machine whose intricately organized spaces encompass activities ranging from the most innocent to the most suspicious moves down a river that grows in the absorption of its tributaries. The activity of the voyage itself is defined by assimilation and exchange:

> Though her voyage of twelve hundred miles extends from apple to orange, from clime to clime, yet, like any small ferryboat, to right and left, at every landing, the huge Fidèle still receives additional passengers in exchange for those that disembark; so that, although always full

of strangers, she continually, in some degree, adds to, or replaces them
with strangers still more strange . . . . (12)

It is appropriate that the movements of an enterprise largely consisting in the effacement of the ideal should be able to unite widely
divergent climates and geographical regions. The business of persuasion is no place for fine distinctions. For this reason, within the
novel's symbolism, polar opposites merge. East can be superimposed on West, and the difference between black and white is by
no means obvious.[2]

Just as the river expands by absorption, the boat receives an endless flow of persons increasing only in their strangeness, their being
alien from each other in the sense of the French *étranger*. A catalogue of the different types of strangers fills out the second chapter.
But more important than their variety is the fact that the voyage,
the river, and the exchange of passengers all proceed by a movement of assimilation. On the most literal level, this is the historical
assimilation of the American population. If Melville introduces the
confidence game by associating it with a kind of interchangeability
in language enabling its chalked-in ideal to be modified by a multiplicity of predicates, he devotes the second chapter to establishing
the capacity of the game to be all-encompassing, to assimilate
everything. Just as the boat traffics in "a piebald parliament, an
Anacharsis Cloots congress of all kinds of that multiform pilgrim
species, man" (14), the confidence game will absorb every type of
individual, both as operators and targets. It will appeal to dowager
widows, college students, and coonskin adventurers. It will employ
smooth business types and wretched juveniles.

The name of the boat is *Fidèle*, and while the craft may wander,
it is forever oriented to the *fides* that is both the North Star and
center of *confidence*. The array of operators will invoke an equally
variegated assortment of ideals in exhorting to action. There will be
rough correspondence between the nature of the pitch and the ideal
invoked. The herb-doctor, for example, who peddles homeopathic
remedies for all ailments, will extol the virtues of nature, while the
"man in a tasseled travelling-cap," an agent of the Black Rapids
Coal Company, will stress the need for business confidence. But
the meta-ideal of the novel, the ideal that directs the targets' response to all other appeals, is confidence itself. The slave trader

whose profession is described as "philosophical intelligence" places confidence in its widest context: "Confidence is the indispensable basis of all sorts of business transactions. Without it, commerce between man and man, as between country and country, would, like a watch, run down and stop" (178). If a target *confides* (verb: intransitive), he will do whatever he has been exhorted to do, whether to contribute to a charity, buy a stock or medicine, or make a personal gift. By invoking confidence as the indispensable basis for social order, the operators, who all descend from that writing specialist, the mute, shame their auditors toward a moment of dull, nonresilient collision with their directives. Down the all-encompassing Mississippi floats a boat on which numerous writers attempt to influence the public with their texts. The stylized interaction between writers and readers becomes a game that in turn encompasses not only all players but all terms deployed in the interchanges. The term common to all rounds of this game, the meta-ideal of confidence or literal acceptance of the word, encompasses all other ideal structures both invoked and emptied by the fiction-makers in the novel. "Here reigned the dashing and all-fusing spirit of the West, whose type is the Mississippi itself, which, uniting the streams of the most distant and opposite zones, pours them along, helter-skelter, in one cosmopolitan and confident tide" (14).

2.

The present reading of *The Confidence-Man* assumes in large part the structural scheme clarified by H. Bruce Franklin in his edition of the novel. According to this scheme, the novel is divided into two halves—the daytime and night of the unspecified April Fools' day on which the action takes place.[3] The text consists of forty-five chapters. Twilight occurs at the beginning of Chapter 23.

The Confidence Man thus joins that significant body of literature in which the text releases the negative potential of its irony against itself. As in *Faust* and *Ulysses*, the nighttime of the work's temporal setting is the night for the determinations crystallized earlier, under conditions of ostensibly greater lucidity. An obscuring and ultimate violation, in the second half, of the patterns at times arbitrarily and mechanistically laid down in the first becomes the culmination of the novel's irony as it sets into play the self-deconstructive potential of language. For the moment, however, we are concerned with delineating the mechanisms crystallized in the first half of the novel, knowing that they will be exploded. For it is precisely such willful patterns that comprise the rules of the confidence game in general and provide for the variants manufactured by such a matrix.

Judging from the mute's entrance onto the stage of action, it is not difficult to understand why, two chapters later, Black Guinea's appeal for alms should find both its sympathizers and its skeptics. Numbered among the former are two clergymen and a country merchant, who is soon to become the novel's first major dupe. What is most important about the doubts concerning Black Guinea's authenticity is not merely that they are expressed—but that they initiate a search for references.

"But is there not some one who can speak a good word for you?" asks an Episcopal clergyman (19). Black Guinea can indeed furnish a list of references, one broad enough to encompass virtually all the operators in the novel and then some. And three chapters later, when the Episcopalian succeeds in finding one of the characters that Black Guinea mentioned, "a gem'man in a gray coat and white tie" (43), this character not only confirms but also bemoans Black Guinea's destitution. This is merely the first of many instances in the novel when the operators assist each other by confirming each other's claims. This happens either retrospectively, as in the case just mentioned,[4] or prospectively, as when the agent of the Black Rapids Coal Company, approaching a sick old miser, wishes that the herb-doctor were there (101).[5] (The herb-doctor later appears and exhausts the miser into buying his Omni-Balsamic Reinvigorator.) Like the uncannily repetitive *dramatis personae* that populate contemporary American television commercials, the operators collectively contribute to a mutually confirming fictive utopia.[6] The operators are interreferential. Suspicions aroused by one operator can be displaced along a chain of reference until they can be "corrected" by someone appearing more solid. The interpretative crisis initiated by an operator's claims can itself be displaced elsewhere in the same network until the hermeneutic energy is dissipated in the public consideration of some tangential issue or anecdote. Thus, a target known as the "good merchant" opens for general discussion a sob-story about an early operator, the "man with the weed," whose tale he had heard in passing from yet another operator, the "gem'man in a gray coat and white tie." The story relates how that first unfortunate's bizarre and dirt-eating wife, Goneril, unjustly turned the law against him and initiated his wanderings along the Mississippi. The filial ingratitude of *King Lear*, from which Goneril derives her improbable name, is transmuted into a marital infidelity assuming the form of both the "mysterious touches" (85) that she gives other men and the legal machinations by which she usurps custody of the couple's children. By engaging the good merchant in a critical evaluation of Goneril's story, yet a final operator, the "man in a travelling cap," is able to divert the good merchant's suspicions regarding *his* intentions. The tangential narrative of Goneril thus connects three operators by bonds of mutual substantiation and also dissipates suspicion along a potentially endless interpretative regress. In their interreferentiality the confidence-men cooperatively fabricate a self-enclosed fictive domain, a utopian *world apart* oriented to the meta-ideal of confidence. The transtemporal quality of the references provides for the endurance of the game. The game has a momentum, a mechanism of its own that is independent of particular participants, themes, or results.

In the first half of the novel the fraud-episodes follow upon each other with the rapidity of slapstick gags. Out of Black Guinea's catalogue of references emerge five operators who fill out the daytime of the novel, occupying the stage for differing lengths of time. Each of these characters bears a unique "trademark," represents an interest, chooses corresponding metaphors and themes for his discourse, and deploys characteristic ploys or gimmicks. The movement that may be extrapolated from the repetitive structure of the fraud-episodes and from the interreferentiality of operators is that of a machine—a language machine dovetailing with a capital machine. It is a language machine because the raw material of the fabrication process is words, more specifically rhetoric. It is a capital machine because it is powered by the constant thrust of the interchanges toward a one-sided exchange of money or its equivalent. As the worldwide vision of the charity business conjured by the "gem'man in a gray coat and white tie" makes clear, the capital machine assembled by the novel proceeds by a logic of endless accumulation. The interreferentiality of the operators in the first half of the novel makes the machine, whose input is words, whose product is money, one with interchangeable parts—a creation of the assembly line and the age of mechanical reproduction.[7] It is not accidental, then, that the Missouri bachelor who deflates the herb-doctor's claims for nature before he succumbs to the analogies of the philosophical intelligence officer—and buys slaves—is a technocrat. "Machines for me," he declares (160).

In the sense that the novel consists of a chain of fraud-episodes, it may be described as a sequence of Wittgensteinian language games.[8] While always reducible to the predatory pursuit of a target by an operator, the fraud-episodes in the first half of the novel vary in their complexity, the degree of their resolution, and above all in the massive battery of ploys available to the community of operators. At their most basic and mechanical, the fraud-episodes are hit-and-run affairs in which the targets are simply bowled over by the operators. The first time we meet the college student, he is reduced to speechlessness by the deluge of verbiage unleashed at him by the "man with the weed." The demand to "drop Tacitus," both the book he is reading and his silence, only renders the collegian more helpless. The operator's exhortation to replace Tacitus with Akenside is a demand to suppress the historical consciousness exemplified by the *Annals* and to cover it over with the circumlocutory exaltation in humanitarian ideals that fills *The Pleasures of Imagination*. The "man with the weed" thus weaves into his appeal a typical American antihistoricism, the belief in an ongoing state of newness that need not be fettered by precedent.[9] If history cannot be renovated to fit the times, it is best ignored.

Such stripped-down episodes as this one may be complicated by a variety of factors. Debunkers, for example, compound the logical structure of the episodes. Although a debunker may impede an operator's delivery, establishing the veracity of the debunker becomes as serious an interpretative problem as ascertaining the operator's claim. A model debunker in the first half of the novel is the "soldier of fortune" who comes face to face with the herb-doctor. The autobiographical narrative provided by this cripple, one Thomas Fry, is in direct antithesis to the unmitigated optimism displayed by the herb-doctor, who professes "confidence in everybody" and designates himself "the Happy Man—the Happy Bone-setter" (131). The story, like the Goneril episode, demonstrates that laws are not necessarily tantamount to justice. Fry's downfall begins when as a cooper he testifies against a gentleman who murdered a pavior in a street fight. Naturally it is Fry who, as a consequence of his lower class, is "fried" by the judicial system. He ends up in prison while the gentleman goes free. His crime: "While I hadn't got any friends, I tell ye. A worse crime than murder, as ye'll see afore long" (133). Although friendship here has the connotation of crude influence and connections, it will be elevated in the second half of the novel into a fundament of the ideology of confidence.

Thomas Fry's travails go only from bad to worse. His experience is a living example of the hollowness not only of the herb-doctor's discourse but of all of the ideals invoked thus far by the operators. Friendship is not love of one's fellow human beings but influence. Justice is defined by class distinctions. The herb-doctor's response to the tale is characteristic: "I cannot believe it" (135)—a profession of total ignorance of those chinks in the ideal that are the very mortar of language and rhetoric.

But the story's final turn, itself a debunking of several varieties of the ideal, is yet to come. Thomas Fry, the cynical penetrator of the optimism claimed to be indispensable to the social order is himself an operator, a minor one, but one who reaps a "pretty good harvest" (136). In the encompassing operation of confidence, the debunkers who arise to battle the operators' claims turn out to be fellow operators, just as the most duplicitous discoursers profess the most extreme sort of prudery. The confidence game not only extends itself temporally in the interreferentiality of the operators: Within a given episode its roles are interchangeable.[10] With great fluidity its characters change—or are engineered into changing—their roles. Bystanders can be appropriated by the operators as model dupes. Valiant debunkers can become fellow operators or dupes. And the operators can be the most implausible pollyannas. Thus the Methodist minister, one of the clergymen who supports Black Guinea—and we will never know his "true" allegiance—assumes the characteristic pose of the operators. First he shames, then he forces the cynical customs house official into charity (20–21). Such relative, situational roles are fully in keeping with a confidence operation passing with facility from one theme and social context to the next.

There is no fuller measure of the variety afforded by the operational matrix delineated in the first half of the novel than the array of ploys at the operators' disposal. These range from the bluntest acts of appeal and shaming[11] to highly intricate performances. More conventional ploys include the following: renouncing payment for wares[12]; serving as a model of charitable acts by conspicuously giving donations to fellow operators[13]; and the operators' casting aspersions on their own enterprises and "relenting" as the targets refuse to entertain such doubts.[14] Faced with the failure of their ploys, the operators prove skillful at sloughing off their own errors and resilient to resistance. The herb-doctor turns an expectation that slips out—that he does not expect the old miser to whom he has just sold medicine to live long—into a warning that the compound will be difficult to find elsewhere (114). Felled by the "sudden side-blow" of the Missouri bachelor, the same operator "recovers" himself with hardly an interruption (122). In so doing he literally demonstrates the capacity of an ideology in which differences are blurred to right or reorient itself in spite of whatever criteria of consistency are applied to it.

The culmination of the operators' nerve in the first half of the novel, the ploy of ploys, occurs when the herb-doctor, encountering resistance from the Missouri bachelor, accuses his debunker of precisely the sort of language play that has characterized the discourse of all operators. "Yes," says the herb-doctor, "I think I understand you now, sir. How silly I was to have taken you seriously, in your droll conceits, too, about having no confidence in nature. In reality you have just as much as I have" (148). In the same gesture in which the herb-doctor professes his naive veneration for nature, he projects his own drollery onto his interlocutor, the Missouri bachelor, whose literality is symbolized by his name: "My name is Pitch; I stick to what I say" (162).

The first half of the novel, in the rapid pace of its episodes, in the division of labor that makes its operators representatives of specialized interests, and in the compartmentalization of themes by operator, invites comparison and the type of structural analysis generated by such comparisons. After Black Guinea we meet, in order, the "man with the weed," the "gem'man in a gray coat and white tie," who represents the Seminole Widow and Orphan Asylum, the "man in a tasseled travelling-cap," an agent of the Black Rapids Coal Company, the herb-doctor, and the philosophical intelligence officer, who sells slaves. Although the highest interest represented by the "man with the weed" is his own desire for money, his anti-historicism and antiintellectualism will be the basis for the claims made by all subsequent operators. The "gem'man in a gray coat and white tie" represents "the charity business . . . in all its branches" (54). Advancing his philanthropic ideal with the rhetoric of evangelism, he envisions a worldwide welfare institution that enriches itself from a universal tithe. What philanthropy is to this cosmic fundraiser, business confidence is to the agent of the Black Rapids Coal Company, who rails against the "destroyers of confidence and gloomy philosophers of the stock market" (68):

> Why, the most monstrous of all hypocrites are these bears: hypocrites by inversion; hypocrites in the simulation of things dark instead of bright; souls that thrive, less upon depression, than the fiction of depression; professors of the wicked art of manufacturing depressions; spurious Jeremiahs; sham Heraclituses, who, the lugubrious day done, return, like sham Lazaruses among the beggars, to make merry over the gains got by their pretended sore heads—scoundrelly bears!

Bullish on America, this character senses that the diametrical opposite of the ideology of confidence, with its duplicitous profession of well-being, is financial depression, or translated into another context, *hypochondriasis*, the claim of nonexistent damage. Hypochondriacs, such as the "spurious Jeremiahs" of the above passage or the dusk giant (119, 122), one of the novel's most outspoken debunkers, intuit harm precisely where an operator sees a panacea. And for the herb-doctor, confidence in nature is the panacea for all earthly woes. "Trust me, nature is health; for health is good, and nature cannot work ill. As little can she work error. Get nature, and you get well" (112). It is the herb-doctor, with his appropriation and disfiguration of Wordsworth ("Nature delights in benefiting those who most abuse her" [151]), who most fully demonstrates the natural affinity of the ideology of confidence for the Romantic code.[15]

Although less specific than the cure-alls peddled by the other operators, the ideal advanced by the philosophical intelligence officer is of the widest philosophical scope. His "doctrine of analogies"—sometimes invoked, sometimes retracted in guaranteeing the quality of the slaves that he sells—is no less than a model of representational thought; it finds its practical application in the slave market and in the trader's need to claim that a child's present physical attributes necessitate his future superiority as a slave. Such a claim must be able to proceed, by analogy, "from the physical to the moral" (167), from physical traits to overall superiority. Within this type of argumentation, the physical trait must function as a thoroughly dependable and stable sign. Zeroing in on the penis, the operator holds firm to the capacity for "anticipation" that it embodies:

> The man-child not only possesses these present points, small though they are, but, likewise—now our horticultural image comes into play— like the bud of a lily, he contains concealed rudiments of others. . . . (168)
>
> Can it now with fairness be denied that, in his beard, the man-child prospectively possesses an appendix, not less imposing than patriarchal; and for this goodly beard, should we not by generous anticipation give the man-child, even in his cradle, credit? (169)

And yet, a complementary posture necessitated by the slave trade demands that the philosophical intelligence officer also adulterate this pure phallocentrism. For while the trader must be able to proceed in an unproblematic fashion from the child to the man and from the physical to the moral, he must also be able to assert that "blemishes" in a young slave will not necessarily continue in adulthood. Hence the questioning of analogical thought—the repudiation of the Wordsworthian dictum whereby the child is "the father of the man" (165)—is as necessary to the philosophical intelligence officer's posture as the transparent model of representational thought. His attitude toward language is thus a double bind. In his own use of language he cannot abide by the notions of causality and referentiality that he must nonetheless presuppose in formulating his sales pitch. Quite typically, this character empties the ideal he represents—that of representational language—in the same gesture by which he invokes it. The philosophical title of the trader, the philosophical nature of the problem he poses, is one of the novel's most direct intimations of the collusion between the critical skills and political repression.

The first half of the novel is an arena in which we observe metaphysical structure—the ideal—and a linguistic structure— the confidence game—pass through a sequence of settings and characters, accruing themes and variations all the while. This schematic effort reveals the power of the scheme, in business and in fiction. In the fate of this scheme will reside many of the resources of the novel's economy.

3.

In postulating a model of the confidence game, the double gesture by which the operators espouse certain ideals while violating them in their actions has afforded a stable point of departure. Yet the manner in which the operators *represent* the ideal is not nearly as transparent as has thus far been implied. While wondering at the operator's efficacy, the novel nonetheless mocks the pettiness of their crime, the triteness of their machinations. And the ideals propounded by the operators are implicated—by association—as targets for the satire.

By assimilating the transcendental concept in so many of its manifestations or guises, whether charity, philanthropy, or nature, the novel becomes an encyclopedic shooting gallery for the puncturing of the ideal. The only factors mitigating the overall nihilistic thrust of this debunking are the affiliations linking the operators to specific social institutions. The component of the novel that asks to be read as an ultimate Nietzschean emptying of the ideal is thus coupled with a concrete social satire or criticism. At the same time that the novel offers a critique of the political uses of the critical skills and acts as a public disclaimer of the linguistic competences at the basis of manipulation, it is also a satire of its characters, the dupes as well as the operators, and, ultimately, of itself.

The continental divide down the center of the text becomes one of the most effective instruments of the novel's irony and self-irony. The adjustments made in the pacing of events, the structure of episodes, and characterization in the second half of the novel are too conspicuous to be overlooked.[16] Both a release of structure and a new wealth of associations are made possible by the eclipsing of daylight in the temporal setting. Episodes become fewer and more attenuated. The stream of targets slows down. The encounters between the cosmopolitan and his various interlocutors become digressive. The naked economic motives propelling the exchanges are obscured and to a certain extent effaced by philosophical speculations.

If, as H. Bruce Franklin suggests, the operators of the first half of the novel merely anticipate the cosmopolitan, the novel leads up to a massive anticlimax, for in terms of the novel's religious symbolism, the cosmopolitan is more lamb than lion.[17] He is a born loser.[18] The exchanges he enters are reciprocal battles of wits, not economic abductions of passive victims. The two interlocutors who eventually assume the name Charlie Noble—suggesting *their* interchangeability—are no less suspicious, cagey, and manipulative than he is. The single weapon in his arsenal is charm; his only strategy seduction. Hence the importance of wine and tobacco in his encounters. The cosmopolitan has no gimmicks or trademarks at his disposal. Consequently, the neat division of labor of the operators in the first half of the novel, the compartmentalization of theme by character, disappears and is replaced by much more fluid convergences of theme. The digressive quality of the cosmopolitan's encounters marks a shift of emphasis in the confidence operation from rhetoric to storytelling.

Obviously, then, in comparison with previous operators, the cosmopolitan undergoes a reduction in stature. The satire of the second half of the novel thus moves in a double direction, on one hand extending the assault on the ideal, but on the other shifting the thrust of the satire toward the novel itself. The cosmopolitan's failure with both characters named Charlie Noble and the fact that his major triumph consists in conniving a twenty-five-cent haircut demonstrate the novel's application of its satire to its antihero and hence to itself.

The novel's second half divides itself into three main scenes. In the initial segment, after an inconclusive foray on the Missouri bachelor, who is the only carry-over from the first half of the novel and a means of affording some continuity, the cosmopolitan falls in with an "acquaintance" who occupies him for some ten chapters and who turns out to be the first Charlie Noble. In the course of this interview, the lineaments of the ideology of confidence fill out considerably. The abstract notion of confidence as the indispensable basis of social interaction in any context is now amplified by its *behavioral* dimension—hence the emphasis on conviviality and congeniality.

Strangely enough, the expansionist racism brought to light in the story of the exemplary Indian-hater, Colonel John Moredock, narrated by the cosmopolitan's interlocutor in these chapters (25–35), goes hand in hand with a social code of friendship and amiability. The Indian-hater is characterized by the same inconsistency that was manifested by the operators who disclaimed their rhetoric in the same act in which they deployed it. "Moredock was an example of something apparently self-contradicting, certainly curious, but at the same time, undeniable: namely, that nearly all Indian-haters have at bottom loving hearts; at any rate, hearts, if anything, more generous than the average" (218). The Indian-hater is an example of the capacity to displace violence, to externalize it, to turn it on *another*, precisely for the purpose of protecting an atmosphere of stability, whether described as peace or confidence, closer to home.[19] This perpetuates the pattern established by the herb-doctor, who externalizes his drollery, his language play, by displacing it to *his* other. The pattern also occurs on a far wider scale in an anecdote introduced into the narrative as a rationalization for Indian-hatred. Chief Mocmohoc suddenly, and for no overt reason, terminates his hostilities against the colony of Wrights and Weavers and offers a truce, one of whose conditions is that "the five cousins should never, on any account, be expected to enter the chief's lodge together. . . . Nevertheless, Mocmohoc did, upon a time, with such fine art and pleasing carriage win their confidence, that he brought them all together to a feast of bear's meat, and there, by stratagem, ended them" (209–10).[20] The Indian chief entertains his neighbors with an ultimate irony. Mocmohoc mocks them with an overt demonstration of the discrepancy in public discourse dramatized repeatedly by the operators in the first half of the novel. Instead of dissimulating this credibility gap, he gives it its most positive—and negative—statement. The anecdote continues the novel's questioning of the status of legal language. The genocide that the anecdote justifies is a means, on a societal level, of liquidating a segment of the population onto which the duplicity of language in civil life has been projected and externalized. The Indian accoutrements for the taking of wine and tobacco appear four times in the last half of the novel (185, 214, 228, and 240) and suggest, in a way reminiscent of the human lampshades of World War II, the form in which awareness of this operation filters through to the domestic front. The violence translates into absurd Indian baskets and calumets.

Indian-hating, then, is the primary instance of the novel's disclosure of the *other*, that is, the usually concealed but complementary side of the ideology of confidence. In the figure of the Indian-hater, the novel comes closest to the obsessive personality whose most developed example in Melville's fiction is Ahab of *Moby-Dick*. Whether the quest is for the Indian or the "deep-sea denizen" (*CM*, 213), a split personality underlies the seemingly monomaniacal project. The hunt is an attempt to restore consistency, to quell an internal discrepancy, whose model is language, by projecting and eliminating an external quarry. The hunter teeters between obsession and schizophrenia.

It is in the cosmopolitan's encounter with Charlie Noble, his first main interlocutor, that the ideal finds its social applications or manners. Considerable attention is paid to conversation itself as the occasion for the always polite transactions of confidence, as the medium of social interaction. And the conversation between the cosmopolitan, alias Frank Goodman, and Charlie Noble passes with facility from one subcategory or theme of confidence to the next. Over a bottle of bad port, which these two house-friends abstain from drinking as they urge each other on to greater libations, they entertain such topics as the nobility of the human heart (230) and the need for humor (232), congeniality (241), and the trite cultivation that prolongs the conversation accompanying the transactions of confidence. This literate veneer is exemplified by the extended discussion of Shakespeare (242–49). Even when the interlocutors seem to argue energetically, their respective positions presuppose the necessity of confidence—as when Charlie Noble scores the Missouri bachelor and Polonius for their skepticism and the cosmopolitan defends them in the name of charity.

The effusive friendship between the cosmopolitan and his interlocutor is interrupted only when the former transgresses the single norm in the code of congeniality and appeals to Charlie Noble for money. The cosmopolitan placates his companion's anger long enough to narrate the tale of yet another character who undergoes abrupt changes of personality: Charlemont, the gentleman-madman. If the figure of the Indian-hater may be described as a paranoid-schizophrenic in the discrepancy between his homicidal isolation and his occasional outbreaks of soppy friendliness, Charlemont is a manic-depressive version of the same incongruity. At the age of twenty-nine, this St. Louis businessman turns morose and begins to fail in his endeavors. He disappears, and his friends speculate that he may have committed suicide. Years later, he returns, "Not only . . . alive, but he was himself again" (262). His restoration is described in terms of a code that is by now well established in the novel. He can now give himself over to "genial" friendship; his "noble qualities" enable him to prosper "in the encouraging sun of good opinions"; "under the influence of wine" he relates to an acquaintance the secrets of the intervening years. The moral of this *mise en abîme* of the situation in which Frank Goodman and Charlie find themselves is, predictably, never to "turn the cold shoulder to a friend— a convivial one" (264); for Charlie, it is also to donate the previously requested contribution. Yet the widest speculative horizon for such instances of discrepancy in character, whether schizophrenic or manic-depressive, is the issue of discrepancy itself—of how both the masquerade and the text in which it is narrated depart from the norms of consistency and representation on which they depend for their effect.

In the second segment of the narrative focusing on the cosmopolitan (Chapters 36–41), he encounters two characters whose personalities are also marked by inconsistency. Espousing the ideals of the American transcendentalists, they nevertheless betray a Yankee pragmatism (265) beneath their admiration for beauty and nature.[21] Just as the philosophical intelligence officer found it necessary both to advance and refute the claim of representation in his discourse, Mark Winsome vacillates between a representational "doctrine of labels" and a "doctrine of triangles" that denies the possibility of "forming a true estimate of any being" from "the data which life furnishes" (271). When encountering Mark Winsome and his disciple, Egbert, the cosmopolitan shifts from being the operator to the straight man. Winsome and Egbert themselves expose the chinks in the ideals they espouse. At no time is this more evident than when Egbert, now as the new Charlie Noble, narrates the story of China Aster in order to deflate the ideal of friendship that the cosmopolitan holds up to him in pressing yet another appeal for money.

The third and concluding installment, both of the cosmopolitan's experiences and the novel, in many senses brings the text full circle. The cosmopolitan's involved haggling with the barber over the price of a haircut returns us to the novel's ur-cynic and to its earliest testing of the status of signs. Hair, which is the barber's business, is a universal human denominator, and the debate about it brings the discourse to the level of the anthropological study of man attained earlier in the philosophical intelligence officer's remarks. The novel's final scene recrystallizes a familiar configuration. The cosmopolitan's representations to a venerable old man who sits reading the Bible under a solar lamp, a recurrence of the sun dawning as the novel begins, are punctuated by a voice of cynicism emanating from an invisible source among the berths. The novel ends as yet a final operator, this time an impoverished boy, peddles "security" devices "the traveller's patent lock" (341), money-belts, a carry-over from the novel's first scene, and *Counterfeit Detectors*.

Of the various scenes and anecdotes in the novel's second half, and in fact in the text as a whole, none provides us with a more heavily coded and ironic self-allegorization than the story of China Aster, the simple candle-maker whose fate is sealed when, in an exploration of usury anticipating *The Cantos of Ezra Pound*, he accepts an unnecessary loan from his friend, Orchis. China Aster, whose name means the star of China and reflects the illumination business, shines and is then eclipsed over Marietta, Ohio, "at the mouth of the Muskingum" (291). The name China Aster endows a story of small-town usury with an exotic aura and with the remote setting of parable. The star of the orient is displaced to Ohio, and the Muskingum—combining musk, essence of the male organs, and the lingum of Indian erotic literature—is an additional instance of the novel's assimilative economy. Although a man, China Aster is endowed with the fragility of fine china. And in the course of the story, he is "screwed," allegorically as well as economically, by his less delicate male associate, Orchis, whose name signifies not only a plant but also a testicle. While China Aster pursues the implicitly speculative *métier* of providing light, Orchis, a shoemaker, attends to the concrete matters under foot.

Having improved his station by winning a "capital prize in a lottery" (292), Orchis sets out to convince his friend of the need for additional capital and to "drop this vile tallow and hold up pure spermaceti to the world" (242). Echoing the "man with the weed's" demand to "drop Tacitus" and the evangelical vision of the "gem'-man in a gray coat and white tie," Orchis compels China Aster to accept unnecessary capital on the basis of an artificial consumer demand for spermaceti rather than tallow candles. And repeating previous operators' dissimulation of their motives, notably the herb-doctor's refusal of payment for his wares, Orchis secures China Aster's commitment in a most offhanded manner:

> "By-the-way, China Aster, it don't mean anything, but suppose you make a little memorandum of this; won't do any harm, you know." So China Aster gave Orchis his note for one thousand dollars on demand. Orchis took it, and looked at it a moment, "Pooh, I told you, friend China Aster, I wasn't ever going to make any *demand*. . . . You see I'll never trouble you about this . . . give yourself no further thought, friend China Aster, than how best to invest your money." (294–95)

China Aster's compliance with the scheme, however, is not entirely without conflict. Two of the old geezers in town, "Old Plain Talk" and "Old Prudence," serve as China Aster's alter egos and voice their reservations. Orchis instinctively senses enemies in these skeptics, just as the agent of the Black Rapids Coal Company was down on "bears." What we have, then, is the "classical" configuration of the confidence game. Orchis, the operator, exhorts China Aster to accept unnecessary credit, while the two "straight men," as simple and direct as their allegorical names, offer some resistance. It can therefore hardly be surprising that Orchis addresses to China Aster the following speech, which condenses an ideology that has elsewhere demonstrated a protean capacity to change forms:

> "Why, China Aster, you are the dolefulest creature. Why don't you, China Aster, take a bright view of life? You will never get on in your business or anything else, if you don't take the bright view of life. It's the ruination of a man to take the dismal one." Then, gayly poking at him with his gold-headed cane, "Why don't you, then? Why don't you be bright and hopeful, like me? Why don't you have confidence, China Aster? (295)

The machine of capital accumulation is once again greased by the language of effusive optimism. But the story of China Aster introduces a new dimension and level to the functioning of this category. For the first time we have an inkling of the psychological manifestation of confidence, both private and mass psychological, an anticipation of the Freudian notion of the dream as wish fulfillment:

> But as destiny would have it, that same night China Aster had a dream, in which a being in the guise of a smiling angel, and holding a kind of

cornucopia in her hand, hovered over him, pouring down showers of
small gold dollars, thick as kernels of corn. "I am Bright Future, friend
China Aster," said the angel, "and if you do what friend Orchis would
have you do, just see what will come of it." With which Bright Future,
with another swing of her cornucopia, poured such another shower of
small gold dollars upon him, that it seemed to bank him up all round,
and he waded about in it like a maltster in malt. (296)

This capitalist reverie achieves the deepest penetration of the ideology of confidence, invading the inmost sanctuary of the psyche.
Attacking China Aster in the defenseless state of slumber, it evades
the resistances mounted both by his own good sense and the detachment of Old Plain Talk and Old Prudence, who induce him,
like psychoanalysts, to interpret the dream. But to no avail. Having
succumbed to the dream, with its images of fertility, abundance,
and drunken abandon (the maltster), China Aster is unable to return
the check that Orchis has pressed upon him. And when the point-
lessness of the loan and the discomforts it causes begin to haunt
China Aster, the now obsessive dream of ever-increasing prosperity
returns and reinforces the debtor's compliance with the understated
conditions of the loan (299).

Thus begin two countertrajectories, both deriving their drift from
the original friendly loan. For China Aster, the path is of uninterrupted, almost mechanical decline. Unable to keep up with payments on the loan, he must assume greater debts. The battle to keep
pace with payments on the principal becomes an equally futile attempt to pay off the interest. Reversals within the broader system
of speculation make China Aster's failure inevitable:

he did not try his hand at the spermaceti again, but . . . returned to
tallow. But, having bought a good lot of it, by the time he got it into
candles, tallow fell so low, and candles with it, that his candles per
pound barely sold for what he had paid for the tallow. Meantime, a
year's unpaid interest had accrued. . . . (301)

Yet the obvious way out of this trap, simply defaulting on the loan,
eludes China Aster, for he is too honest, he has internalized too
well the ideals of politeness and decency promoted by the operators
throughout the novel: "had China Aster been a different man, the
money-lender might have dreaded" (300).

But Orchis is a *different* man. There is no consistency to his meanderings. Like his fellow operators and the narrator, Orchis is free to be inconsistent. Of a suspicious temperament, like one of the earlier debunkers, he is a hypochondriac. Illness takes him to Europe. Like Charlemont, he returns from his travels a changed man, but in the opposite direction, "sallow in cheek, and decidedly less gay and cordial in manner" (302). Having converted into a religious "or rather semi-religious" (301) Come-Outer, Orchis demonstrates once again how popular religion, with its evangelical impulse, interlocks with capitalism and its logic of accumulation. In his final manifestation, Orchis, the civilized operator, the operator as good citizen, is both hardened and religious, superstitious and skeptical. He has aspired to and attained the level of big-time capitalism. For it is through "a breach of trust on the part of a factor in New York" (303) that he must subject China Aster to the crushing and final pressure that will result in the latter's fatal sunstroke. China Aster dies, the candle of his mind extinguished, the sun of optimism within eclipsed by the external sun of harsh economic facts, his children public charges. "The root of all," as is dutifully recorded by Old Plain Talk and Old Prudence on his gravestone, "was a friendly loan" (303).

This story insinuates a sexual dimension into the manipulation that has taken place throughout the novel and suggests the wider psychological impact of the confidence game. Yet the story's primary contribution is not so much to elaborate as to combine details disseminated loosely throughout the novel into a precise allegory. Beneath the hilarity of the story and the provincial travesty contained in the characters' names, a refined economy is operating. The textual economy of this internalized theater runs parallel to the machine operation of the confidence game in the first half of the novel. To the extent that the story parodies the confidence operation outlined in the novel's first half, it is allegory, self-irony, self-deconstruction. But in the sense that it recalls the ongoing machinations of confidence in all its interlocking domains, it is social criticism and mass psychology.

4.

If confidence is ultimately a metaphysical category, implying a relation of optimism and unquestioning belief, consistency is its homologue within the sphere of fiction and representation. What confidence is to belief, consistency is to logic and representation—a guarantee of authenticity, a moratorium on fluctuations of meaning or value. It is fitting, then, that the category of consistency should come into play not only in the three chapters that the narrator explicitly appropriates for himself but also in the occasional narrative descriptions that get out of hand and betray some tampering with narrative "objectivity."[22]

And in his direct entrances onto the stage of the fiction, the narrator provides the operators with cover-fire, for if they are walking embodiments of a basic contradiction, a simultaneous profession and emptying of the ideal, the narrator challenges the worth of consistency in a work of fiction, be it the consistency of the characters to themselves or the "severe fidelity" of the work to "real life."[23] Not only do predictable characters and realistic works lack "the play of invention" (94), but there is a certain order of "facts" (95) to which they are not equal and that they finally betray. As positive models for his fiction, the narrator invokes the "duck-billed characters" for which no classification is readily available (97) and "the best false teeth . . . those made with at least two or three blemishes, the more to look like life" (197). In promoting the cause of fictive inconsistency, the narrator becomes the voice of the text, its house organ. He verges on his own brand of idealism by contending that, in serving concrete reality, a work of fiction betrays a profounder one. But the overall thrust of his remarks is toward a declaration of independence from representation and realism made by and for the fictive work (260). Ostensibly "outside" the text, then, and lending it a dimension of credibility missing from its proper domain, the narrator is assimilated by the masquerade staged by the novel, its array of costumes,[24] its side show of freaks,[25] its menagerie of animals,[26] and its herbarium of flowers.[27]

Viewed as the theater of the unmasking of the ideal, the text could continue endlessly in a joyous demolition derby, with each successive incarnation of the ideal shattered in the textual machinery. Yet there is one small catch to this freeplay, one small rider on the declaration of fictive independence. And the catch is, precisely, the unholy place where language games border on power, where the voices of the operators declaim in the interest of identifiable institutions that exist in some form or another to this day. Note that this catch, this bordering, does not reduce or impose closure upon the general debunking. The puncturing of the ideal and the social critique are simultaneous. Melville thus provides us with a compelling variation on a critical program edging closer to established authority. The Nietzschean-Heideggerian-Derridean isolation and triggering of a violence pent up within master texts or attitudes that were, by implication, too obtuse, inflexible, or blind to account for it—in Melville's version, this disclosure of the duplicity of language moves, from the morally superior position of the pale or margin to the center of collusion, the seat of power. According to this novel, the critics *are* the politicians. The wielding of power is inseparable from the critical awareness of the duplicity of language. In *The Confidence-Man,* the neat division of labor—whereby the literary or metaphysical fatcats *harbor* the violence while the critics *unleash* it—breaks down. Only within a confected discourse several removes from the facts of political life could the utilization of language in suppression and violence be an item of unexpected news.

Under the master rubric of *confidence* a veritable menagerie of ideals ambles through the novel. There are the great ones and the little ones. Of the wider ideals, we have observed: nature, man, charity, philanthropy, and speculation. Of the narrower: friendship, humor, politeness, generosity, nobility, the human heart, patriotism, and, paradoxically, class privilege and racial dominance. Yet we have reserved for last the ideal category perhaps closest to home: "original genius." Melville underscores the importance of this term when he has the narrator, intruding into the action for the last time, emphasize these words: "QUITE AN ORIGINAL" (329), the only instance when the narrator offers a direct gloss upon the text. "Quite an original" is the term that occurs to the barber when he describes his fleecing by the cosmopolitan. But that original operator, the mute, was already an "original genius" upon stepping aboard the *Fidèle* (4). Its trajectory encompassing the entire novel, the term "original genius" is vital not only to the text's historical program but also to its economy of the ideal. To be sure, "original genius" is a function of the novel's concern with various types of origins. There is the demographic origin of the "strangers" intermingling on the boat along the Mississippi and forming a microcosm of the American population. And there is the origin of the language consisting of images, terms, and usages unique to this novel. While *confidence* in its various forms is the most prevalent term in the novel—its meaning runs from self-assurance, hope, and optimism through trust, discretion, privacy, and secrecy, and on subterfuge and trickery—important word plays exploit the variations on words less conspicuous and decisive to the overall scheme: *spectacle-speculate-suspect-suspicion*,[28] *extreme*,[29] *strange*,[30] *frank*,[31] and the *press*.[32] In the widest sense, the concern for establishing origins of all kinds belongs to the program of cultural epigenesis in American letters outlined by John Irwin.[33]

But the originality whose importance is marked throughout the text is coupled to "genius." This word explored in the transcendental investigations of Kant's *Critique of Judgment*, reaches back to the very roots of life but also up to the concept or spirit, a spark conducted back to this world only by the fit few.[34] Among the definitions of the word offered by the *Oxford English Dictionary* is the following:

> 5. Native intellectual power of an exalted type, such as is attributed to those who are esteemed greatest in any department of art, speculation, or practice; instinctive and extraordinary capacity for imaginative creation, original thought, invention, or discovery.[35]

Yet this supersensible gift, somehow finding its way to "native" soil, also adapts itself to the ideology of confidence. For there is a touch of genius in "geniality," the social skills, the conviviality, in which the always polite transactions of confidence are surrounded. It is in this sense that the operators translate their genius so well into the practical interests and activities of business. The initial Charlie Noble is particularly frank regarding the collusion between genius and geniality:

> Fill up, up, up, my friend. Let the ruby tide aspire, and all ruby aspirations with it . . . be we convivial. And conviviality, what is it? . . . A living together. But bats live together. . . .

> Bats, though they live together, live not together genially. Bats are not genial souls. But men are; and how delightful to think that the word which among men signifies the highest pitch of geniality, implies, as indispensable auxiliary, the cheery benediction of the bottle. (250)

> Geniality has invaded each department and profession. We have genial senators, genial authors, genial lecturers, genial doctors, genial clergymen, genial surgeons, and the next thing we shall have genial hangmen. (251)

And here we are indeed closest to home. For in addition to suggesting the spiritual dimension of genius, Melville implicates here, in a remarkable gesture of authorial frankness, both his own work's pretensions to genius and the entire complex of institutions dedicated to the recognition, preservation, and generation of original genius, of which the university is a primary installation. Although unstated in the interest of confidentiality, original genius is the metaphysical orientation of the university and major artistic institutions. It is in the name of original genius that academic recognition and promotion are bestowed. It is around this term that the neutral space is opened in which "any department of art, speculation, or practice" may operate. This neutrality is secured by the protective discursive tariffs that make the various disciplines inaccessible to outsiders. Concurrent with the operators' pursuit and profession of their respective discursive lines is the encompassing institutional aim, that "each department" be invaded by "genial authors . . . lecturers . . . doctors . . . surgeons," and the like. The university is to the individual disciplines what the cosmopolitan is to the singular operators: the sublation of a system of speculation to a higher level, to the universal. As a sanctuary of original genius, the university provides the social systems of government, finance, defense, health, education, and welfare with the security that their operations are backed by the highest emanations of inspiration.

What does it mean, then, for critics to release the play of language within the text when the audience is the university? What can this mean when the debunking takes place *on campus,* within the insulated zone that is protected in exchange for self-administered neutrality? Within this space, critics are recognized as the final authorities on language and reading in the land. But what does it mean to teach the critical skills within the temple of original genius when the moves breathlessly announced by contemporary rhetoricians are near-timeless principles in the rulebooks of political power *out there*? To be sure, there is a politics of the university proper, but its implications are minor in comparison with the collusion between the critical skills and mass manipulation *out there*. From our earlier discussion, television emerges as a powerful instance of a mass medium assuming the characteristic pose of the confidence man. While a complex form of visual and aural language itself, it systematically tends toward the obliteration of difference, an erasure of the political, social, and intellectual discrepancies that discontent the audience. Television's *resolution* of all possible sources of tension at all levels of programming is the mass medium's equivalent of the operators' unsinkable optimism and the processes of assimilation dramatized by this novel. The coordination by which television's programs and commercials mutually confirm and arise out of each other is a contemporary version of the interreferential links by which the operators support each other's claims. A challenge to the ideology of television is a blow to the metaphysics orienting a culture of near-global proportions. But the deconstructive awareness facilitating such an attack has not yet sufficiently wandered *out there*. The principles of sound capitalism dictate a reinvestment of such gains back to the "original" enterprise, the pursuit of original genius. This chapter joins the Melville literature generated by the university and as such is offered upon the altar of original genius.

There is no more striking example of the assimilative neutrality of the university than its reception of deconstructive criticism. Though it may also demonstrate historical rigor, scholarly comprehensiveness, and technical facility, deconstructive criticism primarily bases its appeal not on these types of guarantee but on a bearing, a contrapuntal rhythm to deterministic operations, a characteristic posture or voice of irony.[36] Given the claims of deconstructive criticism to undermine a two-thousand year epoch of Western culture, it is remarkable how, in a few year's time, "critical theory" has become a category to be placed alongside thematic, historical, biographical, formal, and linguistic studies,[37] with its own claims to authority. The untoward posture of deconstructive criticism becomes merely one more commodity among a vast array of skills and wares peddled along the arcade of the academic bazaar. This institutionalization suggests that deconstruction's emptying coincides with its elaboration and entrenchment. The most fruitful avenue for deconstruction may well lie *out there*, beyond the campus, where neutral language gives way to hard language,[38] where the determinisms we observe on an ever-widening *general* scale affect the material, cultural conditions of life. I place *material* and *cultural* in *a*pposition, having no reason to oppose them.

Just as the flaxen-haired mute who emerges out of nowhere on an unspecified April Fools' day anticipates the course of the novel, *The Confidence-Man* has proven prophetic. A product of the age of mechanical reproduction, it plants the seeds of the manner in which communications and mass language will function long beyond its time. In its critical scenario, it is also beyond its day. Not only does it provide a highly sophisticated and comprehensive mechanism for the debunking of the ideal, but it also places the critical skills made accessible by deconstruction in the widest social context. It suggests an alternative to the self-serving configuration in which the critic and the assertion of power are always on opposite sides of a pre-given and mystical bar. It demands of those who would trace out the configurations implied by its internal critical scenario a fresh evaluation of positions—positions within the contemporary critical scene, the position of that scene within the academic supermarket, and the overall social setting of the university. Although in a small way, it is for us to determine what "further may follow of this Masquerade" (350).

4

The University of Verse: The Economies of Modern American Poetry

On the Dump[1]

The major American novelists of the nineteenth century from Hawthorne to James were drawn to Europe as an intriguing setting for their fiction and as a source of information to disseminate to their audience. The twentieth-century poets in their tradition dramatized in the convolutions of their verse parallel interests no less intense. Although their verse is at times fragmented, impenetrable, abstruse, and whimsical, such poets as Ezra Pound, Wallace Stevens, and William Carlos Williams were as committed to the education of a readership as were the great pedagogical epic poets Homer, Virgil, and Dante.

The educational vocation of modern American poetry is as much by necessity as choice. If Pound, Stevens, and Williams were to be assured of a readership, they had to assist in its training. They began their literary careers when the voices of Stephen Crane's street characters rang as loudly in the American *patois* as the precisions of Henry James's narrative. While the methods of these poets often more closely approximated "the fascination of what's difficult" than "the ABC of reading," an obscurantist tendency meriting consideration in its own right, there is little doubt as to the persistence of a didactical thrust throughout their work.

Two of the most fruitful approaches to these poets, exploring the conceptual contours of modernism and the technical innovations of its poetics, are in fact interlocked. Seminal assessments of modernism from Benjamin's[2] and Adorno's[3] through more recent ones by Kristeva,[4] Derrida, Miller,[5] Riddel,[6] and Kenner[7] approach it as a poetics, a rhetoric of disjunctive effects. A rare affinity between theoretical models and the aesthetic objects that they illuminate and subtly influence characterizes twentieth-century poetry. Precisely because the material of twentieth-century poetry is so much imbued with its theoretical qualities, however, it seems fitting, if our broader purpose is to penetrate the economies implicitly inscribed in this body of works, to begin with a poem. The text to which we turn is exemplary, not merely for its turns of phrase but also for its location: at the site from which a large segment of modern American poetry draws its inspiration and derives its form.

THE MAN ON THE DUMP

Day creeps down. The moon is creeping up.
The sun is a corbeil of flowers the moon Blanche
Places there, a bouquet. Ho-ho . . . The dump is full
Of images. Days pass like papers from a press.
The bouquets come here in the papers. So the sun,
And so the moon, both come, and the janitor's poems
Of every day, the wrapper on the can of pears,
The cat in the paper-bag, the corset, the box
From Esthonia: the tiger chest, for tea.

The freshness of night has been fresh a long time.
The freshness of morning, the blowing of day, one says
That it puffs as Cornelius Nepos reads, it puffs
More than, less than or it puffs like this or that.
The green smacks in the eye, the dew in the green
Smacks like fresh water in a can, like the sea
On a cocoanut—how many men have copied dew
For buttons, how many women have covered themselves
With dew, dew dresses, stones and chains of dew, heads
Of the floweriest flowers dewed with the dewiest dew.
One grows to hate these things except on the dump.

Now, in the time of spring (azaleas, trilliums,
Myrtle, viburnums, daffodils, blue phlox),
Between that disgust and this, between the things
That are on the dump (azaleas and so on)

And those that will be (azaleas and so on),
One feels the purifying change. One rejects
The trash.
          That's the moment when the moon creeps up
To the bubbling of bassoons. That's the time
One looks at the elephant-colorings of tires.
Everything is shed; and the moon comes up as the moon
(All its images are in the dump) and you see
As a man (not like the image of a man),
You see the moon rise in the empty sky.

One sits and beats an old tin can, lard pail.
One beats and beats for that which one believes.
That's what one wants to get near. Could it after all
Be merely oneself, as superior as the ear
To a crow's voice? Did the nightingale torture the ear,
Pack the heart and scratch the mind? And does the ear
Solace itself in peevish birds? Is it peace
Is it a philosopher's honeymoon, one finds
On the dump? Is it to sit among mattresses of the dead,
Bottles, pots, shoes and grass and murmur *aptest eve:*
Is it to hear the blatter of grackles and say
Invisible priest; is it to eject, to pull
The day to pieces, and cry *stanza my stone?*
Where was it one first heard of the truth? The the.

This 1938 poem by Wallace Stevens[8] draws its affective force
from its affirmation of poetic productivity in spite of. . . : in spite
of the reduced condition of the contents of the dump, the incoher-
ence of its melange of living, dead, organic, and inorganic matter,
and the indifferent succession of time. In spite of the confusion and
difficulty, the poem argues—and its progression does indeed incorporate an argument—the poet bravely continues his work, like
the U.S. Postal Service, under all, even humble, conditions:

One sits and beats an old tin can, lard pail.
One beats and beats for that which one believes.

The insufficiency or meanness of the dump as the birthplace for
POETRY is essential to the dramatic, or rather melodramatic, tension of the poem. Poetry springs from humble origins. Yet the dump
is also "full of images." It is a linguistic entity, a site where linguistic transformations, which cannot be fully explained, take place.

The entire poem hinges on this ambiguity. On the one hand, it contains an only partially realized wish for poetic process to effect a sublime apotheosis of the material and the banal. A number of elements in the poem are there to effect "the purifying change," the redemption of the objects in the dump: the freshness brought in by the wind, the sensuous covering provided by the dew, the spring flowers that take root even in the material graveyard. At the same time, there is a dead cat in a bag in the dump. Picturesque activities like the puffing of the wind and the smacking of the water—and sensuous interludes, like imagining women's bodies covered with buttons, dresses, and chains of dew—prevent the material from sinking into inertness and horror. In one of its scenarios, the poem dramatizes the sublimation of poetry out of things, with ample assistance furnished by a cooperative nature. This redemption occurs by virtue of a willful receptivity and a resolute act.

> One feels the purifying change. One rejects
> The trash.
>   That's the moment when the moon creeps up
> To the bubbling of bassoons.

The poet of grand flights may reject the trash, infuse a collation of inert objects with reassuring motion, rise above the setting to the accompaniment of bassoons. But the speaker of the poem, and the reader of modern American poetry, will circle back to the dump, and not only for divine inspiration. The dump is also the location for linguistic transformation, a process of digestion. "The dump is full/ Of images. Days pass like papers from a press." The dump is a metonymic manifold. It incorporates objects associated with a wide range of human activities, some called, like the Estonian teachest, from exotic settings. The dump is heavy in papers, wrappers, and forms. The pear wrapper, the corset, the tea chest, and a dead cat's paper shroud all signify and contain.

Only within the scenario of indifferent juxtaposition does the wonder of the fifth and final stanza make any sense. If we read the poem solely as a credo, an affirmation of persistent poetic composition, the poet will beat at his old lard pail in any event. But as a linguistic repository, a scene of writing,[9] the dump sustains a transformation—from raw to finished poetic material. Although any number of linguists and theorists of poetry in our century have devoted their energies to postulating exactly how "mattresses of the dead,/ Bottles, pots, shoes and grass" might become "aptest eve," the poem, in order to sustain its culminating wonder, leaves the rules and grammar of its transformation ineffable, even inarticulate, if "The the" is the final word on poetry. By a certain logic, then, the poem must culminate in awe and wonder. There, in the dump, coexist the panoply of things and the products of poetic condensation: aptest eve, invisible priest, stanza my stone. In the abandonment of the quest for transformative laws to explain the metamorphosis of substantives into verse, there can only be a certain mystification. The wonder with which the poem ends is the highest resolution that its wish can reach, the wish to define poetry as the sublimation of the banal. "The the" is a variation on the "vital, arrogant, fatal, dominant X" of metaphor,[10] a vocal cul-de-sac lodged somewhere between the teeth and the tongue, an utterance of the inarticulate as much as of articulate precision.

There is, of course, no dump. And the objects that supposedly comprise it are not objects but names. The dump is a fictive setting for an allegory of poetic production. The poetic allegory of "The Man on the Dump" is a relatively simple one: Qualified by motion and sublimated by long-standing conventions surrounding nature and time, poetry can be generated out of the metonymic manifold of things. Stevens, Pound, and Williams, to the extent that they assume an epic vocation, all engage in poetic allegory. The allegory to which I refer is situated between the moral symbolism of naive allegory and the complex ironic interplay of text and interpretation best characterized by Paul de Man as the allegory of reading.[11] The epic poetic allegory in which Pound, Williams, and on a miniature scale, Stevens engage, and which may well be characteristic of modern long verse, involves several elements: a historical argument, whose culmination is the production of the work at hand and the fictive "present" of writing; the incorporation of "the scene of writing"; a functional or structural account of the operating principles of the text; and the appropriation of work settings and methods of manufacture, often from beginning to end, as metaphors for poetic production. In this sense, the poetic allegory intimated on a small scale in Stevens's poem is not far from an economy.

The speaker of Stevens's poem may reject the trash, but the corpus of his poetry is drawn to the setting of the dump as a source, an explanation, and a scene of writing. Pound exploits the international flavor of the dump, here intimated by Cornelius Nepos[12] and the Estonian tea chest to its full extent, and when he does he reiterates the fascination elicited by Rome's ruins from the characters of Hawthorne's *The Marble Faun* early in that novel. Despite a professed receptivity to "One's grand flights,"[13] modern American poetry seldom strays far from the setting of the dump, the preserve of objects emptied of their contents and significance. Geographically, the dump is situated on the margin; economically, it resides within a domain of excess and superfluity.

American culture, as well as American manufacture and economics, has thrived on the throwaway. An object whose exhaustion is part of its use makes way for a new object and a new cycle of expenditure. The depletion of such an object and its discarding on the dump does not, however, terminate its existence. In the repository where time figures its passage as the fulmination of sheets from a printing press, the fragmentary discard begins an afterlife, where it becomes the raw material of synthetic art. Its aesthetic properties may differ markedly from those that defined its use. The world of Stevens's poem, Pound's *Cantos,* and Williams's *Paterson* is but a stone's skip away from the twentieth-century art forms based on waste products: collages made with wrappers and newspaper scraps, sculptures fashioned from machine parts and scrap metal.[14]

America was not only, as Gertrude Stein wrote, the first country to enter the twentieth century[15]; it was also the first culture to accord garbage and other waste products their true centrality in the age of mechanical reproduction. The New World not only rests securely on ascertainable origins; its vast and, within recent memory, almost infinite extension has also preempted the need to reprocess, digest, assimilate, or even hide waste. Automobile graveyards and junkyards have become prominent features in the landscape of the American cinema and fiction. What may well stand as the most poignant summation of throwaway culture derives its inspiration, however, more from the Brazilian jungle than from the industrial sprawl of New Jersey:

> Some mischievous spirit has defined America as a country which has moved from barbarism to decadence without enjoying any intermediary phase of civilization. The formula could not be more correctly applied

to the towns of the New World, which pass from freshness to decay without ever being simply old.. . . In the case of European towns, the passing of centuries provides an enhancement; in the case of American towns, the passing of years brings degeneration. It is not simply that they have been newly built; they were built so as to be renewable as quickly as they were put up, that is, badly. When new districts are being created, they are hardly integral elements of the urban scene; they are too gaudy, too new, too gay for that. They are more like stands in a fairground or the pavilions of some international exhibition, built to last only a few months. After that lapse of time, the fair closes and the huge geegaws lapse into decay; the facades begin to peel, rain and soot leave their grimy trails, the style goes out of fashion, and the original layout disappears through the demolitions caused by some new building fever. The contrast is not between old and new towns, but between towns with a very short evolutionary cycle. Certain European cities sink gently into a moribund torpor; those of the New World live feverishly in the grip of a chronic disease; they are perpetually young, yet never healthy.[16]

While treadless tires and empty soup cans present themselves as the stereotypical throwaways, the byproducts of American culture attain the dimensions of entire towns and implicate macroscopic social phenomena such as land use and population movements. The prominence attained by waste products in the poetry of Eliot, Pound, Stevens, and Williams is intimately related to the characteristic attitudes in American culture toward its origins and ends, its cosmology and teleology, and the assumptions regarding time and history that they imply. No single event in the history of American culture may have been more expressive of these attitudes than the moon landing of July 20, 1969.[17] At that moment, both for the political leaders and poets of the United States, the nation fulfilled its potential for groundbreaking innovation and eternal, unaging newness. Although an anthropologist, Claude Lévi-Strauss, the author of the above passage, may also be regarded as an important theorist of modern poetics. The notion of *bricolage,* another of his models that can be applied productively to this field, will be considered below.

The objects in the dump exist at the extremes of the cycle of production, at the final stage of the process that yields goods and at the first stage of the synthetic recycling that takes place in certain art forms. These leftovers, whether as large as a city or as small as a used light bulb, thus join a thoroughly marginal economy, a black market of nonessential goods. Philosophically speaking, the dump resides in the site that systematic Western thought has reserved for writing and poetry. Jacques Derrrida, throughout his writing but particularly in "Plato's Pharmacy,"[18] formulates the conditions of this marginality. In keeping with the Platonic notion of the *pharmakon* that Derrida meticulously elaborates, the dump is toxic. Its contents are at once poisonous, nonessential, corrupting, artificial, and delusory. Plato's drug is a poison, a medication, and a gift. Its attributes derive from the role played by the joker-god Thoth in an alien pantheon dedicated to the Greek, the Egyptian. Pound situates the dump of modern American poetry in the Hades of production. Its artifice substitutes the dead for the living and contributes to the demise of internal memory. Because of its implicit deceit, the dump and its contents are subject to the punishment meted out to the scapegoat: banishment and oblivion.

The dump of cultural remains is the oracle and future for modern American poetry, a fate that in different ways Stevens, Pound, and Williams struggle to avoid. It is in this regard that these poets have a stake, a very direct investment and interest, in their audience's literacy, even if their approaches to its attainment vary. Of the three, Stevens is by far the most musical poet.[19] Music is an emanation of the wonder that reaches a crescendo at the end of "The Man on the Dump" and that flavors much of Stevens's poetry. He is a master at devising musical accompaniments appropriate to the specific moods and concepts deployed in his language. The measured couplets of "The Man with the Blue Guitar" (1937), and the equally careful pauses between them, comprise an accompaniment of strummed chords that the poem generates for itself as it pursues a number of variations on the relation between Being and poetry. This quiet and pensive music contrasts sharply with symphonic flourishes in rhythm and rhyme sustained throughout "The Idea of Order at Key West" (1934). Stevens devises no less than four musical settings for "Peter Quince at the Clavier" (1915), one for each of its main sections, ranging from the ineffable to the clamorous:

She searched		Soon with a noise like tambourines,
The touch of springs	AND	Came her attendant Byzantines.
And found		
Concealed imaginings.		

One could well argue that musical variation is as much responsible for the expansiveness of perspectival works, including "Thirteen Ways of Looking at a Blackbird" (1917), "Study of Two Pears" (1938), and "Someone Puts a Pineapple Together" (1947), as their conceptual elaboration.

It is treacherous, as Nietzsche demonstrated, to reduce music to a determinate ideological content,[20] to impose upon it a representational purpose. Music comprises both the vestige of a sublime poetic vocation, which Stevens never fully relinquishes despite his infatuations with the techniques of modernist art, and an insight into the didactic dimension of his poetry. Stevens educates by means of a musical variation on names, images, and metaphors, which he initially releases into his work devoid of any meaning whatsoever. It is questionable that we ever finally determine the identity of Crispin, the significance of palm trees or blackbirds, or the location of Key West or New Haven on any map of meaning. What Stevens does offer the reader, American or otherwise, is a freshness of idiom, mood, and perspective almost *sans pareil*. Coffee and oranges can comprise the menu of anyone's breakfast, but set in apposition to the "Complacencies of the peignoir" and "the green freedom of a cockatoo" at the beginning of "Sunday Morning" (1915), they acquire a unique flavor. Stevens's "technique" consists in the accretion of meaning to initially empty signifiers and images through musical variation. The components that undergo this process range from the small (blackbirds and pineapples) to the large (the idea of order). In pedagogical terms, Stevens's poetry constitutes a primer whose terms are metaphors. Its operating principle is a verbal cubism by which each X or unknown term is qualified by the particularities of its context and by a relativity in which the unknown influences its own present and future meanings.

Stevens, by virtue of the minute attention that he pays to the context and perspective of his emergent poetic vocabulary, thus becomes a poet of exquisite precision. Just as "The deer and the dachshund are one,"[21] the poet of sublime modernist music is also a poet of logical analysis. Such texts as "Thirteen Ways of Looking at a Blackbird," "Study of Two Pears," "Connoisseur of Chaos" (1938), "Variations on a Summer Day" (1939), and "Notes Toward a Supreme Fiction" (1942) impress upon us the minimalism of their articulation, the qualification and revision of the various positions that they posit, and the logical play that this effort involves. These works may also be regarded as extensions of Wittgenstein's practices of philosophical investigation. In both Stevens's poetry and Wittgenstein's discourse, the meaning of terms derives only from the contexts in which they are framed and the perspectives from which they are viewed.[22] Signification emerges only from a sequence of logical and aesthetic tests. Wittgenstein and Stevens both engage in a close but nonidentical paraphrase of earlier formulations for the purpose of analyzing their linguistic and logical differences. In this regard, they function as philosophers of difference.

Stevens's music is a local phenomenon that depends on the particularity of finished and discrete works, and of their subdivisions, for its maximal effect. While Pound and Williams are hardly deaf to the effects of poetic music, they devote more of their attention to the possibilities and limits of poetic space than Stevens. A poetry taking advantage of the full page as a field for diffusing its traces will necessarily obscure, to some degree, the repetitive patterning at the basis of rhyme and meter. In opening up the poetic page, Pound and Williams explore the effects of interjections, the interpolation of "foreign" material, and the possibilities for logical and semantic juxtapositions and discontinuities—somewhat at the expense of the integrity of separate works and of their internal visual and sonorous patterns.

To be sure, the poetic projects of Pound and Stevens are marked by their own significant differences. Above all, Williams eschews Pound's mimetic practice of assuming and abandoning the guises of personae and favors synthesizing a more consistent poetic voice in the everyday American idiom. Williams seeks a linguistic directness praised as well by Stevens in "The Man on the Dump": the simple style of Cornelius Nepos, the desire to "see/As a man (not like the image of a man)." On the other hand, even where he avoids certain forms of the grafts and suturings that fill the *Cantos,* Williams feels free to continue Pound's practice of incorporating seemingly incongruous remains from the repositories of culture and history. "Voices" other than that deriving from "the persona" are free to enter the text in the form of these extracts.

In their common exploration, what the French would call *ouverture* of poetic space, Pound and Williams continue an experimentation initiated in the previous century by Stéphane Mallarmé. Jacques Derrida's lengthy essay on Mallarmé, "The Double Session," and a roughly contemporaneous piece on the novelist and poet Philippe Sollers, "Dissemination," are instructive in elucidating the philosophical significance of certain literary works.[23] They also delineate a poetics of space and time, of the very page and the movement of words upon it, in modern and post-modern poetry. These essays thus contribute as much to the theory of poetics as to philosophy and criticism.

Derrida devotes considerable attention to the composition of Mallarmé's poetry, and examines how it is sutured together by means of grafting and how it is folded upon itself. This verse is inscribed on a page whose whiteness is not to be mistaken for an absence of qualities. Although these attributes are implanted within the nearly invisible layers of whiteness, thay are quite specific and are closely related to the textual functioning of Mallarmé's poetry:

> The blank—the other face of this double session here declares its white color—extends between the candid virginity (*"fragments of candor."* . . *"nuptial proofs of the Idea"*) of the white (*candida*) page and the white paint of the pale Pierrot who, by simulacrum, writes in the paste of his own make-up, upon the page he is. Through all the surfaces superimposed white on white, between all the layers of the Mallarméan make-up, one comes across, every time, on analysis, the substance of some *"drowned grease paint"* (*The Chastised Clown* [*Le Pitre châtié*]). (*Dissemination,* 195)

The virginity of the page affords it a certain poignancy that is not, however, destined to endure. Upon this prepared surface, the movement away from a self-contained to a more diffuse display of poetic lines is not indicative of any loss of rigor; rather, it reveals lines of stress within the poetry, the multiple ways in which its segments and vectors of force join each other and diverge, Like the figure of the fan, Mallarmé's poetry is at once expansive and subject to many folds.

Nowhere in his writing is Derrida more concerned with the tactile qualities of writing and text, its weave, membrane, and vibration, than in his discussion of Mallarmé. As in some other essays, Derrida gleans from the text under consideration a figure not only illustrative of it but whose richness and complexity supplement the interpretation materially. In the case of Mallarmé, the figure of the hymen—which Derrida locates in the *Mimique,* among other places—

dramatizes the tenuous relation between Mallarmé's language and the truth, spans the figural and performative levels of the text, and indicates the complexity of its spatial relations. While it may be excessive to claim that Pound and Williams address the hymen frontally or incorporate it literally in their poetry, their poetic practices surely implicate the issues that it raises.

> To repeat: the hymen, confusion between the present and the nonpresent, with all the indifferences it entails within the whole series of opposites . . . produces the effect of a medium. . . . It is an operation that *both* sows confusion *between* opposites *and* stands *between* the opposites "at once." What counts here is the *between*, the in-between-ness of the hymen. The hymen "takes place" in the "inter-," in the spacing between desire and fulfillment, between perpetration and its recollection. But the medium of this *entre* has nothing to do with a center.
>
> The hymen enters into the antre. *Entre* can just as easily written with an *a*. . . . The *interval* of the *entre*, the in-between of the hymen: one might be tempted to visualize these as the hollow or bed of a valley . . . without which there would be no mountains, like the sacred vale between the two flanks of the Parnassus. . . .
>
> We are thus moving from the logic of the palisade . . . to the logic of the hymen. The hymen, the consummation of differends . . . merges with what it seems to be derived from: the hymen as protective screen, the jewel-box of virginity, the fine invisible veil which, in front of the hystera, stands *between* the inside and outside of a woman. . . . Neither future nor present, but between the two. It is the hymen that desire dreams of piercing, of bursting, in an act of violence that is . . . love and murder. . . .
>
> The hymen is thus a sort of textile. Its threads should be interwoven with all the veils, gauzes, canvases, fabrics, moires, wings, feathers, all the curtains and fans that hold within their folds all—almost—of the Mallarméan corpus. We could spend a night doing that. The text of *Mimique* is not the only place where the word "hymen" occurs. (*Dissemination*, 212–13)

The hymen is a figure emerging out of the hollowness of poetic space, spanning it and indicating certain of its qualities. It is a sounding board for the music, a tissue sample of the fabric, and a tremor in the sexuality of modern poetry. It encompasses, for Derrida, two vital scenarios: the logical and epistemological indeterminacy that dense poetry unleashes against systematic truth, and the sexual play implicit in poetic inscription. In Derrida's terms, the hymen is an almost nonexistent tissue suspended in negative space, destined to be violated. It is most powerful symbolically, that is, when no trace of its actual existence remains. As a result of its suspension between protuberances and conceptual assertions, it becomes resonant. As a membrane, web, tissue, petal, wing, or feather, the hymen is a prototext installed within the very space that modern poetry will inhabit.

That space is not homogeneous or reducible to uniform segments. Like functional architecture or the schematic paintings of Klee, the space of modern poetry reveals its stresses and inconsistencies rather than absorbing them. While this space may be configured by the ambivalence between sexual provocation and rejection and between absence and presence, it is maintained or held together by the practice that Derrida calls grafting (*la greffe*). The graft is the process implicit in writing itself that encourages, even demands, poetic condensation and metonymic commotion; by means of it, the space in which Mallarmé, Pound, and Williams inscribe their verse can be populated by formulations and things related by incongruity and some violence.

> Margueritte's booklet is thus, for *Mimique*, both a sort of epigraph, an hors d'oeuvre, and a seed, a seminal infiltration: indeed both at once, which only the . . . operation of the *graft* can no doubt represent. One ought to explore systematically not only what appears to be a simple etymological coincidence uniting the graft and the graph (both from graphion: writing implement, stylus), but also the analogy between the forms of textual grafting and so-called vegetal grafting. . . . It would not be enough to compose an encyclopaedic catalogue of grafts (approach grafting, detached scion grafting; whip grafts, splice grafts, saddle grafts, cleft grafts, bark grafts; bridge grafting, inarching, repair grafting, bracing; T-budding, shield budding, etc.); one must elaborate a systematic treatise on the textual graft. (*Dissemination*, 202)

The graft bridges the operation and composition of the text. It is both an activity, which may or may not be exploited, and a property that modern poetry installs within the poetic space. Derrida convincingly demonstrates how the text of Mallarmé's "Livre" is folded upon itself, where its fragments of inscription join and diverge. The folds demarcated in the "Livre" have their counterparts on virtually every page of Pound's *Cantos* and Williams's *Paterson*.

As we will explore in greater detail below, the sexuality of the

Cantos is a curious on-again, off-again affair. A particularly volatile strand of oedipal concern attains prominence in Pound's references to the encounter between Odysseus and Circe in Books X–XII of the *Odyssey* and to the sexual exploits, and occasional recriminations, enjoyed by the troubadours of Aquitaine and Provence. This particularly attractive and dangerous sexuality is compartmentalized, however, to one layer of the text. One might say, in Freudian terms, that elsewhere in the *Cantos* Pound's sexual interest exceeds this repression in a promiscuity of allusion, in a nearly endless receptivity on the part of the poetic space to anything it might assimilate. The jousting of male poets with father figures is qualified by this pronounced receptivity to penetration by extraneous allusions and material. The space of the *Cantos* thus resonates with the activity of the poetic hymen.

Williams's poetry, like his life, may well have benefited from a simpler and more direct expression of sexual energy. The Beautiful Thing of *Paterson*—an imaginary woman or rather a woman of the imaginary that Williams loves as intensely as any of his actual loves— is, however, adorned with the diaphanous petals of the flowers that he explores throughout his poetry, particularly in "Asphodel, that Greeny Flower."[24] When the conflagration breaks out in the library of *Paterson,* a scene every bit as formative to the development of American poetry and modern poetics as Odysseus's encounter with Elpenor in Hades, the energy of books and of a woman's sexuality are being released. Like so much of subsequent American poetry and criticism, we will return to this scene.

Poetic Stuff

Pound and Williams were concerned with the production of poetry at least as much as they were with its textual conditions. Their own practices of grafting and the implicit sexuality of their compositional techniques exerted profound effects on modern poetry—on its density and texture, its logical and rhetorical relations, and on its surface, space, and frames. Stevens's reference to Cornelius Nepos in "The Man on the Dump" is merely one instance of the assimilation of matter foreign to the text at hand, whether in the form of literary allusions, of historical references, names, and citations, or of fragments of documents, records, and literary works. It is a practice that becomes rampant in Pound's and Williams's poetry. The foldlines discernible on the surface of their—and other's—modern poetry follow the borders between grafts of initially extraneous matter. In this sense, Mallarmé is not at all out of place in Stevens's dump.

The empty spaces incorporated into works such as the *Cantos* and *Paterson* may at first glance suggest a thinness of consistency or vacuity. The manner in which Pound and Williams space out more conventional patterns of versification indeed enables them to experiment with poetic density, to explore at the polar limits of minimalism, floridity, and in the more temperate zones in between. In the degree to which such texts are receptive to unlikely interjections, however, they become dense composites of drastically different textures. Like the detritus of Eliot's London and Stevens's dump, these poems, and with them a large portion of modern American poetry, are distinguished primarily for their qualities as a written substance. In this poetry, the nature of the message ostensibly represented, or the uniqueness of separate works, is secondary to the tactile qualities of poetry as substance, or stuff, or the German *Stoff*.

With a few notable exceptions, Pound's individual Cantos offer little to set them apart. The uniqueness of the *Cantos* as a whole derives from the consistency, density, and texture of the poetic discourse that Pound synthesized as their medium. Pound's favorite troubadours, such as Sordello, Guillem da Cabestanh, and Pieire de Maensac, may avail themselves of their lords' wives and may thus violate the conventions of social and conjugal authority. In a similar fashion, Pound's attention to the stuff of poetry lays waste to the feudal authority exercised by discrete poems over their particular semantic and musical fiefdoms. The allocation of resources in modern poetry is less to individuated works than to a characteristic material or stuff.

From the perspective of its grafting, modern poetry synthesizes a stuff remarkable for its density, its concentration, and its weight. The German critic, Walter Benjamin, characterized this gathering of cultural fragments into a synthetic art object as the composition of a mosaic. Concerned with the relation between the fragment and the whole of the artwork into which it is assimilated, Benjamin writes.

> The value of fragments of thought is all the greater the less direct their relation to the underlying idea, and the brilliance of the representation depends as much on this value as the brilliance of the mosaic does on the quality of the glass paste. The relationship between the minute precision of the work and the proportions of the sculptural or intellectual whole demonstrates that truth-content is only to be grasped through immersion in the most minute details of subject-matter. In their supreme, western, form the mosaic and the treatise are products of the Middle Ages; it is their very real affinity which makes comparison possible.[25]

The quality of the mosaic, like the interest of the synthetic artwork, depends on the glue that holds it together. This glue is a common substance. Its adhesive capability depends on the closeness with which the fragments are read. The Middle Ages that Benjamin selects as a high point of hermetic study is no further from the Italian Renaissance in which Pound isolates the origins of the modern political organization, finance, and art patronage than Ravenna is from Rimini, Florence, or Siena.

In their own ways, the *Cantos* and *Paterson* share the fragmentary and scholastic quality of Benjaminian mosaics. In keeping with the modernist practice that I elsewhere characterize as superimposition[26] and that is also at play in the temporal setting of Hawthorne's *The Marble Faun*, Pound retrospectively aligns four historical and literary contexts behind the composition of the *Cantos*: the history of the Chinese emperors, the *Odyssey*, the Italian Renaissance, and the American Revolution. Pound is, then, rather far-reaching in the terrain from which his fragments derive. One finds among them "primary" Greek, Chinese, and Italian sources from the pertinent eras, materials from the secondary literature with which Pound familiarized himself, and a sequence of citations and references, some still unidentified, that concern events occurring and individuals encountered during the composition of the *Cantos*.

Williams is more circumscribed thematically, historically, and geographically in the fragments that he incorporates into *Paterson*. More often than not, the subjects of the American historical materials, news clippings, and letters that he weaves into his text are monstrosity and unrequited desire. *Paterson* Book One, entitled "The Delineaments of the Giants," is embellished with documents of the apocrypha surrounding the Falls of the Passaic river. The accounts of the monster of the Falls, the disappearance there of Mrs. Sarah

Cummings, and Sam Patch's often miraculous leaps into other rivers (the Niagara and the Genesee), all contribute to the wonder necessary for the fulfillment of the work's mythopoetic program, itself
an act of superimposition, to elicit a man, a body, and a city. The
letters from several individuals that achieve increasing prominence
in the course of *Paterson* play on certain distinctions—between public
and private, aesthetic and "natural" or "everyday" expression—that
were not terribly important to Pound. The dramatic effect of the
extracts and the texture of the poetic material resulting from them
is, however, similar in the work of both poets.[27]

From Ashbery to Zukofsky to Stein, the poets who succeeded
Pound and Williams concentrated as much on the accretion of poetic
substance as on the integrity of discrete artworks. Eliot, Pound, and
Williams, following Mallarmé, ushered in an era dominated by the
tactile qualities of aesthetic material comprising modern and post-
modern culture.

The Savage *Bricoleur*

The preceding discussion has thus far attempted to articulate certain
aims of modern poetry, the techniques it devised in order to achieve
them, and the qualities of the resultant poetic text. An examination
of the process of poetic production from the perspective of the poet
may also prove worthwhile, in terms of the functions and guises
that he or she had to assume in order to meet the demands of modernist composition. As in the case of the mentality of refuse so
prominent in American and twentieth-century cultures, it is again
an anthropologist, Claude Lévi-Strauss, who uncannily anticipates
the climate in which modern poetics arise.

In performing the activity of fieldwork and in transmitting its results, the cultural anthropologist must engage in a multifaceted process of translation. The terms and symbols of the culture under study
must be rendered into a vocabulary comprehensible to the culture
that has, in a sense, dispatched the social scientist. The researcher
"in the field" must also master the transformational systems inherent in the various cultures that he or she represents and mediate
between them.

It would be difficult to articulate the grammatical rules and cognitive principles of the so-called "primitive" mind with greater sensitivity to the biases of Western science and to the limits of the analogies inevitably invoked in such studies than has Claude Lévi-Strauss. A certain condescension invades any attempt to explain the simple in terms of the ostensibly more complicated or advanced. Lévi-Strauss nonetheless struggles to avoid reducing the conceptual systems of "primitive" peoples to a level of primitive oversimplicity. "This thirst for knowledge is one of the most neglected aspects of the people we call 'primitive,'" he writes in "The Science of the Concrete," the introductory essay in *The Savage Mind* (1962).[28] "Magical thought is not to be regarded as a beginning, a rudiment, a sketch, a part of a whole which has not materialized. It forms a well-articulated system, and is in this respect independent of that other system which constitutes science, except for the purely formal analogy which brings them together" (*SM,* 13). In the context of this effort to translate or to present the operating principles of primitive thought, it is most striking that Lévi-Strauss, when he assembles aesthetic examples to support his assertions, has recourse to an environment in which Pound, Stevens, and Williams are quite at home:

> From this point of view, it would seem that impressionism and cubism are not so much two successive stages in the development of painting as partners in the same enterprise, which, although not exact contemporaries, nevertheless collaborated by complimentary distortions to prolong a mode of expression whose very existence, as we are able to appreciate today, was seriously threatened. The intermittent fashion for "collages," originating when craftsmanship was dying, could not for its part be anything but the transposition of "bricolage" into the realms of contemplation. (*SM,* 30)

In two pregnant sentences, Lévi-Strauss compresses the development of three important moments in impressionist and modern art. Impressionism and cubism coexist rather than negate each other because they both constitute a moment within the traditional handiwork of the painting when the object and its representation are broken down into the fragments, whether of light in the former case or perspective in the latter, that comprise them. The mentality of the synthetic art object such as the collage, argues Lévi-Strauss,

arises at a moment when the fragmentation common to impressionism and cubism is still current but when the age of craft (echoes of
Walter Benjamin) has been radically transformed, if not definitively
terminated. The figure of the maker that Lévi-Strauss invokes in
this essay straddles the worlds of modernist innovation and the "savage mind" and is called the *bricoleur*.[29] As the translator notes, this
term "has no precise equivalent in English. He is a man who undertakes odd jobs and is a Jack of all trades or a kind of professional
do-it-yourself man" (*SM*, 17). *Bricolage* is also the French term for
all sorts of repairs done by nonprofessionals in their homes and for
the stores where the tools and materials necessary for this activity
may be purchased. As we examine Lévi-Strauss's characterization
of the figure and activities of the *bricoleur* in a "primitive" setting,
we should bear in mind that in real life Ezra Pound was an accomplished cabinet-maker and wood-worker.

There still exists among ourselves an activity which on the technical
level gives us quite a good understanding of what a science we prefer
to call "prior" rather than "primitive," could have been on the plane of
speculation. This is what is commonly called "bricolage" in French. In
its old sense the verb "bricoler" applied to ball games and billiards, to
hunting, shooting and riding. It was however always used with reference to some extraneous movement: a ball rebounding, a dog straying
or a horse straying from its direct course to avoid an obstacle. And in
our own time the "bricoleur" is still someone who works with his hands
and uses devious means compared to those of a craftsman. The characteristic feature of mythical thought is that it expresses itself by means
of a heterogeneous repertoire which, even if extensive, is nevertheless
limited. It has to use this repertoire, however, whatever the task in hand
because it has nothing else at its disposal. Mythical thought is therefore
a kind of intellectual "bricolage"—which explains the relation which
can be perceived between the two.

Like "bricolage" on the technical plane, mythical reflection can reach
brilliant unforeseen results on the intellectual plane. Conversely, attention has been often drawn to the mytho-poetical nature of "bricolage"
on the plane of so-called "raw" or "native" art, in architectural follies
like the villa of Cheval the postman or the stage sets of Georges Méliès,
or, again, in the case immortalized by Dickens in *Great Expectations*
but no doubt originally inspired by observation, of Mr Wemmick's suburban "castle." . . . The "bricoleur" is adept at performing a large
number of diverse tasks; but, unlike the engineer, he does not subor-

dinate each of them to the availability of raw materials and tools conceived and procured for the purpose of the project. His universe of instruments is closed and the rules of the game are always to make do
with "whatever is at hand," that is to say with a set of tools and materials which is always finite and is also heterogeneous because what it
contains bears no relation to the current project, or indeed to any particular project, but is the contingent result of all the occasions there have
been to renew or enrich the stock or to maintain it with the remains of
previous constructions or destructions. The set of the "bricoleur's" means
cannot therefore be defined in terms of a project . . . or "instrumental
sets," as there are different kinds of projects. . . . It is to be defined
by its potential use or, putting this another way and in the language of
the "bricoleur" himself, because the elements are collected or retained
on the principle that "they may always come in handy." (*SM*, 16–18)

In light of the decisive role played by myths and mythology in
the literature and scholarship of modernism (Pound, Joyce's *Ulysses,* Curtius, Cassirer, Kafka's fragmentary fiction, and Hermann
Broch's *The Death of Virgil* are merely a few examples),[30] Lévi-
Strauss's appeal to *bricolage* as a model for primitive mythmaking
is particularly striking. The *bricoleur* is a "generalist." His craft
may not be as systematic or verifiable as the engineer's technology,
but he maintains an especially tangible relationship to his materials
and his work. His interventions are situational, and his decisions
derive from a sense of an ongoing role or social function rather than
from the logic and division of labor imposed by particular projects.

The *bricoleur* in "primitive" society is nonetheless capable of
"brilliant unforeseen results." Of crucial importance to this work,
which explains the distortions and permutations of myths, is the
bricoleur's relationship to his materials and the past from which
they emerge. When we imagine the activity of composing such works
as the *Cantos* and *Paterson,* Lévi-Strauss's image of the *bricoleur*
at work is hardly far afield:

> His first practical step is retrospective. He has to turn back to an already
> existent set made up of tools and materials, to consider or reconsider
> what it contains and, finally above all, to engage in a sort of dialogue
> with it and, before choosing between them, to index the possible an-
> swers which the whole set can offer to his problem. He interrogates all
> the heterogeneous objects of which his treasury is composed to discover
> what each of them could "signify" and so contribute to the definition

of a set which has yet to materialize but which will ultimately differ from the instrumental set only in the internal disposition of its parts. . . . But the possibilities always remain limited by the particular history of each piece and by those of its features which are already determined by the use for which it was originally intended or the modifications it has undergone for other purposes. The elements which the "bricoleur" collects and uses are "pre-constrained" like the constitutive units of myth, the possible combinations of which are restricted by the fact that they are drawn from the language where they already possess a sense which sets a limit on their freedom of manoeuvre. . . . It might be said that the engineer questions the universe, while the "bricoleur" addresses himself to a set of oddments left over from human endeavors, that is, only a sub-set of the culture. (*SM,* 18–19)

Now, the characteristic feature of mythical thought, as of "bricolage" on the practical plane, is that it builds up structured sets, not directly with the structured sets but by using the remains and debris of events: in French "des bribes et des morceaux," or odds and ends in English, fossilized evidence of the history of an individual or a society. The relation between the diachronic and the synchronic is therefore in a sense reversed. Mythical thought, that "bricoleur," builds up structures by fitting together events, or rather the remains of events, while science, "in operation" simply by virtue of coming into being, creates its means and results in the form of events, thanks to the structures which it is constantly elaborating and which are its hypotheses and theories. But it is important not to make the mistake of thinking that there are two stages or phases in the evolution of knowledge. Both approaches are equally valid. . . . Mythical thought for its part is imprisoned in the events and experiences which it never tires of ordering and re-ordering in its search to find them a meaning. But it also acts as a liberator by its protest against the idea that anything can be meaningless with which science at first resigned itself to a compromise. (*SM,* 21–22)

The precise locus of the activity of mythical *bricolage* is indeed "on the dump" of cultural remains. Like the angel of history in Benjamin's philosophical fragments on the subject,[31] the stance of the *bricoleur* is essentially retrospective. The past is the home from which emanate the elements of a set whose coherence is in a state of perpetual emergence. While not necessarily teleological, the creation of synthetic art is invariably cosmological and historical. In *bricolage,* the variables are the odds and ends that can be glued and tacked together, and the constant is the makeshift expectations of

the work. Western science, on the other hand, comes with a conceptual orientation and metaphysical world view built into it; its
variables are the abstract principles that must be adjusted in keeping
with the emergent facts. In the absence of such an orientation,
mythical thought and improvisational art proceed by combination
rather than evolution. The *bricoleur* plays jazz on the instrument of
his fragments. The type of growth predicated by this productive
model indeed comprises "unforeseen results." Achievement consists in the brilliance, innovation, and unexpected quality of a composition made up of known elements.

Lévi-Strauss is rather insistent in his assertion that the *bricoleur*
can dispense with the totalization from which scientific investigation proceeds, if only as an illusion. The *bricoleur,* he states, is
content to work with a subset, to build upon a fragmentary inher-
itance. And in renouncing the desire for totality, either in the composition or the effect of the artwork, the figure of the *bricoleur*
shares his closest affinity with the modern artist. Indeed, the desire
to break away, in varying degrees, from the formal requirements of
completion, resolution, and sublimation is arguably one of the few
attributes shared by modern productions from a wide range of media.

The figure of the *bricoleur* sheds much light on the poetics of the
Cantos, Paterson, and the verse that they inspired. Both works achieve
epic dimensions and tone through their recourse to mythic elements.
Both are willing to work with a subset of remains at hand. In both
cases, the marbled texture of the grafts that hold the fragments together is as meaningful a feature of the text as the contents themselves.

It is somewhat ironic to note, then, that the yearnings for purity
of origin and completion of design survive more persistently in the
poetry of Ezra Pound than in the mythmaking of the primitive *bricoleur.* In the following analysis of the *Cantos,* it will become evident that Pound's joyous patchwork is counterbalanced by a desire
for a reinstatement of a primordial linguistic and economic purity
whose loss occasions genuine anguish on the part of the poet. Poetic
and economic purity enters the complex economies of the *Cantos*
in several forms: in a strand of nature lyric often with the terse
statement of the haiku[32]; in a sequence of poetic pastiches inspired
by the classical epics, predominantly though not exclusively the *Od-*

yssey; in the evocation of a natural, by which Pound specifically means allegorical, landscape; and in a string of references to encompassing features of the "natural" world such as the sea or the wind.

In recoiling from his own inclination to break the impetus of totalization, Pound is not an aberrant modernist but a modernist *par excellence*. When treated as a composite whole, modernism is distinguished from post-modernism precisely in the gravitational sway still exerted upon it by the mythical unities and nostalgia from which it flees. In different ways, James Joyce and Wallace Stevens are precisely in this position; Jorge Luis Borges is not; and Franz Kafka is in the noman's land in between. Williams is willing to watch his yearnings for completion and consummation burn out on the sacrificial pyre dedicated to the Beautiful Thing. In this sense, he remains more firmly ensconced in the workplace of *bricolage* than Pound.

Language as the Currency of Poetry: The Economies of the *Cantos*

> The iron coin of Lycurgus was distempered so that it cd. not even serve as industrial iron or be beaten back into plowshares.
> —Ezra Pound, *Guide to Kulchur*[33]

Ezra Pound's literary contribution will always be muddled by his own confused role in the major historical events of the twentieth century. It was, however, the same sociopolitical interest underlying some of his most outrageous pronouncements and acts that enabled him to discern the economies of energy and resources that engender poetry as much as they give rise to tyranny and war, opulence and poverty.

With few exceptions, the major modern poets came to grips with the fact that, in the twentieth century, the great dreams of the "tradition" either had been forced into an intolerable mockery of the actuality of material conditions or, when realized, had resulted in an apocalypse more horrific than the imagination could postulate on its own. Yeats died just at the moment when international events eclipsed his vision of "The Second Coming," devaluing, if not abolishing, the need for such an aesthetic postulation. As we have seen, Eliot, Stevens, and Williams all made room in their poetry for the refuse and rubble necessitated by the economics of expansion violently turned in upon itself in war or in the accumulation of vast heaps of terminal byproducts. There were, however, means to resist the horrible picture. Eliot aligned himself with the vision of Catholicism to see his way through the wasteland; Stevens converted the dump into something sublime or at least conceptually intriguing; and Williams luxuriated in a multiplicity that ceased to identify garbage as garbage because it telescoped all objects into a single, indifferent perspective. Of his immediate poetic colleagues, Pound alone elected to remain in the repository of cultural remains and to make political economy the subject, indeed a decisive organizing metaphor, of his poetry.

It would be an oversimplification to suggest that the poet suddenly converted to a materialist grounding. Pound began not with systems of economy but with the remnants of former cultures: Greece, Provence, and China. The emphasis in *Personae* (1908–10) and *Lustra* (1916) is not upon the cultural machinery but on the artifacts themselves for their internal beauty. Pound preserves Provence by capturing the idiom and syntax of its songs. The personae that Pound assumes in his shorter poetry become the voices both of particular personages and of historical and cultural moments. The early Pound combines the dramatic play in Browning's dramatic monologues and Proust's pastiches with the historical program of Borges's Pierre Menard,[34] to recreate, by means of an acute ear and style, the conditions under which a text from a remote time and place was composed. Through his earlier poetry, Pound thus joined the other major modernists who knew that any momentous stylistic or aesthetic innovation must be accompanied by historical awareness and a serious rehauling of historiographical principles and methods.

Poems from *Personae,* such as "Sestina: Altsaforte," "Marvoil," and "The Flame," and from *Lustra,* such as "After Ch'u Yuan," "Ts'ai Chi'h," and "The Tea Shop," are most successful in evoking the poetries that inspired them and the wider cultures from which they derive.[35] Textual fragments are, however, merely the first of the components to be claimed and assimilated by Pound's unique adaptation of *bricolage.* In the *Cantos,* scraps of old utterance, as well as mythical and legendary characters, historical personages, cities, dates, documents, and statistics, have all attained the same status—membership in the lexicon of a transformative poetic language.[36]

In the *Cantos,* the functions of economics and the state constitute a pivotal metaphor for Pound's thinking and writing. In terms of the economic allegory that prevails there, language is capital, with a value deriving from the wealth of the old cultures whose utilizable remains it comprises. Language is currency to be invested productively by the poet, so that it will be invested with currency.[37] Bad poetry results in depression, insolvency, and bankruptcy, the inability of a culture to contribute to successive stages of cultural evolution. The implicit economic model at the base of the *Cantos* is simultaneously progressive and retrogressive; it converts the byproducts of extinct cultures into currency but demands a counterevolutionary adaptation to enable the reader to digest the fragmentary remains of old culture.[38]

The reader of the *Cantos* must go to some lengths to assimilate the incredibly diverse assortment of cultural fragments that Pound has assembled. Like Joyce's *Ulysses,* the *Cantos* predicate in their very design the various scholarly instruments that will be necessary for identifying its references.[39] Whether intentionally or not, the reader who braves Pound's challenge enrolls in an exceptionally broad do-it-yourself curriculum encompassing, among other subjects, Greek mythology, the history of Renaissance art, and American and Chinese histories.

Early in the *Cantos,* Pound depicts his encounters with two of his teachers, Professor Rennert of Romance Philology at the University of Pennsylvania and his counterpart at Freiburg, Emile Lévy.[40] In these episodes, the speaker appears thirsty for learning but uncomfortable, to say the least, with academic authority.[41] By his own self-representation, Pound is the student who will outdo his professors and discredit their rank and professional trappings through a highly esoteric erudition. Pound is a self-taught academic who designs a difficult but comprehensive home-study program for his unseen students. Like him, these students may be long in ancestry and historical pedigree but short in inherited wealth and social status.

Pound's program for the *Cantos* is thus endowed with pedagogical, political, and aesthetic dimensions. Its ideological orientation is rooted in an American conservatism whose populism, isolation-

ism, and resentment both of old and new wealth, run deep. Pound
was at the same time willing to dislocate his activities considerably
in order to gain direct access to what he thought were the authentic
sources of world art and culture. There is a curious fusion, then,
between the xenophobic and comparative impulses in Pound's aesthetic politics; at their intersection is a struggle not only for his own
erudition but also for that of a hypothetical common reader. Pound's
populist allegiances greatly explain the "plain talk" that he insis-
tently inserts in the *Cantos* and his prose. This assumes several forms:
intentional misspellings, as in the *Guide to Kulchur*; contractions
of auxiliary verbs, such as "cd." and "wd."; and certain instances
of ventriloquism that we will have occasion to examine below.
Pound's forced pedestrianism of expression, if I may coin a phrase,
hits at the economic privilege underscored by verbal cultivation while
it reaffirms his loyalty to the particular readership with which he
identifies.

If any scenario for long-term cultural profits exists within this
account of Pound's research and labor, he would undoubtedly take
offense. Pound himself espouses an economic system in which wealth
is distributed according to communal need by some benevolent ty-
rant of impeccable character. The positive moments in the histories
of Chinese and American leadership that Pound splices into the *Cantos*
invariably occur when taxes are reduced and rulers renounce their
own perquisites and those of their class. While mismanagement is
relative and variable in the cultures touched upon by the *Cantos,*
economy is inevitable. By frontally engaging the economic sphere
rather than transforming its less repulsive byproducts into aesthetic
decorations, Pound commits himself to a rigorous, if unpredictable,
ethic whose existence we must acknowledge regardless of what we
think of the ideologies he espouses or the means by which he advances his opinions.

The *Cantos* not only engage the political economy in which they
and their privileged precedents are produced; they also constitute a
highly intricate poetic economy, or confluence of economies, in their
own right. Their value cannot be appreciated unless the play of forces
that they sustain is read. In light of the open poetic field in which
Mallarmé, Pound, and Williams inscribed their verse, any attempt
to exhaust the economies of the *Cantos* would be ill conceived. The
challenge facing the reader of the *Cantos* is not so much a comprehensive interlinear gloss as a general and always provisory un-

derstanding of the text's discursive modes and the principles of their interaction. The ultimate exegesis of the *Cantos* may well assume the form of the ideogram of their dynamic forces.[42] For this reason, the text is often most intricate and interesting at the nodes of convergence between its different types of discourse and their cultural sources. The following observations will therefore focus more on transitional moments in the text, where a broad array of forces, themes, and discursive levels are at play, than on particular digressions that Pound elaborated. The *Cantos* cannot be sensitively read unless their interpretation is implicated by the allegorical shorthand of the Chinese written character.

The Zero-Degree of Nature

The outrages of history, the follies of lust and greed, are set in the *Cantos* against a backdrop of nature imagery that might naively be regarded as a nature incorporated into the poem itself. In any text, nature of course is not a material or ontological grounding but a perspectival element that is seemingly more stable and enduring than others. A text is free to incorporate more than one nature; the nature or natures of a text are free to change in themselves and in time. We may encounter in the *Cantos* such a passage as the following:

> The reeds are heavy; bent;
> and the bamboos speak as if weeping.
>
> Autumn moon; hills rise about lakes
> against sunset
> Evening is like a curtain of cloud,
> a blur above ripples; and through it
> sharp long spikes of the cinnamon,
> a cold tune amid reeds.
> Behind hill the monk's bell
> borne on the wind.
> Sail passed here in April; may return in October
> Boat fades in silver; slowly;
> Sun blaze alone on the river.

These lines, from *Canto* XLIX/244, comprise as "pure" a nature poetry as exists in the *Cantos,* if by purity we mean a thematic focus on natural process and a relative dearth of extratextual allusions. If such features as light, the wind, and the sky comprise the accoutrements of the nature in the *Cantos,* its technical specifications are heavily invested in the rhythmical, short lyrical line. The lyric constitutes the technical form of nature in the *Cantos.* Whether inspired by the Greek epic or Chinese verse, this strand of lyrical utterance repeatedly sets the poem's historical events in relief: It surrounds them, softens their contours and harshness, and suggests the existence of a much broader horizon, like the perspective in the Chinese silkscreen, from which the ambitions and deeds of men and women appear as idle vanity. The "big picture" of nature is where the possibility for the Hegelian *Aufhebung,* the transcendental overview, enters the *Cantos.*

Even at this zero-degree of nature, however, a process of imitation, appropriation, and distortion is under way. Such phrases as "Boat fades in silver" and "Sun blaze alone" are free of articles and hence characteristic of the Chinese-inspired verse that Pound fashioned for the recapitulation of Chinese imperial history taking up the bulk of *Cantos* LI–LXI. It is precisely this relative freedom from modifiers and the structure of predication that Fenollosa defined as the dynamic quality which separated the Chinese written language from Western languages more logical and inert.

More typical passages from the nature poetry pervading the *Cantos* are in fact heavy with mythological allusions. This is because the nature for which Pound strives and that serves as a foil to human machinations is not a nature of environmental features and processes. The nature evoked by the lyrical poetry of the *Cantos* is a pristine state of linguistic utterance, which Pound situates in the ur-texts of the various groundbreaking moments in Eastern and Western cultures. In this regard, Pound is not far from the interplay between ground and earth in the very specific senses that Martin Heidegger assigns them in characterizing the origins of the work of art. What holds Homer, Catullus, the Confucian odes, the Provençal lyric, and the haiku together is their status as seminal linguistic moments, moments at which their respective languages opened paradigmatic horizons of possibility.

Ironically, then, the nature that might otherwise seem to undercut and measure the ostensibly more contrived acts of human ambition and greed is itself highly cultivated and artificial. Nature is an allegorical moment in the production of poetry. When the wind blows

its way into the *Cantos* in order to announce the "big picture" of
nature, it is blowing in from somewhere. Where Pound draws upon
the tradition of Western letters, his nature poetry is, more often than
not, literally inspired by Books X–XII of the *Odyssey,* which aptly
serve as the *Cantos'* encompassing mythological framework. It is
in the context of a natural discourse whose origin is not "free" but
instead found in artworks at their "classical" moments of newness
and endurance that we can begin to read some highly characteristic
passages from the nature poetry:

Aye, I, Acoetes, stood there,
            and the god stood by me,
Water cutting under the keel,

Sea-break from stern forrards,
            wake running off from the bow,
And where was gunwale, there now was vine-trunk,
And tenthril where cordage had been,
            grape-leaves on the rowlocks,
Heavy vine on the oarshafts,
And, out of nothing, a breathing,
            hot breath on my ankles,
Beasts like shadows in glass,
            a furred tail upon nothingness.
Lynx-purr, and heathery smell of beasts,
            where tar smell had been,
Sniff and pad-foot of beasts,
            eye-glitter out of black air.
The sky overshot, dry, with no tempest,
Sniff and pad-foot of beasts,
            fur brushing my knee-skin,
Rustle of airy sheaths,
            dry forms in the *aether.*
                  . . . . . .
I have seen what I have seen:
            Medon's face like the face of a dory,
Arms shrunk into fins. And you, Pentheus,
Had as well listen to Tiresias, and to Cadmus,
            or your luck will go out of you.
Fish-scales over groin muscles,
            lynx-purr amid sea . . .

And of a later year,
        pale in the wine-red algae,
If you will lean over the rock,
        the coral face under wave-tinge,
Rose-paleness under water-shift,
        Ileuthyeria, fair Dafne of sea-bords,
The swimmer's arms turned to branches,
Who will say yes in what year,
        fleeing what band of tritons,
The smooth brows, seen, and half seen,
        now ivory stillness.

And So-shu churned in the sea, So-shu also,
        using the long moon for a churn stick . . .
                        (*Canto* II/7–9)

Thus the light rains, thus pours, *e lo soleills plovil*
The liquid and rushing crystal
        beneath the knees of the gods.
Ply over ply, thin glitter of water;
Brook film nearing white petals.
The pine at Takasago
        grows with the pine of Isé!
The water whirls up the bright pale sand in the spring's mouth
"Behold the Tree of the Visages!"
Forked branch-tips, flaming as if with lotus.
        Ply over ply
        The shallow eddying fluid,
        beneath the knees of the gods.
                        (*Canto* IV/15)

The first passage, from *Canto* II, is filled with the fur, noises, and smells of animals, the red glow of Dionysian wine, and the mist of the sea. If these elements comprise nature, then the *Cantos,* propelled forward by the voyage motif, are off to a natural start. The fascination with bodily smells and functions will achieve its full scatological dimension in *Cantos* XIV and XV. By its alternation of short lines with even shorter ones, the passage establishes an ethereal and rhythmic mood for the nature presumably underlying human affairs.

The great leave-taking of *Canto* I, the flourish with which the entire work begins, is not, however, by Dionysus on the way to his

wedding on Naxos but by Odysseus's crew as it departs from Circe's
island for Hades, where it eventually encounters Tiresias and the
ghost of Elpenor. In this way, the beginning of the *Cantos,* which
is narrated by Odysseus, runs parallel to the beginning of Book XI
of the *Odyssey.* The images of the sea wind, bodies, and lyrical
sighs of utterance constitute nature and continue from the first *Canto*
into its successor. How is it, then, that already in the second
Canto we assist at a second voyage? As is asserted by the *Annotated
Index to the Cantos of Ezra Pound* and confirmed by the text, the
narrator of the second *Canto* is Acoetes, the pilot of Dionysus's
ship. There are parallels between the voyages. In the same way that
Odysseus is the only member of his crew invulnerable to the drugs
of Circe and the singing of the Sirens, Acoetes is not deluded by
Dionysus's hallucinations. An "ex-convict out of Italy" (*Canto* II/7),
who also bears resemblances to Pound in his Dionysian fascinations, sets the ship off course.

In its corporeal imagery, expansive setting, and lyrical tone, then,
Canto II continues the voyage, and naturalistic foundation to the
work, initiated in *Canto* I. Strange metamorphoses nevertheless take
place in the passage cited above. Sea nymphs' swimming arms become branches. The transformative environment signals how Pound
is already branching off course and modifying his sources, in a manner akin to the associative chains of the imaginary. If the "trigger,"
so to speak, of *Canto* I and its voyage is the name of Elpenor, the
pedestrian crewman who dies a relatively meaningless death on Circe's
island, *Canto* II sets off from the name of "Eleanor," Helen of Troy,
and the oedipal associations to which she gives rise. The passage
cited above includes a reference to Pentheus, the voyeuristic King
of Thebes, who is surprised during his vigils and dismembered by
female followers of Dionysus. The voyage of conquest, viewed from
a masculine point of view, already encompasses a more heated and
ambiguous war between the sexes than might otherwise appear to
be the case.

The naturalistic voyage lyric thus incorporates and frames textual
superimpositions and variations of a highly complex nature. Nature
is one mood, albeit expansive and incantatory, among others. The
second citation above is, if anything, even more lyrical than the
first. Deriving from *Canto* IV, it combines the crystal of water and
the whiteness of daylight into the sublime image of a transparency

nonetheless folded upon itself. Just as the oriental image in *Canto* II—"So-shu churned in the sea"—is grafted upon the passage concerning a classical Western voyage, the pines of Takasago and Isé (Japan) in *Canto* IV are implanted within this apotheosis of pure light. The ineffable East mystifies an already sublime image even further. The "Ply over ply," the manner in which purity surpasses even itself, also describes the manner in which the text of the *Cantos* is fashioned: as an overlay and ramification of themes, allusions, and discursive levels, a modernistic folding within the space of poetry.

Nature in the *Cantos* is, then, not so much a material environment as a moment within an allegory of textual production, a moment of internal expansion and emptying by which the text affords itself new beginnings. Nature is inseparable from myth because both represent pristine states of language. The nature of the *Cantos* is invariably mythological. From the profile that emerges of Pound as a man, it may be said that he yearned, passionately and painfully, for this nature and the purity that it embodied. As a textual construction, however, this nature could only articulate itself through a complex intertwining of fragments and variations. In renouncing the "more natural language" that might get "the Reverend" (T. S. Eliot) "through hell in an hurry" (*Canto* XLVI), Pound acknowledges the futility of his retrogressive wish.

Pure Language and Zero-Interest Banking

For a poet with such expertise in nature, "love and idleness," and the Dionysian pleasures, Pound devotes a rather large portion of the *Cantos* to a body of historical minutiae whose significance is not always self-evident. The populist home-education course of the *Cantos* informs us of such details as the sexual preferences of several Chinese emperors, the circumstances surrounding the construction of the Tempio in Rimini (1446–55), the founding of a Sienese bank, the Monte dei Pasche (1624), and John Adams's European itinerary (1780–84). Pound's considerable interests in economics and politics help endow the *Cantos* with their epic scale. It is in the context of his futile but nonetheless powerful yearning for a linguistic nature that the hodgepodge of his themes and allusions acquires some meaningful coherence.

Purity in language—that is, language which remains within the pristine state of an ongoing poetic tradition—is tantamount to incorruptibility in government, the renunciation of self-interest in the service of the people, and, in economics, to the distribution of wealth devoid of the accretion of profits through interest. In *Canto* XIII, Confucius characterizes the nature that Pound would reinstate (and whose violation he condemns with rage) as an order or equilibrium:

> Kung walked
> > by the dynastic temple
> and into the cedar grove
> > and then out by the lower river,
> > > . . . . . .
> And Kung said, and wrote on the bo leaves:
> > If a man have not order within him
> He can not spread order about him;
> And if a man have not order within him
> His family will not act with due order;
> > And if the prince have not order within him
> He can not put order in his dominions.
> And Kung gave the words "order"
> and "brotherly deference"
> And said nothing of the "life after death."
> And he said
> > "Anyone can run to excesses,
> It is easy to shoot past the mark,
> It is hard to stand firm in the middle."
> > > > > (*Canto* XIII/58–59)

Pound's attitude toward order could hardly be called casual. Confucius's reflection on this term would be, in its Western emanation, no more exotic than the golden mean, but endowed with the remoteness of the East, this regimen discloses itself within the poem like some long-suppressed revelation. This chaste measure and control, which function as a degree-zero of their culture, are only pages removed from Pound's first, and perhaps most vivid, image of the corrupt and execrable in the *Cantos*.

In *Cantos* XIV and XV, the ribald corporeality, which at the beginning of the work is among the properties of sensual ecstasy, has become something else: a Spenserian-Boschian landscape where deformed creatures deposit waste and other excretions without control or order.[43]

> Above the hell-rot
> the great arse-hole,
>   broken with piles,
> hanging stalactites,
>   greasy as sky over Westminster,
>   . . . . . .
> The slough of unamiable liars,
>   bog of stupidities,
> malevolent stupidities, and stupidities,
> the soil living pus, full of vermin,
> dead maggots begetting live maggots,
>   slum owners,
>   usurers squeezing crab-lice, pandars to authority, . . .
>   (*Canto* XIV/62–63)

This Slough of Despond is the purgatory relegated to those who lose their self-control and parasitically live off excess. It is dedicated to the usurers, the Chinese emperors' eunuchs, who usurp power when it is not formally invested in them, to the Jews, and to women (for the landscape of excrescence symbolically resides in feminine sexuality). When Kung's order is violated, a hell breaks out exceeding anything that Spenser could conjure up for us in viciousness and disgust. In addition, language becomes denatured, perverted, put up for hire:

> And the betrayers of language
>   . . . . . . n and the press gang
> and those who had lied for hire;
> the perverts, the perverters of language,
>   the perverts, who have set money-lust
> Before the pleasures of the senses; . . .
>   (*Canto* XIV/61)

Although brief, this is a capital and decisive passage in the *Cantos,* intertwining Pound's political and economic ideologies inextricably with his poetic aspirations. Language is the cultural capital that must be kept pristine and invested wisely. Usury is not a banking practice limited to rapacious governments and Jews; it is the very adulteration of value and language.[44] The history of China intrigues Pound because out of its byzantine corruption occasionally arise leaders who reinstate the order of Kung: They renounce their privileges, lower taxes, and avoid the dissipation of their energy and purpose in sexual deviance. For Pound, the exemplary leaders in Chinese history not only exercise sound political, economic, and military judgment, but as patrons of literature and the arts, they also publicly demonstrate their stake in literacy. The lasting impression left by this history is its nearly endless alternation between moral and intellectual brilliance and their inverse. The tragedy of emperors such as Ouen-Tsong, Hi-Tsong, and Tchin-Tsong is their abdication of their moral vision and strategic function, an act that Pound describes as a giving in to women or to feminine impulses alien to Kung's pristine order. The power accruing to the eunuchs throughout Chinese history clearly fascinates Pound as much as it revolts him.

Usury is to purity of value what philandering is to the sanctioned bond of marriage: adulteration. Pound's strong interest in the troubadours thus shares in the ambivalent attraction-repulsion characterizing the sexual economy of the *Cantos* as a whole. The love poetry of Aquitaine and Provence owes its vitality to the indiscretions that it celebrates. Pound pursues this lust through the rivalries that divide and align such major Italian houses as Malatesta, Medici, Sforza, and Este during the Renaissance. The conquests of the love poets of the late Middle Ages transmuted into the *Realpolitik* of the Renaissance thus set the stage for two of the *Cantos'* major developments: the institutionalization of usury in the emergence of modern banking in seventeenth-century Siena; and the unfolding of Renaissance warfare as a backdrop for the present-day setting of the work's composition, the long sequence of events linking the First and Second World Wars.

The few pages around *Canto* XLV, the so-called "Usura Canto," thus serve as the thematic and economic crux of the *Cantos*. Late in *Canto* XLII the Monte dei Pasche, whose stable and low interest rates Pound admires but which is nonetheless a paradigm for modern banking, is founded. *Canto* XLIV, which involves a kaleidoscopic variation on the Ferdinands and Leopolds who governed Tus-

cany and the Holy Roman Empire, dramatizes the effect of Napoleon
on eighteenth- and nineteenth-century Florence. This *Canto* links
the rise of institutionalized capitalism to the French and American
revolutions, a constellation exploited fully (and updated to Franklin
Delano Roosevelt) in *Canto* XLVI. During the course of this pregnant transition, the "Usura Canto" and *Canto* XLVII offer the transcendental overview announced whenever the poem's elevated lyrical voice is invoked. If the "Usura Canto" irrevocably declares the
financial practice of interest-charging and all associated forms of
the adulteration of value to be "CONTRA NATURAM," it does so
by celebrating a small group of untainted artists and their productions: Piero della Francesca, Giovanni Bellini, St Trophime of Arles,
and Saint Hilaire of Poitiers. The other lyrical interlude in this momentous passage, *Canto* XLVII, reinscribes the work's encompassing mythological framework: Odysseus imbibes the moly that
will spare him from Circe's charms, while the Fates bemoan another
instance of frustrated female desire, Aphrodite's loss of Adonis.
Immediately following this lyrical interlude, the four *Cantos* that
round out *The Fifth Decad Cantos* are a crossroads for the work's
most compelling concerns. *Canto* XLVIII presents a picture of cap-
italistic excess between the World Wars. It is succeeded by a Chinese
lyric (*Canto* XLIX) and a global overview of the political and economic forces at play early in John Adams's career. Adams, Napoleon, eighteenth-century Florence, and the Jews all converge in
Canto L, which revolves around the Battle of Marengo, while *Canto*
LI, a reprise of the "Usura Canto," reiterates its cry for nature in
art and economic value.

   The historical watershed of the *Cantos* is thus a moment late in
the eighteenth century when the cultural and political fate of the
United States will be decided by its government's response to the
divergence between inflated and natural values, between fidelity to
a predetermined measure and adulteration. Pound's foray into Chinese
history and poetry is a contrapuntal accompaniment to the history
of Western value, in the literal and metaphoric senses. Although
remote and sublime, China is a stage where a drama parallel to the
Western triumphs and delusions plays itself out, perhaps on a slightly
different level. China functions as the internal imaginary of the *Cantos*. Its abrupt rebounds between nobility and corruption heighten

the tension surrounding the decisions faced by John Adams and his colleagues.

Democracy—according to the American model and the European antecedents selected by its major ideologues, such as John Adams and Thomas Jefferson—is the political analogon to nature. Because Adams and Jefferson explore the European roots of American culture, Pound is happy to claim them as his predecessors. British excesses such as "taxation without representation," Writs of Assistance (*Canto* LXIII/352–54, LXXIII/420), and restrictions on free expression and assembly correspond to the governmental corruption at the low points of Chinese history. The early American debates that Pound pursues—between loyalists and revolutionaries (*Canto* LXIV, LXV) and over governmental involvement in private investment and the status of the Second National Bank of the United States (*Canto* XXXVII)—have a place in the wider meditation on the partnership between true art and natural measure. As Adams muses, retrospectively reviewing his political career:

> No indian's hatchet raised while I was president
> Nor has nature nor has art partitioned the sea into empires
>   or into countries or knight's fees
> on it be no farms ornate or unornate, no parks and no gardens
>   (*Canto* LXXI/418–19)

Art and nature are tantamount to each other, joined in apposition. Both nature and art are inimical to the boundaries, claims, and profits of empire.

The crisis posed not only by conflicting values but also by the issue of value itself proliferates from setting to setting, producing increasingly striking resonances. Borso d'Este's inability to keep a peace between the Malatesta and Urbino houses becomes, in *Canto* XXI, a striking analogon to the outbreak of World War I. The inquiry into British democracy, constitutional history, and taxation that begins in Canto XLVI is aligned by the phrase "OB PECUNIAE SCARCITATEM" with the founding of the Monte dei Pasche in Siena and the Chinese ideogram meaning "to regulate the name" (*Cantos* XLII/213, XLIII/216, XLVI/382). Pound recapitulates the rhetorical history that the founding fathers had to assimilate and address. He pursues John Adams's own investigations into British legal history in search of the legal precedents for the powers asserted by England at the time. Such items as Sir J. Pilkington's case, which established Ireland's constitutional autonomy under King Edward I (*Canto* LXVII/389), "Coke upon Littleton" (*Canto* XLIII/352), and Hales' case, in which King James II, having failed to gain dispensing power for the Crown from Parliament, tried to wrest it from the judiciary (*Canto* XLVI/386), are not merely historical commonplaces but stages in the evolution of American rhetoric and ideology.

American history is, of course, the "operative element" in the constellation of backdrops that Pound assembles for his poetry. Renaissance Italy and imperial China are over, terminated, while the crystallization of American values and policies is still in flux, even with its origins in the eighteenth century and after. Beyond Pound's self-dislocation to the European repository of Western culture, it is toward an American setting that his ideological as well as aesthetic interventions are geared.

The nostalgia for a measured nature, then, masculine in its control but feminine in its steadiness and accessibility—and the opposition between this nature and a variety of political and economic contrivances—do indeed bridge the *Cantos'* remarkable array of settings and contexts. As I have suggested above, Pound's nature is deceptively simple, being inevitably textual in its constitution.

Even with this allowance, the conflict between the naturalistic zero-point and the excesses that corrupt it proliferates itself from theater to theater. The threat to nature is largely what ties such disparate elements as Emperor Yu, "Cabestan's heart in the dish" (*Canto* IV/13), the XYZ Affair, and Walter G. Hinchcliff's ill-fated transAtlantic flight together with Elsie Mackay on March 13, 1928 (*Canto* XXVIII/140). The threat, conspiracy, and perversion of something intimate and familiar extend themselves obsessively.

It is economy—sexual, fiscal, and textual—that gives an otherwise amorphous sequence of fears and associations their form. With the Florentine wars and the artworks commissioned by the Malatestas (*Canto* XVI/69) as their background, *Cantos* XVII, XIX, XXXV, and XXVII attempt to furnish a history of the chief capitalist interests at play in World War I. Pound reads the Great War as a conspiracy of bankers and munitions-makers, some but not all Jewish, including Sir Basil Zaharoff, Schneider-Creusot, and Mitzui of Japan. He refers frequently in these Cantos to economists such as John Maynard Keynes and Dexter Kimball, and at one point he incorporates extracts of economic theory into his text:

> A factory
> has also another aspect, which we call the financial aspect
> It gives people the power to buy (wages, dividends
> which are power to buy) but it is also the cause of prices
> or values, financial, I mean financial values
> It pays workers, and pays *for* material.
> What it pays in wages and dividends
> stays fluid, as power to buy, and this power is less,
> per forza, damn blast your intellex, is less
> than the total payments paid by the factory
> (as wages, dividends AND payments for raw material
> bank charges, etcetera)
> and all, that is the whole, that is the total
> of these is added into the total of prices
> caused by that factory, any damn factory
> and there is and must be therefore a clog
> and the power to purchase can never
> (under the present system) catch up with
> prices at large, . . .
>
> 					(*Canto* XXXVIII/190)

The above passage, according to the *Annotated Index* modeled after Clifford Hugh Douglas (1879–1952), describes the economic cycle in which a factory's purchasing power forever lags behind "prices at large." Such social scientific documentation not only enriches the allusive texture of the *Cantos,* but it also presumably lends credibility, if not credit, to a far less measured ideological strand of the text.

Predictably enough, Pound's economic ideal corresponds to a natural economy, in which nature furnishes the collateral behind financial transactions. As one might expect, history does not abound in natural economic institutions. In his *Guide to Kulchur,* Pound praises the Spartan coin for its "MEASURE," gold discs for their universality, and Charlemagne for the stability of the price structure that he established for grain.[45] Pound's ideal for a financial institution is the Monte dei Pasche, whose credit was literally backed by a piece of nature, the fields around Siena:

To pay 5% on its stock, Monte dei Pache
and to lend at 5 and 1/2
Overplus of all profit, to relief works
and the administration on moderate pay..
     that stood even after Napoleon.
                (*Canto* XLI/205)

Charging only 1/2 percent for its money and founded on "natural"
currency, the "Mountain of Pastures" achieves enduring stability.
It is, however, also the model for subsequent institutions and, for
Pound, graver violations of natural measure. A charge of even 1/2
percent deviates from Pound's ideal; poetic utterance in its pristine
state, culture devoid of accumulation. The Monte dei Pasche of Siena,
nearly attaining the heights of Pound's purism, nonetheless falls back
into the slough of a comprehensive ambivalence.

Graft and Ventriloquism

For a work that struggles on several levels with the notion of purity,
the *Cantos* are strongly marked by a form of comic relief based on
its antithesis. At several points in the *Cantos,* Pound's humor assumes a ventriloquism in which an incommensurate voice is projected from the mouth of an unlikely speaker:

And he went down to the old brick heap of Pesaro
     and waited for Feddy

And Feddy finally said "I am coming! . . .
     . . . to help Alesandro."
And he said: "This time Mister Feddy has done it."
He said: "Broglio, I'm the goat. This time
     Mr. Feddy has done it (*m'l'ha calata*)."
And he'd lost his job with the Venetians,
And the stone didn't come in from Istria:
And we sent men to the silk war;
And Wattle never paid up on the nail
     Though we signed up with Milan and Florence;
And he set up the bombards in muck down by Vada
     where nobody else could have sent 'em

and he took the wood out of the bombs
and made 'em of two scoops of metal
And the jobs getting smaller and smaller,
Until he signed on with Siena;
And that time they grabbed his post-bag.
And what was it, anyhow?
Pitigliano, a man with a ten acre lot,
Two lumps of tufa,
and they'd taken his pasture land from him,
And Sidg had got back their horses,
and he had two big lumps of tufa
with six hundred pigs in the basements.
And the poor devils were dying of cold.
And this is what they found in the post-bag:
Ex Arimino die xxii Decembris
"Magnifice ac potens domine, mi
singularissime
"I advise yr. Lordship how
"I have been with master Alwidge who
"has shown me the design of the nave that goes in the middle,
"of the church and the design for the roof and . . ."
"JHesus,
"Magnifico exso. . . ."

(*Canto* IX/36–37)

There is a certain hilarity in Pound's placing twentieth-century jive-talk in the mouths of fifteenth-century Italian magnates. Federigo Urbino (1444–82) becomes "Feddy." "Sidg," Pound's nickname for his central Renaissance doer and shaker, Sigismondo Malatesta (1417–68), conjures up a cigar-smoking stockbroker or insurance agent. Pound's game, in the above passage, is to place a "low" dialect in the mouths of the venerable and venerated. Expressions such as, "Broglio, I'm the goat," and "JHesus" graft a very specific, populist Poundian rhetorical landscape upon what might otherwise be construed as an elevated cultural ambiance.

Pound's humor here runs parallel to the experiments in the representation of consciousness and the distortion of dialogue conducted by James Joyce in *Ulysses*. It is also classically American. As the culture that has enlarged itself through the open-ended assimilation of linguistic traces deriving from virtually every coordinate of the globe, America has prided itself on its ability to flatten preexisting distinctions within a common plane. Assimilated into the cultural clearing-house of the *Cantos,* Urbino and Malatesta speak an American dialect.

The outrageous instances of linguistic imperialism in the above citation implicate the larger issue of the methods by which Pound appropriated his cultural sources. Appropriation is a kind of theft in its own right.[46] For a poet obsessed with certain forms of purity and governmental rectitude, Pound filches what interests him with remarkable ease.

The prestidigitation by which one's own voice appears to emanate from someone or something removed is a form of ventriloquism. The grandiose Italians issue forth in words and intonations that Pound gives them. This trick is, of course, the inverse of assuming "personae," in which the self-effacement accrues not only to the sources but also to the poet, who in effect relinguishes his "self-expression" to the composite voice of a cultural setting whose remains he or she has gathered. Assuming cultural personae is a variation on the comic act of imitating foreign accents or "doing impressions." In Pound's early poetry and elsewhere in the *Cantos,* he externalizes himself to a remote setting, crystallizes its "voice," both recording and playing it through the medium of his poetry, which in this instance functions as a historico-anthropological tape recorder. Pound's "personae" are in the tradition of Yeatsian masks. In Borgesian fashion, Pound immerses himself in a particular culture by extrapolating the composite mask that it presented to history and by standing behind that mask. In so doing, he accomplishes a consummate act of translation: He speaks the Provençal, the Greek, or the Chinese.

While ventriloquism projects or externalizes the here and now, the play of "personae" internalizes the preexistent, and hence the arbitrary, at the expense of the "self." These inverse practices of appropriation thus involve considerable disfiguration, whether to the poet or his historical sources. Although the identification of the greatest Malatesta as "Sidg" stands out, it is the "self"-effacement behind personae that nonetheless predominates in the *Cantos.* This self-abdication shares a passivity with the posture assumed by "observers" of primal scenes.

One could well argue that alongside the expansive, naturalistic voice of lyricism recurring throughout the *Cantos* runs an entire discursive strand of instances when Pound's intonation assumes the voice and intonation of other cultures. Pound's pastiches of the Homeric epic, the haiku, and the Provençal refrain all belong to this stratum of the text. For particularly striking instances of vocal graftings from remote settings into Pound's poetry, one gravitates to the chorus, "It is Cabestan's heart in the dish" (*Canto* IV/13), Dave Hamish's account of his dealings with Sir Basil Zaharoff (*Cantos* XVIII, XIX/82–84), the remarkably pure Chinese lyric of *Canto* XLIX, and the letter of sea captain Tching Mao to Emperor Kang Hi (r. 1662–1722, *Canto* LX/331). One of the *Cantos'* densest confluences of personae, discursive modes, and artifacts from widely dispersed points of the globe appears in *Canto* LXXIV, first of the *Pisan Cantos,* which we will be examining later in some detail. The only moment of equal textual density in the *Cantos* may well be *Canto* LII/257–61, where "Between KUNG and ELEUSIS" and within five pages, the speaker rails against Jews and usury, consults the zodiac, invokes Leopold II, Grand Duke of Tuscany, Palmerston, and Manes, utters a lyric whose rhetorical thrust counters the excesses of usury, and inscribes the Chinese ideogram *chih,* whose translation is "to stop" or "to desist."

One senses that Pound luxuriated in the despair that the profusion of Austrian and Tuscan Leopolds and Ferdinands in the *Cantos* would bring to his future readers, not to mention the complex recycling of names such as Liang, T'ang, Chin, and Chou in Chinese imperial history. Particularly in the *Chinese Cantos* (LII–LXI), the recapitulation of dynasties and their more notable events is somewhat tedious. The repetitive-variable play on names by royal houses serves as an insignia for the manner in which the *Cantos* function as a brokerage house for the artifacts and poetic modes of divergent cultures. Pound remorselessly pursues the lines of several dynasties, because after a while the uniqueness of the leaders and the "high deeds" of their reigns dissolve into a certain indifference. The traces left by the emperors fade into a historical manifold whose substance is as characteristic as the texture of a voraciously assimilative poetic stuff.

Odysseus and Oedipus

We are indebted to Freud for establishing incontestably that mythology, if not oriented toward psychological explanation in itself, is nonetheless a human production uniquely privileged in its psychological intuition and intensity. In our earlier discussion of the topology of the *Cantos,* we have often been confronted by the psychosexual traits of their constitution. The obsessiveness of Pound's pursuit of the deflowering of purity emerges; the cultural detritus in which he submerges himself is a kind of excrement; he cheers oedipal troubadours on to their conquests but worries about female secretions.[47] Homer's *Odyssey,* between Odysseus's escape from Polyphemus and his arrival on Calypso's island, constitutes the overarching mythological framework of the *Cantos.* (Calypso's island is both the original setting of the text and the destination it reaches after a long digression). In light of the impasses that arise during Odysseus's and Circe's mutual seduction and the various types of sexual joy and threat embodied by Scylla, Charybdis, and the Sirens, the Homeric text is itself highly suggestive on the level of Freudian models of psychosexual evolution and behavior. Before reading one of several possible exemplary passages from the *Cantos* in detail, it should prove informative to review the Homeric antecedents to the work and the emergent psychological profile of Pound—as an additional possible access to the text.

It is perhaps already apparent that the *Cantos* heavily depend on paradigms which nevertheless undergo a serious disfiguration as a result of the text's pervasive climate of ambivalence. We have already observed the proximity of Pound's most intense yearnings for purity to his most bitter railings against corruption. In *Canto XXIX,* Pound articulates a paradigm for the feminine that remains no more stable than any of the other icons installed into the poem:

> Pearl, great sphere, and hollow,
> Mist over lake, full of sunlight,
> Pernella concubina
> The sleeve green and shot gold over her hand
> Wishing her son to inherit
> Expecting the heir ainé be killed in battle
> He being courageous, poisoned his brother puiné
> Laying blame on Siena
> And this she did by a page
> Bringing war once more on Pitigliano
> And the page repented and told this
> To Nicolo (ainé) Pitigliano

Who won back that rock from his father
"still doting on Pernella his concubine"
        . . . . . .
There is no greater incomprehension
Than between the young and the young.
The young seek comprehension;
The middleaged to fulfill their desire.
Sea weed dried now, and now floated,
    mind drifts, weed, slow youth, drifts,
Stretched on the rock, bleached and now floated;
Wein, Weib, TAN AOIDAN
Chiefest of these the second, the female
Is an element, the female
Is a chaos
An octopus
A biological process
               and we seek to fulfill . . .
TAN AOIDAN, our desire, drift . . .
        . . . . . .
She is submarine, she is an octopus, she is
A biological process,
So Arnaut turned there
Above him the wave pattern cut in the stone
Spire-top alevel the well-curb
And the tower with cut stone above that, saying:
    "I am afraid of the life after death."
and after a pause
"Now, at last, I have shocked him." . . .
        . . . . . .
The tower, ivory, the clear sky
Ivory rigid in sunlight
And the pale clear of the heaven
Phoibos of narrow thighs,
The cool cut of the air,
Blossom cut on the wind, by Helios
Lord of the Light's edge, and April
Blown round the feet of the God,
Beauty on an ass-cart
Sitting on five sacks of laundry
That wd. have been the road by Perugia
That leads out to San Piero. Eyes brown topaz,
Brookwater over brown sand,

The white hounds on the slope,
Glide of water, lights, and the prore,
Silver beaks out of night,
Stone, bough over bough,
            lamps fluid in water,
Pine by the black trunk of its shadow
And on hill black trunks of the shadow
The trees melted in air.

                              (Canto *XXIX*/141–46)

This lengthy citation, encompassing four extracts, follows the drift
not only of Canto *XXIX* but also of Pound's sexual ambivalence. In
characteristic fashion, the passage is composed of a montage of
three superimposed women: a historical one, Pernella the concubine, who brings discord and destruction upon the House of Orsini;
a timeless woman, "Weib, TAN AOIDAN," a feminine archetype
who would be at home in the psychology of Sándor Ferenczi[48] (and
as close as Pound comes to Williams's Beautiful Thing); and a contemporary Italian woman concurrent with the time of the poem, who
moves, if not inspires, the "speaker." Pernella concubina, like Helen of Troy and Cunizza da Romano (a second historical female in
the *Canto*), incites men to rivalry; she both arouses their passion
and demoralizes them. There are quite tangible repercussions due
to the loss of control that the women, whether mythical or "real,"
occasion. Perhaps in the *Canto*'s own allegiance to Kung's order,
the image of the woman, in the wake of such peace-shatterers as
Pernella and Cunizza, becomes abstract, general, and eternal. She
is chaotic, ungovernable, and set in the sphere of biological, as opposed to intellectual, process. Through interlinguistic punning, the
Weib (German for woman) is associated with the wine of intoxi-
cation and the waves of the sea. Brainless woman is a thing of
timeless nature. *Canto* XXIX thus ends in a paean to an unidentified
present-day paradigm of beauty sitting on five sacks of laundry by
the road to Perugia; it is a passage cast in the same tense, abbreviated utterance as the other nature poetry running through the *Cantos*. This creature is "Beauty on an ass-cart." She links herself and
Woman to the allegorical slough of excrement, uncontrolled excretions, and usury in *Cantos* XIV and XV.

"Ball-crushers" like Helen of Troy, Circe, Pernella concubina,
and Cunizza da Romano, who has an affair with the troubadour

Sordello and is spirited away by him at the request of her brother, add romantic interest to a history conducted by men of action. Mindless themselves, women function as inert catalysts to historical explosions. When women begin to deploy volition or ruses of their own, they become dangerous. In the *Odyssey,* it requires the bestialization of Odysseus's entire crew and the divine intervention of Hermes to enable one man, our hero, to resist Circe's charms and potions successfully. Indeed, the section of the *Odyssey* that Pound appropriates as the mythological source and framework of the *Cantos* is fraught with the threats of an overwhelming female sexuality. Circe deprives men of their reason, an effect also achieved by the Sirens' song (*Odyssey* XII/39–54); Scylla bites off their heads (*Odyssey* XII/85–100); and Charybdis, in the shadow of a fig tree, sucks them under the sea (Odyssey XII/103–10).[49]

In fact, Odysseus's successful encounter with Circe is described, both in the Homeric text and the *Cantos,* as a war between poisons, a significant image in characterizing Pound's relation to his own poetry. In *Canto* XXXIX, the sex-heavy atmosphere of Circe's island is described as follows:

> When I lay in the ingle of Circe
> I heard a song of that kind.
> Fat panther lay by me
> Girls talked there of fucking, beasts talked there of eating,
> All heavy with sleep, fucked girls and fat leopards,
> Lions loggy with Circe's tisane,
> Girls leery with Circe's tisane
> κακὰ φάρμακ' ἔδωκεν
> kaka pharmak edōken

> (*Canto* XXXIX/193)

Richmond Lattimore translates the Homeric phrase that Pound retains in the Greek as "whom the gods had given evil drugs" (*Odyssey,* X/157). The dissociation of manly will and motivation is described, by Pound as well as Homer, as a toxic contamination. The only antidote for Circe's poisons (*pharmak*) is another poison, the moly preemptively prepared for Odysseus by a male god, Hermes. "By Molü art thou freed from the one bed/ that thou may'st return to another," declares Hermes in *Canto* XLVII/237; in the *Odyssey,* he describes the preparation as "good medicine" (X/287). Pound's transliteration of the Greek, "kaka pharmak," homonymically links Circe's charms and the scene of seduction to the German and French words for excrement.

The toxic effect of medicines, the medicinal quality of poisons, and the significance of drugs as an insignia for the various attitudes toward language in Platonic philosophy and thereafter have been most productively explored by Jacques Derrida in "Plato's Pharmacy."[50] Although an extended recapitulation of the nuances of meaning encompassed by the Greek *pharmakon* is beyond the scope of this chapter, it may suffice to suggest that Pound's ambivalence to feminine sexuality falls well within the purview of the long-standing Western ambivalence toward writing and the figure of the *pharmakon*. For Pound, the seductive feminine sexuality of such figures as Helen of Troy, Circe, and Cunizza da Romano introduces the loss of measure and control, opening a vast, potentially imprisoning slough of indifference before the male adventurer. In the work of Jacques Derrida, the poison is not sex-linked but marks an irreducible double standard in the prevailing relations to the monuments of culture and writing. Pound's ambivalence, if we take into account Derrida's meditations on the figure of poison that Pound incorporates into his text, extends beyond women to his writing and the act of poetic composition. If a wide gradation characterizes the sexual possibilities included in the *Cantos,* this is as much owing to Pound's second thoughts about his own work as to any sexual confusion on his part.

Among several passages from "Plato's Pharmacy" that associate the suspicion toward the *pharmakon* with a characteristically negative view of language is the following:

> Sperm, water, ink, paint, perfumed dye: the *pharmakon* always penetrates like a liquid; it is absorbed, drunk, introduced into the inside, which it first marks with the hardness of the type, soon to invade it and inundate it with its medicine, its brew, its drink, its potion, its poison.
>
> In liquid, opposites are more easily mixed. Liquid is the element of the *pharmakon*. And water, pure liquidity, is most easily and dangerously penetrated then corrupted by the *pharmakon,* with which it mixes and immediately unites. (*Dissemination,* 152)

Derrida's poisonous writing flows within the same liquid medium inhabited by Pound's *Weib*. As we have seen, Pound's purism articulates its own fear and loathing toward artifice and ornamentation for their own sake. Rage and revulsion are responses to a number of specific sexual, political, and economic activities evident in literature and history. What Pound may not realize is that, within his own tradition and psyche, his own artistic production provokes comparable reactions.

In many senses, then, Odysseus, or at least Pound's version of him, is also Oedipus. Pound, like Freud's sexually curious boys, passively assists at some of the climactic sex scenes in Western literature and history.[51] Even more important than the place of Odysseus's encounter with Circe in the Homeric epic is the episode's colossal sexual ambivalence. Circe will give in to Odysseus and serve him but only after he has aggressively rebuffed her sexual wiles. Hermes has advised Odysseus to "rush forward against Circe, as if you were raging to kill her" (*Odyssey* X/294–95). Her favors are offered obligingly but only after Odysseus has heeded the call for sexual hostility. Odysseus mounts the attack after imbibing a drug that acts as an antidote to Circe's potions. Sexual consummation, in the Homeric source, is an act of war, occurring only in the aftermath of checks and balances against provocation. The complexities inscribed in this primal scene continue throughout the *Cantos*.

Some of the troubadours' exploits incorporated by Pound, for example, do indeed regard the sex act from the perspective of Freud's curious but traumatized little boys. In the cases of Pieire de Maensac, the troubadour who runs off with the wife of Bernhart De Tierce (*Canto* V/18), or Sordello (*Canto* VI/22–23), the male interloper gains forbidden attention, presumably at the husband's expense. As often as not, however, the oedipal dramas to which Pound alludes result either in the destruction of the male interloper or in the frustration of the female's desires and plans. Ignez da Castro, the wife of Pedro of Portugal, appears twice in the *Cantos*. Murdered by a distrustful and possibly jealous King Alfonso IV, she exemplifies a woman who vies with a male (of the parental generation) for the allegiance of her beloved and who suffers a brutal punishment. Interwoven into the opening of *Canto* IV are two instances of sexual cannibalism as manifestations of jealous rage:

> And by the curved, carved foot of the couch,
> > claw-foot and lion head, an old man seated
> Speaking in the low drone . . . :
> > > > Ityn!

Et ter flebiliter, Ityn, Ityn!
And she went toward the window and cast her down,
        "All the while, the while, swallows crying:
Ityn!
            "It is Cabestan's heart in the dish."
            "It is Cabestan's heart in the dish?"
            "No other taste shall change this."
And she went toward the window,
                the slim white stone bar
Making a double arch;
Firm even fingers held to the firm pale stone;
Swung for a moment,
                and the wind out of Rhodez
Caught in the full of her sleeve.

                            (*Canto* IV/13)

The wife of Raymond of Château Roussillon commits suicide in
response to her husband's murder of her lover, troubadour Guillem
da Cabestanh—and to having his heart served to her in a dish. Grafted
onto the reference to this grisly, and perhaps gristly, episode is a
mythological allusion. Tereus, King of Thrace, seduces Philomela
and, in order to silence her, cuts out her tongue. His wife, Procne,
is Philomela's sister. In a similar act of revenge, she cooks and
serves the flesh of Itys, the son she rears with Tereus. Itys is thus
eaten (Ityn), echoing the social ostracism suffered by Mrs. Peggy
Eaton, wife of Andrew Jackson's secretary of war, in Washington
D.C. (*Cantos* XXXIV, XXXVII). Eating, then, exists at the climax
of a certain sexual aggression. Oedipal interloping is not only desirable; it is positively threatening. The cannibalism that it provokes
in the *Cantos* violates the only taboo equal to incest in its primor-
diality.

We assist at the sexual odyssey of the *Cantos* from the perspective of Odysseus. The work's breathless lyrical refrains are also a
pornographic accompaniment to love-making. The vantage point of
the observer is, however, undermined by complexity, danger, and
even terror. Since some of the *Cantos'* sexual martyrs are females,
it may be said, from a psychoanalytical point of view, that their
psychosexual orientation is as feminine as masculine. Pound also
embarks upon a female sexual odyssey, one as tenuous as its male
counterpart.

The sexual adventure of the *Cantos* therefore brings us to a land not totally alien to the domain implicated by Freud's classical analyses of obsessive neurosis. Pound goes to rather extreme lengths to defend and preserve an aesthetic and sexual nature, maternal in its purity, and his efforts displace themselves from one remote arena to the next. Pound situates himself in a cultural repository that is also a multipurpose wastesite. He concerns himself a good deal with money. He associates the practice of charging interest with female wiles and seductiveness. Male order (and sexuality) is presumably backed by the collateral furnished by the phallus. Pound witnesses sexual activity both from "male" and "female" perspectives: The *Cantos* provide evidence of male aggression but also of sympathy for "female" frustration and longing. The sexual odyssey of the *Cantos* thus unearths an economy of ambivalence: toward sexual behavior itself and toward the very poetic composition that structures a certain cultural and emotional clutter.

The formal techniques that Pound devises for a modernist poetics are somehow informed by this ambivalence, but they function autonomously from it as well. Pound's techniques of *bricolage*, grafting, and ventriloquism point to a poetic space that sustains an perpetual dance of disequilibrium. We turn now to one of those moments when the *Cantos'* internal economies are particularly revealing of themselves—of their stases and their impasses as well as of the backlog of forces that they bring into play.

The Entropy of Economy: A Frozen Dance

Canto LXXIV transpires at the moment between the breakdown and the halt of the machinery of government, economy, and culture—when the final convulsions of activity only serve to grind the shattered remains into further disrepair. The four winds of the *Odyssey* still sweep over the Disciplinary Training Center near Pisa, where Pound is impounded. Light, a significant image for the *Canto,* pulsates over "the death cells in sight of Mt. Taishan @ Pisa" (427). The *Canto* focuses on the reversal of process into stasis or of freedom into imprisonment but also on involution, the internal self-destruction of machines that have lost their direction, though not their energy. This involution manifests itself in a persistent reiteration of the *Canto*'s central motifs, including wind, light, and voyages, almost out of the lack of anywhere else to turn.

Sudden reversal can be horrifying, but through a literature descended from Indo-European languages that balance subjects against objects on a fulcrum of predicates, we have developed a taste for it. The central ploy of *Canto* LXXIV pivots on this gesture. Pound aligns his current circumstances behind a series of backdrops or tableaux whose historical, aesthetic, and poetic categories we have already surveyed. What these side shows have in common is the theater of activity that they open to our view: The motion of their miniature figures attenuates and freezes from its normal pace into suspended animation. Art historian Léo Bronstein has organized the contorted abstraction of so-called "primitive" representations into a tradition of "mobile rigidity" recurring throughout the history of art in nomadic and declining cultures, most recently in our own modernism.[52] "Mobile rigidity" is distinguished by its capacity to capture a motion in the instant of its "aboutness" to occur—in the "aboutness" of a wave to break, for example. It is not by accident that there are references to two different masks in the *Canto,* one from the Baluba tribe in Zaire and another from an Australian image of Wanjina, "whose mouth was removed by his father/ because he made too many *things*" (*Canto* LXXIV/426–27). These masks may well convey the fixed horror that Bronstein identifies as the affective content of "mobile rigidity."

Pound repeatedly freezes the dance of his historical figures in a rigid and grotesque parody of motion; he tears our attention away from the side shows to which he has lured us with his Chinese landscapes and the misdeeds of Cunizza da Romano, and he throws us back into the inescapable crudity of a detention camp.

Toward the middle of the *Canto* we arrive at a striking instance of this paralysis. A passage that associates the extinction of the European bison with war profiteering ("and the fleet that went out to Salamis/ was built by state loan," [431]) ends in an implicit comparison between the defenseless herds and Pound, as he "looked on Mt Taishan" from the confines of the DTC (432). From this rather clear elaboration of Pound's impasse, which shares the *Canto*'s emphasis on material conditions, the text embarks on a poetic argosy as full-blown as any in the work.

The escape fantasy indulged by the *Canto* announces its own fantastic atmosphere. It begins with an outright evocation of names and events that have been rendered irrelevant and fictive by World War II:

> but in Tangier I saw from dead straw ignition
> > From a snake bite
> fire came to the straw
> from the fakir blowing
> foul straw and an arm-long snake
> that bit the tongue of the fakir making small holes
> > and from the blood of the holes
> > came fire when he stuffed the straw into his mouth
> dirty straw that he took from the roadway
> > > first smoke and then the dull flame
> > > > (*Canto* LXXIV/432)

Not only do these lines assert a mythical metamorphosis; they also postulate a highly mystified explanation: The magician ignites a fire with the blood from his snake-bitten tongue. The sorcery in this aside describes what is taking place in the *Canto*: From a rather concrete apprehension of the collusion between war and profit, the text withdraws into itself and enters a reverie, situated in an exotic Tangiers populated by characters who are both alien to and somehow responsible for the misery at hand. This brief imaginative escape reenacts and parodies the Homeric odyssey comprising the *Cantos'* mythological superstructure, whose retardation is a primary metaphor for Pound's immediate circumstances.

Adding to this atmosphere of orientalism is the reference to Rais Uli, a Moroccan who, according to the *Annotated Index,* kidnapped three British and American citizens, Walter Harris and Ion Perdicaris (1904), and Sir Harry Maclean (1907). In order to avoid war, the Sultan of Morocco paid their ransom. While the mention of this episode interjects a note of adventure, it also hints at the political and economic underpinnings that the fantasy would appear to evade. Kidnapping is a means by which a private operator profits by usurping, in the most literal sense, control of a person. As a result of Rais Uli's mercenary motives, Morocco almost goes to war. Thus one moral of the story is that the price of profiteering, if not exacted in the booty of war, must be borne by the state.

Through a self-undermining edifice of fantasy, the text of *Canto*

LXXIV has detached itself from the constraints of Pound's untoward circumstances. Despite its exotic setting, the world of fantasy-
adventure is a mere step away from a milieu of civil interaction that
the war has also rendered obsolete. The ambiance of metamorphosis
that facilitated the poetic flight reasserts itself in such phrases as
"the chrysalids mate in the air/ color di luce/ green splendour"
(432), but these in turn give way to a line from *The Seafarers,*
which Pound had translated from the Anglo-Saxon: "Lordly men
are to earth o'ergiven" (432). The "lordly men" turn out to be Pound's
intellectual compatriots: "Fordie that wrote of giants/ and William
[Butler Yeats] who dreamed of nobility/ and Jim [Joyce] the co-
median singing:/ 'Blarrney castle me darlin'/ you're nothing now
but a StOWne'" (432–33). The company includes mathematician
Victor Plarr, who was also librarian of the Royal College of Surgeons, Edgar Jepson, an English novelist, and gossip Urquell Kokka,
who appears both here and in the *Guide to Kulchur* as a migratory
socialite. The pronounced civility of this coterie, suggested most
pointedly by the Joycean dialogue and the personage of Kokka, lends
itself most easily to a pan-European catalogue of fine restaurants:

> Sirdar, Bouiller and Les Lilas,
> > or Dieudonné London, or Voisin's,
> > > . . . . . .
> > the cake shops in the Nevsky, and Schöner's
> not to mention der Greif at Bolsano la patronne getting older
> Mouquin's or Robert's 40 years after
> > and La Marquise de Pierre had never before met an American
> > "and all their generation"
>
> > > > > > > (*Canto* LXXIV/433)

The list of no longer frequented pleasure domes comprises a poignant obituary for a certain European way of gracious living. Order,
etiquette, and irrelevance to the immediate circumstances also stand
behind the inclusion of an episode involving Pound, his housekeep-
er, Mrs. Hawkesby, and Henry James, which becomes a commentary on the academic world:

> Mr James shielding himself with Mrs Hawkesby
> as it were a bowl shielding itself with a walking stick
> as he maneuvered his way toward the door

> Said Mr Adams of the education,
> Teach? at Harvard?
> Teach? It cannot be done.
> and this I had from the monument
> (*Canto* LXXIV/433)

While Pound has allowed himself an aside on elitist education, he has also orchestrated together three side shows reminiscent of the once possible, but now bankrupt, mannered existence: literary society, life at the café, and the academy. With a disconcerting finality, however, the characters and places he has temporarily resurrected from the graveyard of cultural remains melt into surreal deformity when he applies the heat of his confinement to them on, of all days, the anniversary of French independence:

> Under Taishan quatorze Juillet
> with the hill ablaze north of Taishan
> and Amber Rives is dead, the end of that chapter
> see Time for June 25th,
> (*Canto* LXXIV/434)

Among the deaths memorialized in the *Canto,* that of Princess Troubetzkoy, author of *The Quick and the Dead*, epitomizes the death, rather than quickness, of the other figures summoned in the course of the poetic digression, at least in terms of their relevance to the war's devastation. These references do, however, advance the economic allegory. Literary circles, café society, and the academy are all tangential to the economic priorities determined and dictated by the state of war. Those of Pound's *semblables* lucky enough to survive World War I share a marginal relation to the economy, relying on the maintenance of so-called "essential" industries and services, while functioning autonomously of them and the immediate catastrophe. (Pound pays tribute to his less fortunate literary and artistic colleagues in *Canto* XVI.) In a sense, Pound puts, or at least figures, all of his literary *confrères* to death through the abrupt shift from fanciful flight to an ostensibly more material grounding.

The reader's reinstatement to the courtyard of the DTC culminates one exemplary instance of the predominant performative act in the *Canto*: the paralysis of figures who are ironically rendered gratuitous when their animation is suspended. This gesture is compulsive. Its repetition demands intervals when the marginal figures are literally set aside. Between such fanciful flights as the one to Tangiers or the Parisian café life of the 1880s (435), Pound evokes a vivid, almost tactile sense of enclosure, witnessed from the inside, and explores the political, economic, religious, and cultural roots of the war and his ensuing confinement.

The parallelism between Pound's confinement in the heat of summer under "Mt. Taishan @ Pisa" and the wartime experience of millions who entered camps of various types is a phenomenon that skitters on the border between massive psychological repression and irony. The *Canto*'s messianic rhetoric and sacrificial scenarios owe much to Pound's apprehensions in this regard. At the same time, however, it is with impunity that Pound observes the proximity of a Farben chemical factory to the DTC. On the threshold of guilt, he retreats into repression, condemning himself to a Sisyphean track between escape fantasy and self-justification.

The Farben plant is "still intact/ to the tune of Lilibullero" (434). In characterizing the degradation of his position, Pound selects what his bigotry identifies as images of extreme subservience: "the Adelphi/ niggers scaling the obstacle fence/ in the middle distance/ and Mr. Edwards," a black fellow prisoner who warned, "doan you tell no one/ I made you that table" (434). Still secure in his ideology, Pound explores the biblical provisions for usury and unearths the mythological city of Dioce.

This city and the Baluba mask that Pound compares to Mr. Edwards's face are among the objects comprising an archaeological motif that runs throughout the *Canto*. In light of Pound's fascination with cultural remains, it comes as no surprise that he regarded archaeology as among the most productive enterprises of modern science. Archaeology is to knowledge what the ideogram is to language: a means of releasing into the here and now energies that have lain dormant for centuries in the artifacts of old cultures. Among the few individuals unabashedly revered by Pound is Leo Frobenius, the German anthropologist and archaeologist who is best known in the United States for his *African Genesis*[53] and who led the attempts to unearth Atlantis. In one of several tributes appearing in the *Guide to Kulchur*, Pound describes Frobenius's contribution in terms bearing directly on his own poetic enterprise and his particular practice of appropriation. "To escape a work or set of words loaded up with dead association Frobenius uses the term Paideuma for the tangle or the complex of the inrooted ideas of any period. . . . As I understand it, Frobenius had seized a work not current for the purpose of scraping off the barnacles and 'atmosphere' of a long-used term."[54]

The conception of Pound's linguistic economy as a linguistic excavation illuminates not only his archaeological references but also the serenity presumably emanating from the Chinese gods, Mt. Taishan, and the Homeric odyssey. The most significant archaeological objects in the poem are two masks. The image of Wanjina, deriving from an Australian creation myth, suggests a coincidence between the historical events that Pound has witnessed and an ongoing and inevitable chaos of things. The Baluba mask recalls the destruction of African culture by mercantilism; it survives only in the faces of people who, like Mr. Edwards, are the descendents of uprooted slaves. Pound is perfectly capable of bemoaning such cultural cannibalism while nursing his deep-seated prejudices.

The city of Dioce (or Ecbatan), capital of Greater Media, appears twice in the *Canto* as a haven of good taste and culture, even though it is a seat of imperial power. Pound's most extensive debt to archaeology is incurred in the repeated references to "Gassir's Lute," a Sudanese folk legend preserved by Frobenius in his *African Genesis*. The refrain "Hooo Fasa" that Pound incorporates into the *Canto* forms part of the incantation ending each section of the legend. The goddess Wagadu, who embodies the spirit of bravery, splits into four emanations, Dierra, Agada, Ganna, and Silla, and upon these Pound superimposes the four winds of the *Odyssey*, which attain particular prominence at the end of the *Canto*.

Given the extent of *Canto* LXXIV's investment in schemes—the near-symmetrical arrangements dominating its cities, winds, and masks—it can be well argued that the *Canto* is unusually dense in extrinsic structures. Their proliferation is partially responsible for its anthropological flavor. The distinctions drawn by the folk legends are "primitive" both as the term is applied by Lévi-Strauss to the totemic and classificatory systems of native peoples and as Freud elaborates the qualities of childhood obsessive thought. Out of its ephemeral and in some senses frivolous motion, then, the *Canto* precipitates the stability and repression the law.

In so "economical" a *Canto* it is almost predictable that Pound should resume his diatribe against usury, and in so anthropological a one that he should delve into the biblical roots of this practice, as "far back" as he pursues them in the *Cantos*. It is ironic that Pound should cite the prohibitions of *Leviticus* against usury as evidence against the financial practices of the Jews. There is perhaps an even greater irony in the qualitative similarity between the biblical injunctions and Pound's ideological thought:

> and the greatest is charity
> to be found among those who have not observed
>   regulations
>   not of course that we advocate—
>   and yet petty larceny
>   in a regime based on grand larceny
>   might rank as conformity nient' altro
>   with justice shall be redeemed
> Who putteth not out his money on interest
>   "in meteyard in weight or in measure"
>   XIX Leviticus or
> First Thessalonians 4,11
>   (*Canto* LXXIV/434)

Though the Bible shares the old age and pristine expression of the archaeological objects, Pound puts it to quite a different use. A good deal of the power in Australian masks and African legends derives precisely from the fact that they have been lost, have become estranged. The Bible, on the other hand, has had an continuing impact on Western culture. The very continuity of this influence, even upon such matters as capital accumulation, has necessitated its corruption, while Frobenius's finds, precisely because of their disappearance from the sight of culture, are endowed with a primitive innocence.

The grafting of the biblical "source" for economic corruption upon the text during a pause between fantastic excursions is characteristic of the manner in which Pound elaborates his central themes. Economic adulteration is, in terms of Pound's conceptual repertory, what the prison is to the spatial dimensions of the *Canto*; it is a thematic ground where his vituperation eventually settles, just as the inroads of his associations, however flighty, lead back to the DTC. In the same way that he diverts our attention to the prison by attenuating and arresting the motion of figures identified with prison, Pound returns to economic activity as the context of the paralysis that he observes around him. In isolating the biblical precedents for usury, Pound invokes the source of a source, the ancient cultural basis for what, in terms of the poetic economy, becomes its characteristic transaction.

Canto LXXIV has thus far offered us a twofold key into its complex movements: a rhythmic involution of historical vignettes into suspended animation, and a linear expansion, from the perspective of prison, of themes that are associated with the notion of enclosure and that are relevant to its cause. Throughout the *Canto*, however, Pound frames and contrasts this overall motion with a wind and rain that he would identify with natural process. Just after introducing the *Canto* with the sacrificial image of the Mussolinis hanged "by the heels at Milano," Pound embarks on an incantatory celebration of natural process, entering a mode of lyrical utterance that has now become familiar:

> rain also is of the process.
> What you depart from is not the way
> and olive tree blown white in the wind
> washed in the Kiang and Han
> what whiteness will you add to this whiteness,
> > what candor?
> "the great periplum brings in the stars to our shore."
> You who have passed the pillars and outward from Herakles
> when Lucifer fell in N. Carolina.
> if the suave air give way to scirocco
> Oὖ TIΣ, Oὖ TIΣ? Odysseus
> > the name of my family.
> the wind also is of the process,
> > sorella la luna
> > (*Canto* LXXIV/425)

This nature is revered and blessed in all corners of Pound's cultural globe. It transcends the arbitrary distinctions of nationality and religion. It celebrates Odysseus, the universal man. This nature manifests itself in a wind and rain capable of encompassing any historical event. These natural phenomena derive from a temporal order vastly more magisterial and steady than the one governing the war and Pound's particular circumstances.

Behind each of the historical and allusive stage sets constructed for the ironic purpose of being abruptly stripped away to reveal war and destruction stands the *Canto*'s economic function: its operation as a brokerage house for cultural artifacts:

> 4 giants at the 4 corners
> > three young men at the door
> and they digged a ditch round about me
> > lest the damp gnaw thru my bones
> > > to redeem Zion with justice
> sd/ Isaiah. Not out on interest said David rex
> > > > > the prime s.o.b.
> Light tensile immaculata
> > > the sun's cord unspotted
> "sunt lumina" said the Oirishman to King Carolus,
> > > "OMNIA,
> all things that are lights"
> and they dug him up out of sepulture
> soi disantly looking for Manicheans.
> Les Albigeois, a problem of history,
> and the fleet at Salamis made with money lent by the state to the
> > > > > > shipwrights
> > > Tempus tacendi, tempus loquendi.
> Never inside the country to raise its standard of living
> but always abroad to increase the profits of usurers,
> > > dixit Lenin,
> and gun sales lead to more gun sales
> > they do not clutter the market for gunnery
> > > there is no saturation
> Pisa, in the 23rd year of the effort in sight of the tower
> and Till was hung yesterday
> for murder and rape with trimmings   plus Cholkis
> plus mythology, thought he was Zeus ram or another one
> > > Hey Snag wots in the bibl'?
> > > wot are the books ov the bible?
> > > Name 'em, don't bullshit ME.   莫   Oὐ ΤΙΣ
>
> a man on whom the sun has gone down
> the ewe, he said had such a pretty look in her eyes;
> > > (*Canto* LXXIV/429–30)

Encompassing the biblical roots of usury, Greek war profiteering, the African counterpoint to this tradition, an ambivalent citation of Lenin, and a reinstatement to the confines of the DTC, this extended passage is exemplary of the motions and economies sustained by the *Canto*. The "4 giants" from the Gassir legend provide a ritualistic précis to two biblical allusions: one to *Isaiah* regarding the redemption of Zion, and another to the ditch dug by "three young men at the door," which alludes to Elijah's contest against the priests of Baal in *The First Book of Kings*. This latter episode demonstrates the efficacy of Yahweh at the expense of the pagan gods through Elijah's success in summoning a sacrificial flame and through his opponent's failure. Throughout the *Canto*, sacrifice is a condition of unjust enslavement, persecution, and martyrdom; at the very beginning, the executed Mussolini and Clara are described as a sacrificial carcass:

> Manes! Manes was tanned and stuffed,
> Thus Ben and la Clara *a Milano*
>   by the heels at Milano
> That maggots shd/ eat the dead bullock
> DIGONOS, Δίγονος, but the twice crucified
>   where in history will you find it?
>   (*Canto* LXXIV/425)

For Pound, Mussolini's death is sacrificial in the same sense that Jesus, Dionysus, and Manes, founder of the Manicheans, were murdered, as bearers of a controversial New Learning, which could purify human corruption but only at the expense of radical conceptual reorientation. The forebears that Pound selects for himself share a constellation of attributes that include a commitment to literacy, a messianic fervor, and a vivid sense of the threats around them. Erigena Scotus—the freethinking medieval theologian who authored the phrase "*omnia quae sunt lumina sunt*" and was condemned at church councils at Valence and Langres—and the Albigensian sect—targeted for obliteration by a crusade in the early thirteenth century—are included in the *Canto* because they undergo a similar martyrdom.

Pound places himself directly in the sequence that includes the Mussolinis, Dionysus Zagreus, and the Albigenses: At the beginning of the long passage cited above, the sacrificial trench that

Odysseus digs in Hades in *Odyssey* Book XI is being dug around
Pound himself. Pound figures his own imprisonment as an instance
of the betrayal suffered by the other saints in the *Canto*, at the hands
of the very communities that were to be illuminated by a New
Learning. Erigena Scotus's light widens into a rhetoric of natural
illumination that envelops and counteracts the scenarios of destruction incorporated into the text.

The sacrifice of martyrs such as Jesus and Manes is precipitated
through an act of betrayal, whose motives are at least partially economic, on the part of the traitors and the regimes threatened by
illumination. Translated into the operations of statehood, the mercenary handing over of the saintly becomes the triggering of warfare
by the interests that will profit from it. The martyrdom of war is an
extension of messianic martyrdom. The *Canto*'s primitive artifacts,
martyrs, and biblical references thus find themselves subsumed within
an economic argument: Expansionistic wars "increase the profits of
usurers,/ . . . and gun sales lead to more gun sales/ they do not
clutter the market for gunnery."

In light of such patterns, it is fitting that the economic argument
in the passage under discussion should ultimately lead us, on the
twenty-third anniversary of Italian fascism, to the DTC where a fellow prisoner named Till has just been hanged and another is wondering, of all things, about the books of the Bible. When the broken
machinery of warfare finally does bring us back to the barren center,
where even light, wind, and rain are of little recompense, the *Canto*,
and the work of the *Cantos*, are free to recommence, to look toward
even more distant and ancient cultural artifacts, where the fated dance
can run its course again. Other noteworthy economic passages in
the *Canto* perform the function described above—to provide a pro-
cedural frame of reference for images culled from widely diverging
activities; to seek a material grounding for images and metaphors,
in full cognizance of their textual constitution.

It is in the midst of an exchange of energies beyond the speaker's
control—wind, rain, and light, symbolized by the figures of Eastern
serenity and "primitive" contortion—that Pound's poetic economies
function. Their operation is double: archaeological excavation in
search of images retaining some of their power; and the discharge
of this energy in poetry through the activities of conversion, digestion, and translation. This energy, generated by a process of cultural

recycling, impedes, but cannot reverse, the entropy that overcomes culture as it gradually arrests matter. The adulteration of nature in Pound's metaphysics, dramatized in this *Canto* by the suspension of the dance in midmotion, ultimately eventuates at a certain death. *Canto* LXXIV, first of the *Pisan Cantos*, composed at the end of the Second World War when as an old man Pound is imprisoned due to the outrages of his homemade and enigmatic ideology, emphasizes the entropy into which each economic configuration and artwork ultimately lapses.

Entropy is a form of systematic death that proceeds by a spilling off—and gradual loss—of energy, not soul, mind, or Being.[55] It violates those prim and proper laws—of conservation of matter and energy—by which classical physics reassures us that our world, and in some form or another we ourselves, will be here forever. Is there any way that a poetry such as Pound's, and a culture such as the United States', with their fascination for cultural rubble, recycling, and appropriation, could not also yearn for the bleeding of this energy, the inertness and vacuity whose origin is still in relatively recent memory?

In a bizarre sense, World War II culminates Pound's native American, purist dream. The European sources rise to assert, most concretely, their priority and the various forms of their purity. Pound embraces and celebrates this movement, at the cost of a personal social and cultural suicide.

Entropy consummates the death wish not of a person but of a system. It is a hidden wish and eventuality muted by the marvelous energy that American culture spins out of itself—and presents to the world. Pound's poetry thus pursues a rather full segment of the course followed by the cultural fascination with ruins and origins— and with the celebration of novelties never before brought to light. The entropy of the *Cantos* is no small measure of their wish.

No wonder, then, that *Cantos* LXXIV should leave us with a simulated rose made of iron filings. For the moment, the waste material from an altogether questionable industry has usurped the place of roses and natural light; but then again, the poem's odyssey already envisages the other side of death:

> so light is the urging, so ordered the dark petals of iron
> we who have passed over Lethe.

William Carlos Williams: The Conflagration in the Library

> The language is missing them
>   they die also
>   incommunicado.
>
> The language, the language
>   fails them
> They do not know the words
>   or have not
> the courage to use them
>   —girls from
> families that have decayed and
> taken to the hills: no words.
> They may look at the torrent in
>   their minds
> and it is foreign to them.
>
> they turn their backs
> and grow faint—but recover!
>   Life is sweet
> they say: the language!
>   —the language
> is divorced from their minds,
> the language   .   .   the language!
>   *(Paterson,* 11–12)

Early on, *Paterson* marks an estrangement between the community of speakers and the language they use, at least within the climate that William Carlos Williams frequents. The language "is missing them. . . . fails them. . . . is divorced from their minds." As if to emphasize his point, Dr. Williams subtly interpolates a few Germanisms, a foreign element, adding a dimension of alienation (*Entfremdung*). Adjustments for these interlinguistic jokes must be made if the passage is to be read. "The language is missing them" is not a very elegant turn of phrase in English, but its German equivalent, *"Die Sprache fehlt ihnen,"* is perfect, a point underscored when the text specifies, four lines later, "the language *fails* them" (my emphasis).

Williams characterizes this linguistic alienation, this public dyslexia, as a divorce between mind and language, a serious repercussion. The accounts, entreaties, and confessions that the doctor hears from his patients and intersperses throughout this realistic epic are often the children of this divorce, abandoned children without the linguistic key. Their *patois* contrasts sharply with the cultivated discourse, historical documents, and vital statistics preserved in the public library. The doctor's medical children, to whom he attends even after bringing them into the world, suffer from chronic illiteracy.

This linguistic and intellectual deprivation, however, does not cost them any desire, action, or energy. A torrent runs through their minds. The problem is that it is foreign to them, like the German in Williams's English. *Paterson*, whether a place in New Jersey, a text by William Carlos Williams, or an allegorical man in that text, does not suffer from any lack of energy or physical transfer of forces. A good many poetic innovations associated with Ezra Pound are evident in *Paterson*: an "open" arrangement of lines, the incorporation of documents and other artifacts of concrete language, a play between modes of expression (poetic, realistic, "personal," etc.), and a contrast between the poetic potentials released by different line lengths and formats of utterance. The entropy that ultimately takes over the *Cantos* is, however, notably lacking in *Paterson*. A large portion of what is at stake in *Paterson*'s articulation of itself as a text is embedded within the metaphor of physical forces and fields of energy: their storage, containment, divergence, release, and explosion.

The geography of *Paterson* centers around a river, the Passaic, but at crucial junctures, the poem becomes a river of language in its own right. A text with such a heightened awareness of its currents and flow naturally pays careful attention to its sources. It is in the context of the deliberations by an American poetic community on the literary potentials of modernist innovation that we may regard *Paterson* as a derivative work in the most creative sense. Williams read his contemporaries and antecedents, above all Pound, carefully. The discursive modes that he devised and the sources, documents, and fragments that he incorporated into *Paterson* comprise the forces at play in an open-ended economy. *Paterson* is both a new point of departure and a reading of Pound's *Cantos*, one not entirely incommensurate with our own.

Williams's favored metaphors for the energy of poetry may well

be the cyclotron and cloud-chamber of nuclear physics, yet late in
Paterson Book Four, Section II, he makes sure to intertwine this
field with an economy in which money is tantamount to a joke,
usury is a cancer, and in which, to introduce a clinical dimension,
radiotherapy fights the disease (*P*, 182–86). This graft is characteristic of Williams's relation to Pound: he pays almost excessive
obeisance to the ur-explorer of modern American poetic space and
the splices and folds that characterize it. Within Williams's own
poetic economy, however, there is a subtle shift from substance and
value to force. In this sense, it is Williams, not Pound, who fulfills
the prophesy of dynamic energy in verse revealed by Chinese poetry
and Fenollosa.

Williams both opens up the lyrical end of Pound's poetic range
and takes its prosaic potentials at their word. While the lyrical continues to be the mode of sublimity, the blurring of distinction, and
sexual desire in *Paterson*, Williams devises a "metalyric," with very
short-line and fragmentary phrasing, which he adds to his medium-
length, "standard" lyrical line. Williams's hypershort line—which
we find in the Preface ("To make a start," *P*, 3), in the long passage
cited above, and in such lyrics as "Look for the nul" (*P*, 77), "The
rock/ married to the river" (*P*, 107), and "like a mouse, like" (*P*,
116)—creates a tension within the lyric mode itself. This line enables Williams both to concentrate his utterance almost to a point
of saturation and to diffuse this tension when he exploits the full
dimensions of the page. In opening up a fuller range of lyrical potentials than Pound, Williams spares us the jarring shift between
reverie and a domain fictively endowed with the ontological grounding of nature or a natural currency. Except where Williams literally
incorporates a geological survey of the region and its strata (*P*, 139),
the dance between poetic modes that he sustains never eventuates
at a firm bottom.

At the opposite extreme of the poetic repertoire, Williams height-
ens the tension between lyricism and its other by simply incorporating prose, a possibility on which Pound only rarely capitalizes. Prose
fragments display the more concrete utilizations of language and
avoid the lengthy digressions of pseudopoetry into which Pound lapses
when he paraphrases nonpoetic texts such as Chinese histories or
John Adams's biography.

Williams thus continues such Poundian practices as open grafting and activating a poetic economy that serves as an exchange house between contrasting poetic modes, but he shifts the emphasis in *Paterson* toward the display of force and physical vectors. As in the *Cantos*, feminine beauty is at the apex of textual and sexual energy. Williams's Beautiful Thing incites the release of yearning and rage in a way similar to, but still different from, the manner in which Circe's bedding down with Odysseus is both a primal scene and source of lyrical energy in the *Cantos*. Williams retains sexual desire within the field of kinetic energy; Pound transforms this drive into guilt-laden fetishes. *Paterson*, then, is a modern-day American epic aware both of the analphabetic crisis in which it arises and of the physical, sexual, and textual forces that surround, immerse, and inform it. The text stands at the interstice linking the hydraulic force of a river and waterfall, a constant sexual yearning that varies primarily in the explicitness and degree of its satisfaction, and a radioactive energy that becomes an emblem of its times. Not only the generation of forces but also the relations between them, their convergence or dissonance, acquire decisive importance in a work so attuned to physical metaphors.

The physical climax of *Paterson* is a conflagration in a library, a violent release of literary as well as physical energy figured as a fire. Such a book-burning must attain particular significance in a work so intensely aware of the conditions and difficulties surrounding its own reading. The reader of *Paterson* necessarily addresses the physics of the major force-fields that the work sets into play, including the textual.[56] *Paterson*, by means of various energies that it entertains and releases, surpasses the planned entropy of the *Cantos*. In order to appreciate this realization of the freeplay installed in modern poetics, we expose ourselves to its radiation, at whatever the cost.

If the *Cantos* strive, economically, to install themselves within the tradition whose authority and protection they will claim, *Paterson* never fully overcomes the violence with which it is severed from and imposed upon the stately evolution of language. As an allegory of poetic composition, *Paterson* periodically gasps at its own wonder; it marvels at the points of departure, diversions, and inventions of slang that do eventually emerge from systems as slow-moving as rivers and languages. If Williams delves into the geological and

mythical reaches of time in furnishing his epic with an appropriate
time frame, he does so less to play on his audience's patriotic sym-
pathies than to reflect the true deliberation with which language
changes, with which the patchwork of improvisations ventured in
the *parole* are acknowledged and absorbed by the *langue*.

The "elemental character" of a place, even if initially inscribed
with Book One, "The Delineaments of the Giants," does eventually
issue forth in modifications, monstrosities (e.g., the 126 pound 7'
6" sturgeon, [*P*, 11]), curiosities (e.g., Sam Patch), and other ar-
ticulations in its continuity. The poem *Paterson* may be considered
as one additional modulation to the geological and cultural lifespan
of Paterson. Williams pays careful attention to this coming-into-
articulation of the poem. The poem arises as an interruption in a
continuous flow, a diversion from a linear stream, a mutation in the
genetic pool, a long-repressed rape, an eruption of kinetic out of
potential energy, a divorce in a well-established marriage, and an
inbred dissonance capable of unleashing vast amounts of energy (e.g.,
the image of uranium [*P*, 176]). These are all measured metaphors
for the articulation of poetry in general and Williams's text in particular. If the poet fashions a cosmological framework for his poem,
he does so in the interest of pursuing the process of poetic articulation from its origins to its ends in silence and quiescent energy.

The text of *Paterson* thus hovers at the lip of the cataract, well
ensconced in the streambed but about to undergo a cataclysmic change
in level and intensity. This site is akin to the moment, at the outset
of Hegel's *Phenomenology of Spirit*, when organic change reaches
a limit, when growth measured quantitatively produces qualitative
difference, and when time is ripe for revolution.[57] On the thematic
level of the Hegelian text, however, the outbreak of energy will
eventuate in historical progression and higher levels of awareness—
while Williams is content to watch as the Passaic crashes below,
to let'er rip purely for the sake of the riot. The refrain "So be it"
interpolated among the multiple climaxes of Book Three underlines
the indifference and inevitability with which violence breaks out and
poetry is written in *Paterson*. It is in the sense of writing as the act
of violence necessary to interrupt and redirect physical and linguistic processes only too well entrenched that "beauty is/ a defiance
of authority" (*P*, 119). This beauty is both lived and thought. It sets
the guys from Paterson off against the guys from Newark and is

behind a good many of the babies that Dr. Williams delivers. It also defines the power of the Beautiful Thing that serves as the writer's still horizon, a hurricane's eye engulfed by writerly rage. Within a setting of tense stillness—the aboutness to erupt of potential energy—is the poem's consummate lyric, "Is this the only beauty here?" arises.

As such, the poem invests a good share of its resources—and delves deeply into the British Romantic roots of modern individualistic poetic expression—in order to establish the stability, the determined transfer of forces, that poetic composition violates.[58] It is in the context of the effort to develop metaphors for closed and stable circuits of energy that we read much of the poem's hydraulic energy, its motion-language of whirls, eddies, rises, and descents, and an evolutionary rhetoric that marries the movement of natural phenomena to analogous developments in the mind. The poem, in positing its equivalents to Pound's natural and manageable economies, not only alludes to Romantic works; it also incorporates its own Romanticism, as Paul de Man has developed the term: a movable and vulnerable horizon of expectation.[59]

Williams's efforts at his own poetic economics are more impressive than the thematic imitations of Pound that he incorporates into Book Four, Section II and elsewhere. In this regard, four passages, all revolving around the interaction between a stream and its stones, attain particular prominence. The second lyrical passage in the body proper of the poem sets into splendid motion, and apparent commotion, the currents of water and thought whose confluence is Paterson:

Jostled as are the waters approaching
the brink, his thoughts
interlace, repel and cut under,
rise rock-thwarted and turn aside
but forever strain forward—or strike
an eddy and whirl, marked by a
leaf or curdy spume, seeming
to forget   .
Retake later the advance and
are replaced by succeeding hordes
pushing forward—they coalesce now
glass-smooth with their swiftness,

       quiet or seem to quiet as at the close
       they leap to the conclusion and
       fall, fall in air! . . .

                    (*P*, 7–8)

As wild as the action described here may be, it is sobered by its
inbuilt potentials for recollection and reconsideration. Within the
passage's allegory of cognition, advances will be subsequently re-
taken, "lightness lost" (*P*, 8). Any doubts about the sound economic
planning underlying this apparent riot are dispelled by an evolutionary rhetoric in which thought somehow derives its energy from
the flow but is nurtured in detachment and seclusion from it.

           Thought clambers up,
    snail like, upon the wet rocks
    hidden from sun and sight—
              hedged in by the pouring torrent—
    and has its birth and death there
    in that moist chamber, shut from
    the world—and unknown to the world,
    cloaks itself in mystery—

               And the myth
    that holds up the rock,
    that holds up the water thrives there—
    in that cavern, that profound cleft,
            a flickering green
    inspiring terror, watching . .

    And standing, shrouded there, in that din,
    Earth the chatterer, father of all
    speech . . . . . .

                    (*P*, 39)

The snail is a creature of linguistic and evolutionary simplicity. The
development of speech out of inarticulate noise moves forward with
the dogged persistence and inevitability of a snail's progress. The
affirmative thrust of this passage is sustained by the power of the
myth, which, arising out of a Wordsworthian din, achieves an equilibrium. As much force in this passage is devoted to holding up the
rock, balancing it against the water, as is released by the irretriev-
able flow.

    "Sunday in the Park" (in Book Two) is an interlude or Sunday

in the text when human juices flow and energy silently gathers amid
the relaxed commonality whose aptest legend is "Anywhere is
everywhere" (*P*, 235). Williams follows the course of this Sunday.
Still during its morning, just before a seminaked white girl puts
herself on display, we happen upon the following paean to measure,
as close as Williams comes to espousing Kung's order:

> Without invention nothing is well spaced,
> unless the mind change, unless
> the stars are new measured, according
> to their relative positions, the
> line will not change, the necessity
> will not matriculate: unless there is
> a new mind there cannot be a new
> line, the old will go on
> repeating itself with recurring
> deadlines: without invention
> nothing lies under the witch-hazel
> bush, the alder does not grow from among
> the hummocks margining the all
> but spent channel of the old swale,
> the small foot-prints
> of the mice under the overhanging
> tufts of the bunch-grass will not
> appear: without invention the line
> will never again take on its ancient
> divisions when the word, a supple word,
> lived in it, crumbled now to chalk.
>
> (*P*, 50)

This passage, like large sections of the *Cantos*, falls under the sway
of the homemade aesthetics of *bricolage*. The musical numbers of
poetry are *devised*, not written in the stars or spheres. The line, the
unit of measure, is not the precondition of poetry but its aftermath.
At the end of a Sunday that has absorbed and caressed the reader
in a surface dense with familiar pleasures, a carefully modulated
poetic economy has only begun to consolidate its power. The characteristic instruments of its control include a rhythm of rises and
descents and a rhetoric of hovering: between inertia and momentum
and between recollection and experience. Such calibrated movement is typical of the closed energy systems thematized by the text.

An expansive lyric early in Book Two, Section III, which bemoans, "no whiteness (lost) is so white as the memory/ of whiteness" (P, 78), epitomizes the recuperative potentials of *Paterson*
and reassures us:

> But Spring shall come and flowers will bloom
> and man must chatter of his doom   .   .

> The descent beckons
>   as the ascent beckoned
>   Memory is a kind
> of accomplishment
>   a sort of renewal
>   even
> an initiation, since the spaces it opens are new
> places
>   inhabited by hordes
>   heretofore unrealized,
> of new kinds—
>   since their movements
>   are towards new objectives
> (even though formerly they were abandoned)
>   (P, 77–78)

The apparently unproblematical flow of a stream against and around
stones, a literary figure of venerable pedigree, becomes the poem's
predominant sounding board for the reassurances of containment,
measure, and legibility that it holds out to its readers and itself. The
calibrated rises and falls of energy, the recoils of memory and in-
ternalization—these actions may derive from the field of physics,
but their semantic function is to assure measure and hence comprehensibility. A closed circuit of physical transfers of energy is tantamount to the representational infrastructure of a text. The mythical
sedateness surrounding the figure of Paterson (man, city, place),
the historical continuity assured by the myth, and the semiotic control asserted by such closed circuits comprise the field from which
emerge the explosion, monstrosity, and divorce that eventuate when
texts collide and interact.

The role of the ultrashort line in *Paterson* is akin to the function of
the ace in gin rummy: the double terminus of expansion and contraction. As the ace comprehends the upper and lower registers of

value, the ultrashort line signals a poetic discourse that both inten-
sifies and explodes the continuous hydraulic and semantic systems
around it. The evening of "Sunday in the Park," which might otherwise consummate such rejuvenation and recreation, begins precisely with such a metalyric. This text not only reaches for the concentration of a minimalist *line*; it also pivots on a single letter, the
N of nullity, the emptiness at the heart of—and betraying—comprehensive systems, whether of energy or signification:

> Look for the nul
> defeats it all
>
> the N of all
> equations
>
> that rock, the blank
> that holds them up
>
> which pulled away—
> the rock's
>
> their fall. Look
> for that nul
>
> that's past all
> seeing
>
> the death of all
> that's past
>
> all being   .
>   (*P*, 77)

This text marks a significant change in direction, if only pulling out
the supports from the rock which earlier could be sustained by the
myth and hydraulic pressure. Written in the vocative mode, the passage exhorts the reader to find the nothing that betrays the sustaining
power of equations and other myths. The search for the nul will be
in the direction of a *beyond* but specifically not the *beyond* of phenomena (seeing), history, existence, or Being. There is an ultraism
in this passage, a thrust beyond, but it implicates something—or
rather a nothing—falling outside the purview of the directed thought
coalescing in the systems of phenomenology, ontology, and metaphysics. Thought, like the river, must be relieved of its direction if
the associative volatility of its language is to be released. It is during

the conflagration in the library of Book Three that this emptying and release are executed, in keeping with the imperative quest for the nul.

Once again the metalyric marks a serious revision in the interchange between the river and the rock, the natural and physical "sources" of poetic sound. *Paterson* provides us with a rather full snapshot album of this relation (*P*, 7, 22–23, 39, 53, 80–81, 97, 107). The last image in this sequence not only broaches new possibilities but also reaches the limits of hydropower in the work:

> The rock
> married to the river
> makes
> no sound
>
> And the river
> passes—but I remain
> clamant
> calling out ceaselessly
> to the birds
> and clouds
> (listening)
> Who am I?
>
>   —the voice!
>   (*P*, 107)

In this lyric, the water and the rock have lost the primordial status that would be accorded by any naturalistic myth of the origins of poetry as an *ur-Geräusch* or primordial sound. The speaking "subject" is also overcome by an oceanic vertigo and loss of self-identity. The lyric transpires at an uncanny moment of suspense. The image persists, but the "soundtrack" accompanying the flowing river has been "cut." The marriage of rock and water, that union between an immanent subject and the "outside," between language and "mind," whether individual or collective, has suddenly lapsed into silence. The voice of the "I" in the poem, however, continues, "clamant"—clammering but also full of metaphysical claims and questions. A parenthetical stage direction, "(listening)," is marginally inserted into the lyric, but who does the listening is left ambiguous. Is it the "speaker" of the poem, the birds and the clouds, or perhaps the reader? The silence of the image is tantamount to the nothing that undermines the equation. The someone listening, perhaps the voice of the poem, hears silence and does not know itself.

This brief lyric underlines an act of ventriloquism and a persistence of momentum. The image in the text "speaks" only as the speaker throws his "voice." But when the image is exhausted or speechless or has been removed from the sources of its illumination, the structure of the poetic voice continues. The great revelation of this minitext is the automation of the poetic voice. No instrument of a subject, the poetic voice is subject only to its inbuilt structures. The voice of *Paterson* leaves this passage knowing what it is. This knowledge coincides with an apex of hydraulic power in the work. The emphasis in the text subsequently shifts to potential rather than kinetic energy, to invisible rather than visible sources of power, and to expenditure and exhaustion rather than containment.

"It is summer! stinking summer" (*P*, 103), when a fire breaks out in the library, releasing but also spending the energy of texts. Initially, books are presented as a "cool" medium (*P*, 95), the library as a quiet preserve of potential energy and repressed desire. *Paterson* Book Three begins with the considered reconstruction of various functions characteristic of Wordsworthian seclusion. Winds, scents, and roars have been transferred from their "natural settings" to the "subject's" mind ("and there grows in the mind/ a scent" [*P*, 96]). Books, by means of their storage capacity, effect a mimetic transference:

> A cool of books
> will sometimes lead the mind to libraries
> of a hot afternoon, if books can be found
> cool to the sense to lead the mind away.
>
> For there is a wind or ghost of a wind
> in all books echoing the life
> there, a high wind that fills the tubes
> of the ear until we think we hear a wind,
> actual   .
>
> (*P*, 95)

The library is an ambivalent structure for the culture in which it stands. It exemplifies the divorce of langauge from "their minds," yet it constitutes a major resource in effecting a reconciliation. One

must affect an unnatural silence within its confines. Its maintenance, as conventionally represented in the popular media, is en-
trusted to nonfecund women: sexually repressed schoolmarms and
shriveled battle-axes. It is an environment totally hostile to the various forms of release celebrated by Sundays in the park.

A conflagration in a library is, on the one hand, a triumph for
the thoughts and intellectual energies stored there. It is a jubilation,
an orgasm celebrating an allegorical seduction: A sexually as well
as socially forlorn personification of culture is rejuvenated by the
call to nature and the generosity of youth. The apprehensions previously retained by "cool" books in the form of anxiety and potential energy now break out of solitary confinement and expend themselves in a world of concrete acts and events. The river of fire
illuminates "the torrent in/ their minds" (*P*, 12), the linguistic infrastructure of psychological life, whether understood or taken into
account by its "subjects" or not. In one sense, the conflagration in
the library is a Nietzschean revolution, an apocalypse in which language consumes and thereby redeems the metaphysical delusions
constructed to contain and order it.

But the fire is also the burning of the books, the obliteration of
culture's memory files, a deadend for literacy. Nuclear fission may
provide an intellectually ingenious parallel to the dissonance between a community of speakers and a language, and within the signification function of the language itself. Nuclear destruction also
presents itself as a particularly ominous analogon to the fire that
erupts from the books—and is then dissipated.

Paterson is of course destined to join the books on the shelves
of the library. As a work that dramatizes the burning of all books
in the library, *Paterson* ignites the books and initiates the chain
reaction of its own destruction. *Paterson* belongs as well to the doctor's good deeds and contributions, but it is composed in despair at
its literate fate within a dyslexic readership. *Paterson*'s cynicism,
like its flame, spreads to the other works on the shelves of the library.

The wind or its ghost in all books (*P*, 95) may fan the flames of
this catastrophe, but from where does the spark issue forth? Is it
from a hypothetical energy, akin to sexual frustration, latent in the
books themselves? But "The Library is desolation, it has a smell of
its own/ of stagnation and death" (*P*, 100). In one sense, the library

is a thanatopolis, populated by "dead men's dreams" (*P*, 100), and Williams's poem joins the tradition of morbid aversion to writing traced by Derrida and recalled at several points in the present book. On the other hand, the Beautiful Thing, which according to this scenario would breathe life into such morbid self-enclosure, is "a dark flame,/ a wind, a flood" (*P*, 100), all qualities that the text has associated with books. According to this formulation, books configure a nature of their own, the nature recollected in tranquility and seclusion. The nature and activity of books in *Paterson* thus hover on the edge of their own double meaning.

The incriminating spark, however, might well emanate from outside the library and reflect the incendiary wish of a community with little love either for books or for the irresolvable questions that they raise. The burning of the books, then, destroys not only the systems that have indelicately packaged thought but also the ambiguity of the thought itself. An allegorical fire is a cosmological fate that Williams foresees for his own allegory. Is a fire in a library a threat at all to anyone? If it constitutes a danger, does this arise primarily in the Battle of the Books, the disagreements between the practitioners and professionals whose works are enshrined in the library, or is it situated in the volatile space between the language and its community of users?

It is questionable that Williams ever envisaged philosophically rigorous answers to these and related questions. His various positions regarding the status and placement of literature and his own work are as dispersed as the poetic spacing that he adopted from Mallarmé and Pound. To read the fate of writing and literacy in the fragmentary lines (if not tealeaves) of Williams's text is to follow the vectors of its energy, the traces of its atomic charges.

We know, though, that the crisis of literacy arises with some inevitability: Williams intersperses his "So be its" with echoes of Lear's hopeless cries on the heath:[60]

Blow! So be it. Bring down! So be it. Consume
and submerge! So be it. Cyclone, fire
and flood. So be it. Hell, New Jersey, it said
on the letter. Delivered without comment.
So be it!

(*P*, 97)

We know that sexual, nuclear, and textual energies interlace as the tension silently rises, making the catastrophe unavoidable. In a single passage, the text combines an account of a seduction conducted in anger and revulsion ("TAKE OFF YOUR/ CLOTHES! . . . You smell/ like a whore," [*P*, 105]), with "the riddle of a man/ and a woman" (*P*, 107), an inquiry not only into the persistence of marriage but also into the barrage of social, economic, and theoretical constraints emanating from the epistemological equation, and finally, wonder at the "radiant gist that/ resists the final crystallization/ in the pitch-blend" (*P*, 109). The metaphor of nuclear energy plays a role in the transfer of physical forces analagous to the role of the metalyric within the poetic economy. It is both sequential and "wild": It partakes of and destroys the equilibriums of classical physics. The nuclear material incorporates both a pitch—a proposition and an angle—and a blend, a blinding as well as a mix. The coincidence between a fire in a library and blindness has also been explored by Elias Canetti in his novel *Die Blendung*.[61] In Williams's epic, the fire in the library is that element of the text resisting assimilation within its internal economies of force and meaning, evading, like the radiant gist, "the final crystallization."

Thus books for Williams posit their internal systems of exhaustive comprehensibility but also harbor an incongruity that cannot be assimilated. An outbreak of the incommensurate is both a redemption and a threat. The figure of the Unicorn emerges in Book Five as an icon of sublime stability retrospectively applied to the work. Given the explosiveness with which the nul erupts within *Paterson*'s planned economies, the Unicorn arrives hopelessly after the fact.

When the outbreak finally happens, it emanates from the scene of writing itself. Where the conflagration unleashes itself in Book Three, Section II, *Paterson* joins the Western body of literature, from *Faust* and *King Lear* to *The Confidence-Man* and *Ulysses*, that dramatizes the internal derangement of the text's own structures of comprehensibility. The authors of these self-consuming artifacts invariably dispatch a messenger or surrogate to assess the damage, and at the beginning of this section, Williams himself summons someone whose life bears striking similarities to his own and who manages to write despite "a busy life."

Fire burns; that is the first law.
When a wind fans it the flames

are carried abroad. Talk
fans the flames. They have

manoeuvred it so that to write
is a fire and not only of the blood.

The writing is nothing, the being
in a position to write (that's

where they get you) is nine tenths
of the difficulty: seduction

or strong arm stuff. The writing
should be a relief,

relief from the conditions
which as we advance become—a fire,

a destroying fire. For the writing
is also an attack and means must be

found to scotch it—at the root
if possible. So that

to write, nine tenths of the problem
is to live. . . .

(P, 113)

The couplets that introduce this climactic section of *Paterson* view the writing act both as it literally strikes the author and in terms of its social context. But the passage, which might provide a much needed definition regarding the relation between writing and life, is virtually impossible to read. Writing initially appears as a fire that breaks out when the writer's burning desire is fanned by the winds retained, as potential energy, by books. By the end of the passage, it is the "conditions" of life that oppose writing by depriving it of the "relief" it might otherwise provide. Two forces oppose each other in this lyric: The purifying rage of creative activity is met and dissipated by the existential demands of life. Both forces are destructive; the poet gets burned from both ends, a large measure of writing's "cost." Writing is not the problem: "being in a position to write" is "where they get you." The writing is itself "an attack," like a conflagration, and yet is "scotched," dissipated as well as

quenched, by demands personified, in subsequent lines, by the uncomprehending audience, the community of inarticulate speakers.
"How *do*/ you find the time for it in/ your busy life?" this collectively, in its various manifestations, wonders.

> It must be a great
> thing to have such a pastime.
>
> But you were always a strange
> boy. How's your mother? . . .
>
> —the cyclonic fury, the fire,
> the leaden flood and finally
> the cost—
>
> Your father was *such* a nice man.
> I remember him well   .
>
> Or, Geeze, Doc, I guess it's all right
> but what the hell does it mean?
> (*P*, 114)

Caught betwen a vocation—which is, as in Kafka's world, an
unavoidable patrimony—and an uncomprehending audience, the
writer is a privileged candidate for "burnout," in this case a double
liability. Paradoxically, "to live" is the only way to be in a position
to write. There is, however, no stepping back from the congenital
condition of writing. The die is cast. Williams's tragic and self-
dismantling literary sources presage it. How curious it is, then, that
on the lip of the cataract, at the outbreak of the fire, when there is
decidedly no turning back, Williams inserts a metalyric whose distinction consists in its utter inconsequentiality that adds precisely
nothing to the action:

> like a mouse, like
> a red slipper, like
> a star, a geranium,
> a cat's tongue or—
>
> thought, thought
> that is a leaf, a
> pebble, an old man
> out of a story by

Pushkin

Ah!
rotten beams tum-
bling,

an old bottle

mauled

(*P*, 116)

In so wide open a text, this interjection appears as a mere parenthetical remark, a pebble in a chattering stream. Its overall rhetorical
form is that of a simile, a comparison between the small and familiar things of the first stanza and the encompassing physical system of the fire. This quiet and marginal text refuses, however, to
offer itself as fuel for the totalistic conflagration. Its phrasing is
unusually discontinuous and fragmentary, even within the confines
of *Paterson*. At the lip of the cataract, when there is no arresting
the sequential mechanics of motion, this text utters a quiet but ineffaceable affirmation of the fragmentary.

The metalyric's brief Chinese encyclopedia of similes incorporates the living and the inert, the geometrical, the arbitrary (why a
red slipper?), the articulate, and the inarticulate. A cat's tongue may
be inhuman, but it can speak. "Pushkin" furnishes a literary "reference," but it also pushes the text along in its inconsequentiality.

Like a botched fishing expedition, this compact lyric eventuates
at nothing, or rather, nothing more than an old bottle. This figure
is not without its significance. It arises as an artifact, a figure, and
a metaphor for the linguistic residue that cannot be absorbed or dispatched by the constraints of systematic thought or encompassing
composition. One of its preeminent characteristics is simply its remaining: It remains as a pedestrian and inert but nevertheless structured way station in the gregarious stream of *Paterson*. At the moment when the work as a "whole" goes up in flames, when it collapses
under the pressure of the physical cycles and the conceptual systems
that it metaphorically incorporates, the lyric gestically performs the
irreducibility of the fragment in the stuff of modern American poetry. It does, however, eventuate at the figure of a bottle, whose
spatial, temporal, and structural ambiguities summarize Williams's
contribution to the literature that his poem joins.

A direct descendant of Wallace Stevens's "jar in Tennessee,"[62] abandoned to the dump of cultural vestiges, Williams's bottle decants the contours and limits of modernist composition. This poetry celebrates a release of energy in a "drunkenness of flames" (*P*, 117). It resounds in raucous laughter. Modern poetry, like the culture that it joins, celebrates and immortalizes a polymorphic release from inherited forms. But "An old bottle, mauled by the fire/ gets a new glaze,/ . . . the flame that wrapped the glass/ deflowered, reflowered there by/ the flame" (*P*, 118). Modern art, like Williams's fired bottle, surpasses its economies only to witness their reinstatement. The glass, briefly relieved of its glaze, regains its reflexive surface and all the metaphysical and psychological baggage that it implies. A "reflowering" restores an ephemeral abandonment of prudery and constraint. With a clinical detachment, Williams measures the jubilation of the movement and moment to which his own work has lent an important share of its images.

Any measured reassessment of the program, accomplishment, and results of modernism must seek the coolness of libraries and the cool flames that persist in the wake of the conflagration. Following in the footsteps of Mallarmé and the French imagist poets, Stevens, Pound, and Williams explored certain new-found properties of poetic space and innovative possibilities for appropriating and grafting textual resources. Their poetry demonstrates a profound concern with its own textual conditions and with the literate knowledge and skills of its readership. This poetry is, like any form of human communication, susceptible to its own mystifications and ideological and constitutional blindspots. It occasionally falls prey both to delusions operative in the historical and political arenas and to the momentum of its internal economies. We are particularly indebted to the doctor of Paterson for that explicitness with which he adds up the costs of poetry. His persistence in pursuing its fluctuating vectors opens up a panorama from which we may examine his tradition's claims.

5

The Expanding Castle:
The Literature of Literacy

The Expanding Castle

Working with hypotheses, I can at times construct for myself such a minute and convincing picture of the fortress that in my mind I can move through it completely at my ease; whereas the elements I derive from what I see and what I hear are confused, full of gaps, more and more contradictory. . . .

In the early days of my imprisonment, when my desperate acts of rebellion hadn't yet brought me to rot in this solitary cell, the routine tasks of prison life had caused me to climb up and down stairs and bastions, cross the entrance halls and posterns of the Château d'If; but from all the images retained by my memory, which now I keep arranging and rearranging in my conjectures, there is not one that fits neatly with another, none that helps explain to me the shape of the fortress or the point where I now am. Too many thoughts tormented me then—about how I, Edmond Dantès, poor but honest sailor, could have run afoul of the law's severity and suddenly lost my freedom—too many thoughts to allow my attention to concern itself with the plan of my surroundings. . . .

Now that, with the passage of years, I have stopped brooding over the chain of infamy and ill-luck that caused my imprisonment, I have come to understand one thing: the only way to escape the prisoner's state is to know how the prison is built. . . .

Therefore: each cell seems separated from the outside only by the thickness of a wall, but Faria as he excavates discovers that in between there is always another cell, and between this cell and the outside, still another. The image I derive is this: a fortress that grows around us, and the longer we remain shut up in it the more it removes us from the outside. The Abbé digs, digs, but the walls increase in thickness, the battlements and the buttresses are multiplied. Perhaps if he can succeed in advancing faster than the fortress expands, Faria at a certain point will find himself outside unawares. It would be necessary to invert the relative speeds so that the fortress, contracting, would expel the Abbé like a cannonball.

But if the fortress grows with the speed of time, to escape one would have to move even faster, retrace time. The moment in which I would find myself outside would be the same moment I entered here: I look out on the bay at last, and what do I see? A boat full of gendarmes is landing at If; in the midst is Edmond Dantès, in chains. . . .

The concentric fortress, If-Monte Cristo-Dumas's desk, contains us prisoners, the treasure, and the supernovel *Monte Cristo* with its variants and combinations of variants in the nature of billions of billions but still in a finite number. Faria has set his heart on one page among the many, and he does not despair of finding it; I am interested in seeing the accumulation of rejected sheets increase, the solutions which need not be taken into account, which already form a series of piles, a wall. . . .

Arranging one after the other all the continuations which allow the story to be extended, probable or improbable as they may be, you obtain the zigzag line of the *Monte Cristo* of Dumas; whereas connecting the circumstances that prevent the story from continuing you outline the spiral of a novel in negative, a *Monte Cristo* preceded by the minus sign. . . . The decisive difference between the two books—sufficient to cause one to be defined as true and the other as false, even if they are identical—lies entirely in the method. To plan a book—or an escape—the first thing to know is what to exclude.

—Italo Calvino, "The Count of Monte Cristo"

By its very nature, the problem of literacy is not one to be neatly set aside, resolved, or silenced. In "The Count of Monte Cristo," Calvino opens a large interpretative panorama on Alexandre Dumas' novel of the same title and initiates a spiral and labyrinthine interplay between Dumas' text and his own.[1] In a scenario anticipating Woody Allen's film, *The Purple Rose of Cairo,* Calvino releases Dumas' characters from their original roles in Dumas' novel, but a hopeless confusion of their status goes hand in hand with this liberation. Edmond Dantès, the hero of Dumas' "supernovel," is both the narrator of Calvino's allegorical rendition of it and an autonomous third-person character. A metafictive variation on a text not only splits or doubles its characters; it also splits the "original" work into two counterworks, which Calvino relates by a minus sign and zigzags. Calvino's "original" works are fictive rereadings of earlier works. The act of "invention" by interpretation splits the visual and spatial fields of the text, and gives rise to a Borgesian dissonance between counterdomains.

So it is that when Calvino's "Dantès" and "Abbé Faria" survey, measure, and read the dimensions of the prison in which Alexandre Dumas circumscribed them, with a "mind" to escape it, the complexity of their situation increases before the light appears at the end of the tunnel. Calvino's Abbé Faria provides a graphic illustration of this unavoidable confusion, in a passage confronting us with the unique playfulness its author was capable of infusing into theoretical situations and discussions:

> The walls and the vaults have been pierced in every direction by the Abbé's pick, but his itineraries continue to wind around themselves like a ball of yarn, and he constantly goes through my cell as he follows, each time, a different course. He has long since lost his sense of orientation: Faria no longer recognizes the cardinal points, indeed he cannot recognize even the zenith and the nadir. At times I hear scratching at the ceiling; a rain of plaster falls on me; a breach opens; Faria's head appears, upside down. Upside down for me, not for him; he crawls out of his tunnel, he walks head down, while nothing about his person is ruffled, not his white hair, nor his beard green with mold, nor the tatters of sackcloth that cover his emaciated loins. He walks across the ceiling and the walls like a fly, he sinks his pick into a certain spot, a hole opens; he disappears. (*tz,* 141)

In Calvino's hands, Faria becomes a slapstick scientist whose tenuous postures register a growing disorientation. The more avenues of escape that he explores, the greater become his opportunities to arrive at impasses. The involution that he quite tangibly confronts is the often exasperating but irreducible condition of interpreting language. The number of nuances entertained by the text proliferates as the linguistic sensitivity of its interpreters becomes more acute. Clearings, simplifications, and broader perspectives can and do eventuate, but before the prison embodied by any vast and encompassing problem cracks, new levels and impediments of complication are sure to arise.

With breathtaking simplicity, Calvino demonstrates that the problem confronting the unjustly imprisoned Edmond Dantès during his fourteen years of seclusion and confinement is, more than a moral, legal, or existential one, *interpretative* in nature. In Dumas' "original," it is the equally misunderstood and highly articulate and literate Abbé Faria who *sheds light* on Dantès, not by improving prison lighting but by teaching him ancient and modern languages, by imparting an outline and sense of Western history, by sharing his understanding of science, and by reviewing the specific details and circumstances of Dantès' case. In Dumas' novel, Dantès has already inherited his (adoptive) patrimony and treasure before he digs his spade into the sharp angle of the second grotto on the island of Monte Cristo. The precious metals, coins, and jewels comprising the cache in whose existence no one but Dantès would believe play an integral role in the drama of the hero's revenge and further education—but in the most profound sense they do not comprise his treasure.

Because they demand to be *read,* the walls of the Château d'If grow around Dantès and Faria, whether regarded as Dumas' or Calvino's "creations." And just as the dimensions of the prison expand around the fictive characters, so will the attempt to analyze and address the problem of literacy grow around us—initially—until we too can hazard some informed guesses about its scale and some reasonable methods of escape.

Dumas' Château d'If is not the only prison that Calvino incorporates into his fictions, and "The Count of Monte Cristo" is far from the only work in which Calvino raises the question of literacy, both as a social phenomenon and as the precondition for the reception of his fiction. The unforgettable image of the Cottolengo institution in Calvino's 1963 story "The Watcher" is set, like the Italian cinema of its day, in an ambiance of disciplined realism. It might therefore seem remote, temporally as well as temperamentally, from such playful science-fictive innovations as *Cosmicomics, t zero,* and *Invisible Cities*. Cottolengo, however, in its view of the comprehensive political, physical, and mental disability resulting from a certain illiteracy reinforced by ideological cant, is but a stone's throw away from the political and sensory deprivations suffered by Dumas' and Calvino's "Monte Cristo." In "The Watcher," Calvino brings this city of the indigent to light at a moment when it is invaded and polarized by the political process during an election.[2] The protagonist of the story, interestingly named Amerigo Ormeo, is a leftist member of a board of election supervisors drawn from the major Italian political parties. The voice that cautions a calm oversight of possible election irregularities, the voice of resolution, in this case derives from the Catholic church, which founded and maintains the institution. Nothing could be more alien to the inventiveness of Calvino's subsequent fictive settings than our initial glimpse of this subcity of Turin.

> The institution sprawled among poor, crowded neighborhoods, covering as much space as a whole quarter of the city, including a complex of asylums and hospitals and homes for the aged, schools, convents, virtually a city within the city, surrounded by walls and governed by different rules. Its outline was irregular, a body that had become gradually extended through new bequests and constructions and enterprises: from over the walls rose the roofs of buildings, spires, treetops, and smokestacks. Where the public street separated one part of the institution from another, they were joined by overhead passages, as in certain ancient factories, which had sprung up according to the dictates of practical utility and not of beauty; these were the same, bounded by bare walls and gates. The factory idea went beyond the external resemblance: the same practical talents, the same spirit of private enterprise of the founders of the big industries had also inspired—though expressing the succor of outcasts rather than production and profit—the simple priest who between 1832 and 1842 had founded and organized and operated, despite difficulties and hostility, this monument to charity on the scale of the nascent industrial revolution; and even his name—Cottolengo, that simple rustic family name—had lost all individual connotation and had come to denote a world-famous institution. . . .

> In the cruel speech of the poor, that name had become, by a natural process, a mocking epithet, meaning cretin, idiot, even abbreviated, in the Turin way, to its first syllables: *cutu.* In other words, that name

"Cottolengo" united an image of misfortune with an image of comedy, of the ridiculous (as often happens, in popular speech, to the names of madhouses and prisons), and also an image of kindly providence, of the power of organization, and now, too, through its electoral function, an image of obscurantism, of the medieval, of bad faith. . . . (*W*, 6–7)

The institution's name fuses a truncation of competences with the linguistic capabilities attached to the tongue. Calvino's description here is reminiscent of the nondescript and impacted architecture of another monument of modern aesthetics, Kafka's castle. The institution is a dual product of nineteenth-century social theory and church ideology.

Within the context of Calvino's story, Cottolengo registers a broad range of reactions—from gratitude to conflict and exasperation—that takes place when democratic choice is presented to a varied public. The story is set in 1953, still within a decade of the fall of fascism.

Although Cottolengo may comprise an unusually incapacitated segment of the population, the shock—and intellectual readiness—necessitated by democratic elections extend beyond its precincts, at least to the entire Italian voting public. In its widest sense, then "The Watcher" measures the impact of democratic process, and the differential literate skills that it demands of its public, upon a population accustomed to totalitarianism in various forms. At several points in the story, individuals suffering from unconsciousness and other mentally debilitating states vote—with the glad assistance of the nuns and party officials. The image of a "vote"—an ostensible exercise of differentiation and choice—on the part of unconscious patients is merely the extreme instance of a certain miscarriage of political process that results when "universal" suffrage is not accompanied by the dissemination of a high-level literacy to a large population. In this sense, Cottolengo, or "cut tongue," is also Italy and any society whose political forms require upgraded educational institutions and informational media. The narrative of "The Watcher" is explicit about this political dimension of its self-contained allegory of reading. Amerigo

didn't want to succumb to the room's squalor, and to avoid that he concentrated on the squalor of their electoral equipment—that stationery, those files, the little official book of regulations which the chairman consulted at the slightest doubt, and he was already nervous before they began—because, for Amerigo, this squalor was rich, rich in signs, in meanings, perhaps even contradictions.

Democracy presented itself to the citizens in this humble, gray, unadorned dress; to Amerigo there were moments when this seemed sublime; in Italy, which had always bowed and scraped before every form of pomp, display, sumptuousness, ornament, this seemed to him finally the lesson of an honest, austere morality, and a perpetual, silent revenge on the Fascists, on those who had thought they could feel contempt for democracy precisely because of its external squalor, its humble accounting; now they had fallen into the dust with all their gold fringe and their ribbons, while democracy, with its stark ceremony of pieces of paper folded over like telegrams, of pencils given to callused or shaky hands, went ahead. (*W*, 10–11)

Within the economy of this passage, the wealth of democracy assumes the austere trappings of the polling place and the semiological and logical richness of the choices at hand. This modest wealth, a form of understatement and absence, contrasts itself with the pomp and ceremony that, under totalitarian government, directly represent and justify centralized, autocratic power. The symbolic expression of democracy involves the self-effacement of political authorities and an emphasis on the process of choice itself. The diversity of the choice and its implications take precedence over the identity and stability of the current leadership.

For at least one election supervisor, Amerigo Ormeo, the voting scene at Cottolengo dramatizes the expansion of deliberative and structural horizons and a departure from totalitarian thought and government. It is from the perspectives both of literate semiological possibility and of political allegory that we witness and evaluate scenes in which officials of the church and the established political parties only too willingly guide the blind and the otherwise incapacitated.

The abuses to which an opposition party's watcher can usefully raise objections during the balloting at Cottolengo are limited. To become angry because they allow idiots to vote, for example, doesn't achieve any great result: when the documents are in order and the voter is able to go into the booth by himself, what can be said? You can only let it go, perhaps hoping he hasn't been taught well and will make a mistake (though this occurs rarely) and will increase the number of invalid ballots. (Now that the batch of nuns was finished with, it was the turn of a horde of young men, resembling one another like brothers, with their twisted faces, dressed in what must have been their best suits, as they are sometimes seen filing through the city on a Sunday when the weather is fine and people point to them: "Look at the *cutu*.") Even the woman in the orange sweater was almost solicitous with them.

The cases where you have to be more alert are when a medical certificate authorizes a half-blind woman, or a paralytic, or someone without hands, to be accompanied into the booth by an authorized person (usually a nun or priest) who can make the "x" for her or him. With this system, many poor wretches, incapable of discrimination, who would never be able to vote even if they had the use of their eyes or hands, are promoted to the rank of bona fide voter.

In such cases there is almost always a certain margin for doubt and protest. . . .

This was a poor man with a deformed neck and a goiter. The priest accompanying him was large, heavy, blunt-faced, a beret pulled down to his ears; his manner was harsh and practical, not unlike a truck driver's; he had been bringing voters in and out for some while. He held out the palm of his hand, vertically, with the document plastered over it, and he struck it with the other hand: "Medical certificate. It's written here than he can't see."

"He can see better than I do! He took two ballots, and then he noticed there were two of them!"

"You think you know better than the oculist?"

The chairman, to stall for time, pretended amazement. "What's the trouble? What's the trouble?" Everything had to be explained to him again from the beginning.

"Let's see if he can go into the booth by himself," the woman said. The man was already on his way.

"Oh no!" the priest said. "What if he makes a mistake?"

"Ha! If he makes a mistake it's because he isn't capable of voting!" the woman in orange replied.

"Why are you taking it out on this poor unfortunate man? Shame on you!" the other woman official, the one in white, said to the first woman. (*W*, 31–33)

In the most immediate sense, Calvino's watchers may be motivated by the desire for the most advantageous vote-count for their respective parties, but what is being played out at the widest reaches of the story's implications is the differential skills necessary for responsible choices in a democratic context. The above vignette makes clear that it is less taxing, both intellectually and emotionally, to allow the guides' exploitation of the incompetent to go on. Both the onus of disruption and the burden of proof will be borne by those who question the propriety of the election and the literate standards that it imposes. Amerigo Ormeo is driven by two contradictory impulses: to apply rigor to the process and to capitulate to the hopelessness of the situation, the same two options that color, to some degree, the approaches taken by the major contributions to the current literature on literacy. In the end, he objects to the vote of the patient with goiter in the above passage, and he later succeeds in invalidating the vote of a paralytic. He who raises the issues of conceptual discernment and literacy is a disturber of peace. The advocates of a tranquil acceptance of the literate status quo (and of the votes of the incapacitated) base their position on the humanism of pity. For them, voting is like religious ritual in which the participation and acceptance of all is more important than the exercise of competences and wills.

> As for the others at the polls (all of them Christian Democrats, or further to the right), they seemed concerned only with smoothing over the differences: all of them knew that everyone in here would vote the same way, didn't they? Then why become upset, why look for trouble? There was nothing to do but accept things as they were, friends or enemies.
>
> Among the voters, too, the importance of what they were doing varied. For the majority the act of voting occupied a minimal space in their awareness, it was a little "x" to make with the pencil against a printed symbol, something that had to be done, as they had been taught, with great care, like the proper way to behave in church or to make their beds. With no suspicion it could be done any other way, they concentrated their effort on the practical act, which was in itself—especially for the invalids or the mentally deficient—enough to engage their complete attention.
>
> For others, more emotional, or indoctrinated in a different didactic system, the election seemed to take place in the midst of perils and deceit; everything was to be distrusted, a source of offense or fear. Certain nuns in white habits were especially obsessed with the idea of spotted ballots. One would go into the booth, stay in there for five minutes, then come out without having voted. "Have you voted? No? Why not?" The nun would then hold out the ballot, open and unmarked, and point to a little dot, faint or dark. "It's got a mark on it!" she would protest, in an angry voice, to the chairman. "I want a new one!" . . .

They couldn't be convinced that these were only defects in the paper, and that their ballots wouldn't be invalidated because of them. The more the chairman insisted, the more stubborn the little nuns became: one— an old, dark nun, who came from Sardinia—actually flew into a rage. They must surely have been given God knows what instructions about the question of the stains or spots: they were to watch out, at the polls there were Communists who spotted the nuns' ballots on purpose, to spoil their votes.

Terrified, that's what they were, these little white nuns. (*W*, 27–28)

Assuming that no deviation from business as usual is to result from the electoral process, the Christian Democrats speak the *lingua franca* of resolution and "smooth over" the differences (*smussare i contrasti*) along the political spectrum. For their part, the electors transfer onto the act of voting their approaches—metaphysical as well as methodical—to the *tasks* (rather then initiatives) of life. The voters bring their resignation, their terror, their purity, to the ballot box. The nuns who, in the above passage, wish to exorcise every material imperfection from the surface of their ballots, dramatize an intense concern for effacing the conflicts engendered by the electoral process almost before it is over. But the nuns of the story are not the only voters who wish to abolish the fissures and faults in social stratification that electoral issues tend to accentuate.

At the same time that he would warn us away from any quick fixes to our literate problem, Calvino reassures us of its centrality to the quality of contemporary life. Perhaps no writer has so successfully applied a familiarity with science and an inventive humor to the process of illuminating the serious theoretical problems posed by modern literature and of confronting the linguistic status of his own work. In adapting the short fictive form to the demands of theoretical elaboration, he is Borges's *confrère* and Kafka's descendant. If Calvino's characters, like Kafka's, tend to confront the arbitrariness of encompassing systems, successful reading invariably comprises the only escape from the prison. In Calvino's words, "the only way to escape the prisoner's state is to know how the prison is built" (*tz*, 140). This imperative for architectural knowledge echoes throughout Calvino's work. It corresponds to the careful reconstruction of conceptual machines practiced by Derrida and other close readers before the process known as deconstruction becomes productive and revealing. Penetration—whether of walls or texts—through literacy may present a remote, austere, and difficult alternative, but it is, at least, manifestly *possible*. To emerge intact and even victorious from a cat-and-mouse chase played out in traffic jam requires the narrator of "The Chase" to decipher the temporal and spatial principles "of the general system of moving cars" (*tz*, 127). And in "t zero," Calvino qualifies a lion's simple leap through the air by the products, and rhetoric, of meditations on time from Aristotle and Zeno to Heidegger. In both "The Chase" and "t zero," the escape from the encompassing system by reading depends on the discernment of differences, whether "in speed among the various lines" in the former story or between the lion's different agonies, strengths, and directions of attack in the latter. *If on a winter's night a traveler,* Calvino's most ambitious late novel, spins its narrative out of pastiches of the popular narrative styles generated by this genre over the past two centuries. The story does not so much develop as reverberate out of the echoes between different narrative voices and their implicit world views. With manners and conventions that have evolved rapidly since Richardson and Fielding, even the novel can imprison its readers within a certain set of expectations. In *If on a winter's night a traveler,* Calvino achieves an ironic distance from the most powerful forms of the novel by according them equal status and playing them off against each other. In this way, he does not leave even the etiquettes of literature unscathed.

Calvino's fiction demonstrates both the vast scale of the problem of literacy and its inbuilt sources of hope. The fascination, humor, and exhilaration of well-wrought language constitute the implements it offers us for solving the problems it articulates and sets in relief. Contemporary scholarship and research have been considerably enriched by a number of attempts to approach the problem of literacy at its own word. To find any egress from the problems occasioned by the abortive dissemination of the skills of differential literacy, it may prove fruitful to address the literature of literacy itself.

Ongelus Novus: The Orality-Writing Debate

Spanning conceptual, ideological, practical, and political dimensions, the notion of literacy is not conducive to any easy unanimity. Given the difficulties posed simply by defining the term—whether identified functionally, verbally, linguistically, or aesthetically—it is no wonder that a set of coherent prescriptions to address this issue constitutes an awesome challenge. And yet in recent years, a growing literature has attempted to come to grips with the problem, no doubt partially in response to the assimilative force exerted by the electronic media and computer technology, and partially prompted by the declining verbal and attention skills that instructors have discovered in their classrooms.

Keeping books in print is itself problematical in a culture ambivalent about the skills and apprehensions of literacy. And yet the current repository of books available in the United States includes treatments of this topic that range from Robert Pattison's historical survey, *On Literacy*,[3] to Jonathan Kozol's politically activist *Illiterate America*,[4] Walter J. Ong's synthesis of his earlier research on oral culture, *Orality and Literacy*,[5] and Fiske and Hartley's *Reading Television*. Two current collections of essays, *Literacy and Social Development in the West*[6] and *Literacy, Language, and Learning*,[7] present approaches to the topic from historical, cognitive, pedagogical, psychological, and media perespectives. Precisely because the problem and its approaches are still in a state of definition, the issue of literacy elicits responses from virtually every discipline and enterprise implicated in some way by it.

Despite the vastness of the literate *terra incognita* and the plurality of the approaches elicited by the problem, the current literature of literacy is characterized by some astonishing coincidences of theme, concern, and attitude. Virtually every recent approach to literacy acknowledges the impact of the electronic media on the nature and acquisition of language skills and asks if we are not on the verge of a new literacy, conditioned by these very media. Every specific attempt to articulate and confront the problems of literacy implicitly joins a more general inquiry into the nature and deployment of language. The underlying commonality of interest that pervades this relatively recent field of inquiry is all the more striking because it takes off from one of the seminal moments of contemporary critical theory, the distinction drawn by Jacques Derrida, above all in *Of Grammatology* and *Speech and Phenomena*, between the sets of attitudes attached to the voice (or oral culture) and those attached to writing throughout the history of Western thought.[8] Within this tradition, all forms and media of language are suspect, but oral forms and qualities are less so, because they have been associated with divine inspiration and immediacy, as well as with the presence of the speaker and with the production of language by the physical organs of speech. Writing, on the other hand, is detached from the body (and from the spirit often assumed to inhabit it), self-contained, and hence ambiguous in its sources, allegiance, and meaning. The rigor and comprehensiveness with which Derrida has formulated and historically pursued the interplay between these linguistic models comprises no small measure of his contribution to contemporary thought. The theater in which he examines the accommodation of speech and a suspicious contempt toward writing extends as far back as Plato and is as recent as the critique of Lévi-Strauss's implicit attitudes discussed in Chapter 1.

The current literature of literacy, because it acknowledges two historical phenomena—a decline in print literacy and the cognitive impact of the electronic media—is on a collision course with contemporary critical theory's inquiry into the nature of and prospects for language. Recognizing how much TV people watch, how desperate the struggle for remediation has become throughout the educational system, and how great the social cost of massive illiteracy is, the literature of literacy finds itself situated at a crossroads. If it maintains aspirations for the broader differential and cultural literacy—for which a solid foundation in the traditional verbal and quantitative skills is a mere starting point—it must assess the vast damage done to the capabilities of large populations in the United States and now in Europe whose performance was once higher. This position is uncomfortable, for it implies the social criticism of a submerged phenomenon. After all, what is a decline, and on whom can it be comfortably blamed? Social criticism involves a tension with the society that feeds one, and tension, as the movers and shakers of television have long acknowledged, is both unsettling and emotionally draining. Only Kozol, in the idealism of his educational activism, has the stamina for this particular tack.[9]

A path of lesser resistance means accommodating the prevailing historical forces and "broadening" the notion of literacy—not as I have done in terms of *higher* criteria for linguistic training and skills but in terms that accept television, with its cognitive and existential effects, as the source for a "new" literacy. To an astonishing degree, the more forgiving and perhaps more progressive approaches than my own find in oral culture a precedent and model for the impact, and some would say irreversible changes, wrought by television. A large part of the current literature on literacy thus reintroduces the terms and traditions of linguistic ambivalence, which were traced by Derrida in 1967 in *Of Grammatology* and which became a point of departure for much subsequent critical theory. Marshall McLuhan looms as a major figure in anticipating the "new" literacy generated by an electronic age. Under the influence of the electronic media, the world becomes a "global village" whose newfound intimacy harkens back to a primitive time of oral communication (and satisfaction).[10] The expectation of universal print (i.e., written) literacy is reinstated to its traditional status of remoteness, technicality, and questionable allegiances. The notion of new and unprecedented forms of literacy deriving from television offers those of us who teach and were educated in the antiquated universe of written literacy a rationale for embracing the students who enter our classrooms conditioned by three-minute breaks between commercials. Electronic literacy defines the new challenge of our teaching.

There are, then, many good *reasons* for much of the current literature's muted optimism and acceptance of the existing climate of literacy. Yet underlying this bravado lurks an anxiety whose most pronounced manifestation is the near-universal nostalgia for "oral culture," an intimate, maternal free zone somehow protected from the "nuts and bolts," from the difficult prerequisites of differential verbal capability. The longing for this oral environment may be most intense in Ong's *Orality and Literacy,* but it also tempers the studies by Fiske and Hartley, Pattison, and even Kozol.[11] The rhetoric of orality may well satisfy a compelling need quickly, like fast food. Television is increasingly treated as a medium with oral characteristics. Social scientific data can be cited, as in Pattison's book, to support the view that young television watchers make the best readers. On the other hand, if we pursue a "hard line," insisting that differential literacy requires a serious investment from its disseminators and students and that there is no substitute for it, electronic, oral, or otherwise, in articulating the intellectual and behavioral options of individuals and communities, we do so more to establish an *orientation* for educational and cultural institutions than to specify the means of reaching it. Any rigorous pedagogical approach that can enhance, on a long-term basis, the differential apprehensions of its audience merits investigation, if not implementation, regardless of the technical hardware or teaching materials that it may involve.

We are deeply indebted to those scholars and intellectuals who have devoted their labor and professional preparations to defining and addressing the complex problem of illiteracy. Writers such as Pattison, Ong, Gitlin, Fiske, Hartley, and Kozol render the inestimable service of bringing before the public a serious social dysfunction whose most pernicious aspect may well be its submersion. Their work also furnishes us with some of the terms on which countermeasures may be based. Any effective response will of course require some cooperative effort on the part of an intellectual community suffering from a fragmentation described in Chapter 1. In *On Literacy*, Robert Pattison attempts to establish the most constructive and nonpunitive context possible for raising and articulating the issue. He disarms much of the resistance that the topic alone might evoke by providing a broad historical overview that demonstrates the centrality and persistence of societal and philosophical attitudes toward language that have existed at least since Homer. The sweep of his historical argument follows the counterpoint between speech-based and writerly views of language that Derrida pursued at decisive junctures of the Western tradition.

Pattison's notion of literacy is, in its most succinct formulation, "individual and cultural awareness of language and the interplay of this awareness with the means of expression" (*OL*, 7). He arrives at the cultural options available to contemporary readers and agencies by examining two different literate traditions that have prevailed since ancient times: one may be described as elitist, technocratic, and restricted, while the other finds its precedent in the more open, populist, and oral-based literacy that was offered to its adherents by the early church. So far as Pattison is concerned, universal literacy of the rigorous and print-based (and, I would add, differential) sort has never been necessary, desirable, or desired. A technocratic class forms the administrative and communications nexus of every society. Beyond this cadre, what prevails, and needs nurturing and appreciation, is the by no means negligible vernacular of popular culture. Pattison argues that, instead of expecting literate refinement from every individual, intellectuals and educators should accept the more popular literacy on its own terms and work toward its dissemination and refinement. He is particularly sensitive to the bewilderment and loss of face that individuals who will never join the administrative nexus of society suffer when too formal and technical a literacy is imposed on them. On the pedagogical level, Pattison counsels the tolerance and productive use of students' conditioning by television and other electronic media. A wish to temper the condescension between the more and less privileged literate classes colors much of Pattison's book, which implicitly presupposes the uneven distribution of cultural wealth described above in the volume.

Pattison's pedagogical prescriptions are invaluable, and they are based on an unusually frank assessment of his academic formation and classroom experience. They should be taken into account by every intellectual coming to grips with the sociopolitical dimensions of his or her work. To offer such sage advice, however, Pattison has had to engage in a division with a long history of its own: the act, an expression of ambivalence, of separating language (or literacy) into its "good" and "bad" components. The overall drift of Pattison's argument, from its nostalgia for oral culture and the inclusive community of the early church to its distrust for technical language skills and its amelioration of linguistic expectations, emerges in a sequence of extracts from his book:

> Every writing system seems torn by conflicting impulses. On the one hand it wants to include within its scope all the subjects of language itself. Writing means to be the hard copy of human life. But at the same time every writing scheme has its taboos. Much as writing wants to be inclusive, there are some areas of life it either will not or cannot discuss as well as speech. This propriety is clear in traditional and classical civilizations, where certain themes like personal confession are never entertained in writing. (*OL*, 37)

> At heart, the Church's quarrel with the empire was a confrontation of two opposed attitudes toward language. Cultivated speakers of Latin and Greek, on the one hand, had evolved a highly formal literacy that provided the basis of education and of power. This literacy was increasingly stylized, on the Alexandrian model, and as it became artificial, it also became exclusive. . . . Against this ever more rigid attitude toward language, the Church offered a new variety of literacy in which the fundamental sanctity of spoken language was reaffirmed (in this at least the Christian movement was reactionary more than revo-

lutionary) and the idea of correct usage was temporarily discarded. In the Christian scheme, truth once again inhered in the Word, and the truth once again was available to all who had the spirit to listen in faith: "He that hath ears, let him hear," Jesus had said, stressing the ear over the eye. It was a dictum the Church lived by. (*OL*, 72–73)

We have produced two literacies, one of formal language as encoded in grammars and dictionaries, another of the living language found in daily intercourse and in popular art. To some degree every culture faces this split between formal and informal discourse, between the language of power and the language of the streets. But with us the split has assumed troubling dimensions. The best evidence of this is the anxiety expressed about literacy in a succession of books, articles and popular commentaries.

The first Christian centuries have a lesson to tell us. The present crisis will not be solved by better schools, new textbooks, or sterner discipline. It is at heart a struggle between two ideologies. One of these, advocating a formal, correct grammar, is at the moment the ideology of established authority. This literacy becomes increasingly distant from the people controlled by it. The other ideology, the ideology represented by the informal, oral literacy we see growing up around us, is as yet undeveloped. It is at present a movement without a messiah, a doctrine that awaits its fourth gospel. (*OL*, 84–85)

Consider the alternative: a world in which the young are uniformly trained not merely in the mechanics of reading and writing, but in some critical attitude toward language necessary as a first step in the formation of literacy. This kind of educational endeavor has been the dream of visionaries from Plato to Lenin, and, as Lenin observed, it would produce not merely the functional skills requisite to the successful exploitation of a modern economy but the critical insight necessary for popular opposition to stifling institutions and oppressive ideologies. (*OL*, 177)

The new media will not produce a population of non-readers or non-writers. They will, though, change fundamentally the way people regard reading and writing, first, by fostering an attitude toward language that believes in the real, inherent power of the Word and, second, by providing new mechanical means for the expression of literacy.

The new literacy, operating through the electronic media, will compel the established literacy of middle-class authority to become looser and more idiomatic. At the same time the established literacy will assert its claim that it alone provides the social and economic cohesion necessary for a productive society. (*OL*, 206)

These passages make clear that Pattison falls back to a position at least as old as Plato, one that arises when a *need* for writing is established despite the objections that are raised to its impersonality and questionable loyalties. Under these circumstances, as Derrida carefully establishes in "Plato's Pharmacy," a good, vital, and spiritualized writing is precipitated out of the "bad." The ambivalence toward language hovers around the Platonic figure of the *pharmakon,* and in a capital passage, Derrida elaborates its scope. The *pharmakon* encompasses both extremes of writing:

> good writing (natural, living, knowledgeable, intelligible, internal, speaking) is opposed to bad writing (a moribund, ignorant, external, mute artifice for the senses). And the good one can be designated only through the metaphor of the bad one. Metaphoricity is the logic of contamination and the contamination of logic. Bad writing is for good a model of linguistic designation and a simulacrum of essence. And if the network of opposing predicates that link one type of writing to the other contains in its meshes all the conceptual oppositions of "Platonism"— here considered the dominant structure of the history of metaphysics— then it can be said that philosophy is played out in the play between two kinds of writing.[12]

Pattison's technocratic and elitist literacy, unrelenting in some of its demands, smacks strongly of *bad writing.* While reiterating Derrida's overall historical trajectory and acknowledging the decisiveness of his project to a new engagement with the notion of literacy, Pattison offers as a solution to the problem the complex of attitudes falling under the Derridean rubric of logocentrism: a belief in the spiritual constitution, power, and mission of language, language invested with the immediacy traditionally ascribed to the voice. The living Word that should be, for Pattison, the message of a "new literacy" has much in common with the claims against preexisting religions and philosophical positions that were issued by the church and are accorded such a strategic place within his argument. Pattison's Word renounces abstract formality; it is tolerant, accepting, flexible, and nontechnical. His paradigm for literacy is founded, then, on long-standing arguments indeed.

Pattison's receptiveness to the media-conditioning of current students who have grown up with television stems from more than an interest in pedagogical efficiency. The messages that flash instantaneously across the compass of the "global village" share the universality of a living, accepting, and expansive religion. Proponents of media evolution per se and apologists for the media's inevitable propagation seldom stray far from the aspirations to such conceptual and ideological universality. At various moments in his book, Pattison associates the dissemination of a broad and rigorous literacy, and the technical skills on which it is based, with Augustan Rome, the medieval reversion to Latin as a bureaucratic language, the "old boys'" network of elitist colleges in the United States, Communist China, and, in the above-cited passages, Lenin. The early church, the Lollards, and the electronic media, on the other hand, provide examples of a nontechnical and tolerant literacy. An otherwise linguistic and pedagogical exposition thus resonates with religious and political equations and values.

The degree to which, in Ong as well as Pattison, oral communication emerges as the acceptable form of language because of its intimate, spiritual, and body-related nature is significant—especially in light of Derrida's emphasis, still in the late 1960s, on the different expectations invested in oral and written discourses. The current hopes attached to oral culture—by Kozol, Fiske, Hartley, Pattison, and Ong—confirm rather than challenge the substance of the Derridean distinction.

Although explicitly addressed only in specific contexts, deconstruction remains the underlying motive, almost the powering force, of Ong's *Orality and Literacy*. Were one to summarize this work briefly, one could almost say that it embodies Ong's response, after decades of research in oral communication and culture, to deconstruction and other current theoretical approaches. We are particularly indebted to this book for enlarging upon and fleshing out the (conceptual) position of the voice in Derrida's work to the point at which oral culture becomes an actual and substantial phenomenon. To a remarkable degree, Ong successfully extrapolates a model of orality that can stand alongside the Derridean constellation of qualities and attitudes associated with writing in its explicitness and comprehensiveness. The fundamental agreement between Derrida and Ong far outweighs any specific divergence of opinion. *Ecriture,* for Derrida, incorporates what Ong calls the oral. It serves as a rubric for the assumptions, the illusions, and their debunking that coincide in the deployment of language. Orality, on the other hand, represents, for Ong, a stage of linguistic development that is prior to writing, that generates artifacts independently of writing, and that can still be of immense use in the transmission of culture, skills, and information. The coexistence and mutual enhancement of oral and written language-models poses little problem to Ong. While he of course promotes the applications of his oral-oriented research, he finds no particular menace or evil lurking in the upgrading of rigorous literacy skills. Indeed, the relation between the oral and the written is one of his central concerns.

> Language study in all but recent decades has focused on written texts rather than on orality for a readily assignable reason: the relationship of study itself to writing. All thought, including that in primary oral cultures, is to some degree analytic: it breaks its materials into various components. But abstractly sequential, classificatory, explanatory examination of phenomena or of stated truths is impossible without writing and reading. Human beings in primary oral cultures, those untouched by writing in any form, learn a great deal and possess and practice great wisdom, but they do not "study."
>
> They learn by apprenticeship—hunting with experienced hunters, for example—by discipleship, which is a kind of apprenticeship, by listening, by repeating what they hear, by mastering proverbs and ways of combining and recombining them, by assimilating other formulary materials, by participation in a kind of corporate retrospection—not by study in the strict sense.
>
> When study in the strict sense of extended sequential analysis becomes possible with the interiorization of writing, one of the first things that literates often study is language itself and its uses. . . .
>
> Thus writing from the beginning did not reduce orality but enhanced it, making it possible to organize the "principles" or constituents of oratory into a scientific "art," a sequentially ordered body of explanation that showed how and why oratory achieved and could be made to achieve its various specific effects. (*O and L*, 8–9)

Oral cultures indeed produce powerful and beautiful verbal performances of high artistic and human worth, which are no longer even possible once writing has taken possession of the psyche. Nevertheless, without writing, human consciousness cannot achieve its fuller potentials, cannot produce other beautiful and powerful creations. In this sense, orality needs to produce and is destined to produce writing. Literacy, as will be seen, is absolutely necessary for the development not only of science but also of history, philosophy, explicative understanding of

literature and of any art, and indeed for the explanation of language
(including oral speech) itself. There is hardly an oral culture or a predominantly oral culture left in the world today that is not somehow
aware of the vast complex of powers forever inaccessible without literacy. This awareness is agony for persons rooted in primary orality,
who want literacy passionately but who also know very well that moving into the exciting world of literacy means leaving behind much that
is exciting and deeply loved in the earlier oral world. We have to die
to continue living.

Fortunately, literacy, though it consumes its own oral antecedents and,
unless it is carefully monitored, even destroys their memory, is also
infinitely adaptable. It can restore their memory, too. Literacy can be
used to reconstruct for ourselves the pristine human consciousness which
was not literate at all—at least to reconstruct this consciousness pretty
well, though not perfectly (we can never forget enough of our familiar
present to reconstitute in our minds any past in its full integrity). Such
reconstruction can bring a better understanding of what literacy itself
has meant in shaping man's consciousness toward and in high-technol-
ogy cultures. (*O and L*, 14–15)

In programmatic statements of the kind reproduced here, Ong may
well regard oral communication as the "pristine" form of language,
dominated, supplemented, and committed to memory by "literacy."
And yet the constellation of oral behaviors, skills, and attributes that
he assembles throughout the main part of his book constitutes a
major contribution to the theory of linguistic behavior. Within Ong's
scenario, orality and literacy do not so much threaten as condition,
extend, and in some cases stimulate each other. Some of Ong's
ongoing concerns about writing, such as its impact on memory and
memorization, may have been shared by Plato, but the research that
he marshals to support his profile of oral traits is a good deal more
recent. Ong's fascination for his subject has enabled him to explore
a wide range of its conditions—physical, temporal, cognitive, logical, social psychological, and metaphysical. He begins his elaboration with the incontrovertible fact of the "evanescence of sound"
(*O and L*, 31–33) and its temporal implications. Mnemonic devices, such as formulas and other redundant elements, play a prominent role in a culture whose signs are constantly expiring within
the flow of temporal duration. A cognitive correlative to this intense
concern for stability (in the absence of written traces) is a loyalty

to the *aggregate* of a body of information at the expense of its *particulars,* be they exceptions or details. Stylistically, Ong describes the discourse of oral culture as "additive" rather than specific in the interrelation of its details: More attention is paid to the coincidence of events and facts than to their temporal and logical priority. Oral narratives are "copious" rather than spare. Dramatically, they delight in battles and conflicts as means to organize their information. They are "homeostatic," or they slough off memories whose relevance has vanished. When possible, oral culture attempts to ensure the continuity of its traditions, but it does not hesitate to revise earlier accounts in conformity with subsequent developments. In a variety of dimensions, Ong (echoing Lévi-Strauss) stresses the concreteness of oral culture. Its narrative skills are transmitted by apprenticeship or on-site training. Its performances solicit empathic and direct participation. Its logic is "situational" rather than "abstract."

Some of the most memorable passages in *Orality and Literacy* review research on illiterate (i.e., oral and semiliterate) individuals, such as those in A. R. Luria's fieldwork of 1931–32 in Uzbekistan and Kirghizia (USSR). As Ong reports, oral subjects "identified geometrical figures by assigning the names of objects, never abstractly as circles, squares, etc." (*O and L*, 51); they grouped objects not by abstract qualities but by concrete functions; they resisted inferential reasoning and abstract definitions; and they had some difficulty with "articulate self-analysis." (For Ong, intense introspection is a function of the isolation accompanying print culture.) By invoking the epic poets of modern Yugoslavia, Ong demonstrates powerfully that aesthetic values are not contingent on written artifacts and that complex and beautiful poetry can be composed and transmitted by individuals lacking formal literate skills. He also indicates the prominence within this mode of communal existence of what he calls "verbomotor lifestyle," i.e., heavily stylized oral behaviors such as bartering and oaths.

As the result of Ong's exposition, oral discourse, lifestyle, and habits emerge in far greater relief and immediacy than they have in deconstruction's critique of the prevalent suspicions toward language throughout Western thought. But Ong refrains from elaborating in specific detail the application of this cultural model to contemporary theoretical or educational problems. This caution enables

him to circumvent some of the objections that more explicit prescriptions, such as Pattison's, are likely to raise—but it leaves certain fundamental questions open. How much is print culture alone
responsible for the isolation and alienation that Ong identifies as its
sociopsychological effects, ones that for Walter Benjamin coincided
with the advance of "mechanical reproduction" and the rise of the
modern city?[13] Even if oral culture can claim some historical (or
rather prehistorical) priority over writing, even if it then comprises
some sort of cultural "missing link," how does this help us address
the very specific theoretical and social problems posed at the present
time by illiteracy? How specifically useful are the oral behaviors
observed among cultures such as the Gonja of Ghana and the Cuna
of Panama? Can oral culture undo our prior inscription within a
scene of writing?

I have no doubt whatsoever that the distinctive skills of oral culture and the habits conditioned by television can be applied to the
dissemination of the broader, differential literacy whose health is
so essential to our individual growth and our collective wisdom. But
I remain struck by the degree of hope invested in cultural and educational forms whose promises include a circumvention of books
and of the demands of written language. Pattison is explicit in his
messianic hopes for orality. Fiske and Hartley describe television
as the interstice between oral and literate discursive conventions.[14]
Kozol designates oral history as a first step in achieving at least
functional literacy for individuals who have not been exposed to
written traces of their collective past.[15] As Derrida specifies, all language forms are conditioned by the differentiation that pervades
writing and may thus be deployed in the critical function of teaching. But the hope of preempting or circumventing rigorous verbal
training in the upgrading of literate capability may well be symp-
tomatic of ongoing ambivalence toward the full range of linguistic
variation.

The religious rhetoric that enters the statements by those intellectuals and scholars who survey the literate conditions of our age
is a curious phenomenon. It surely signifies, far more than the es-
pousal of any particular doctrine, the gravity with which these men
and women assess the current literate environment and the seriousness of their commitment to its improvement. Perhaps theology furnishes a set of terms and images familiar to a public that has not

yet evolved a commitment to literate formation per se. In reading such statements closely, I risk falling into a regrettable divisiveness and parochialism that I myself have lamented above. The complex socioeconomic, political, and cultural conditions that conspire to produce the current climate of illiteracy surely warrant a plurality of approaches and tools. And yet where the attacks against this dysfunction implicitly harbor the biases that have (both currently and traditionally) produced it, they should beware. It is both the achievement and the burden of contemporary critical theory to have made the at times subtle suspicions toward language an area of its special concern.

At the present moment, then, what one could hope for is a redoubling and a certain abandon. Groundbreaking efforts of the sort made by the authors we have touched upon and by their colleagues in linguistics, educational studies, philosophy, literature, and media studies need to be extended and nurtured by every available means of support. At the same time, the defensiveness and apologetic tone in which approaches to the theoretical and behavioral dimensions of illiteracy have been couched in all likelihood have outlived their utility. Additional work needs to be done in establishing the conditions of illiteracy and the forces that resist its concerted confrontation. On the basis of such understandings, there is considerable room for an integration of the various institutions and enterprises dedicated to the dissemination of literacy.

Postscript and Prescriptions

No document could be more indicative of the current impasses surrounding the public image and policy of literacy than a Letter to the Editor responding to Colin Campbell's article in *The New York Times Magazine* of February 9, 1986, "The Tyranny of the Yale Critics." Campbell's article accorded "front page coverage," in the most widely read Sunday feuilleton in the United States, to the series of intellectual developments summarized in Chapter 1—and to their impact on literacy studies in at least one major American university. Its title, however, belied the article's attempt to present a tempered

view: The "unquestionable" brilliance of Derrida and critics such
as J. Hillis Miller was counterbalanced by the "tyranny" that deconstruction presently exercises in its hold on teaching and scholarship.

Campbell's article accounted for the power of deconstruction and
critical theory in general as a phenomenon of Yale University. In
its need for a "hook," the article devoted some attention to the personalities of critical theory's proponents at Yale, and to a few of
its naysayers as well, such as Harold Bloom. Whatever narrative
and argumentative devices the article chose, it did expand, beyond
the confines of the campus, the public awareness of critical theory
and of the most pressing issues facing literacy studies. It lifted the
debate surrounding deconstruction out of the muffled submersion in
which much academic discourse tends to find itself and raised the
issue to the level of a public concern—of a peripheral nature, perhaps, but on the roster of matters under deliberation nevertheless.

I cite in full a Letter to the Editor from Andrew A. Rooney of
CBS News that appeared five Sundays later in the same magazine:

> There's nothing I like better Sunday morning than to relax over a second
> cup of coffee with an article in The Times Magazine that's smarter than
> I am. "The Tyranny of the Yale Critics" was perfect. It was so cultural
> and so far beyond me I could hardly put it down to spread the mar-
> malade on my toast.
>
> There are some ways I have of determining when an article is beyond
> my intellectual means. Perhaps I could share them with some of your
> readers. "Neo" is a key word to look for. If there are a lot of neo's in
> an article, I don't usually understand much of it. When Colin Campbell
> wrote of "neo-Freudian poststructuralist" something, I knew I was in
> for it.
>
> There are other word clues to a high-class piece of writing. Among
> them are "ethnocentricity," "nihilists" or "nihilism" and, of course,
> references to Rilke, Wittgenstein and Heidegger.
>
> The fact that I never got to understand what Jacques Derrida meant
> by "deconstruction" only heightened the pleasure I got from the article.
> The text in the box by J. Hillis Miller, "How Deconstruction Works,"
> was a good touch, too. At first I thought it was the answer to last week's
> Double Crostic.
>
> One final comment—a sort of personal note. Mr. Campbell said that
> there was "a certain counterlonging for an end to controversy in the air

at Yale." I knew there was something in the air up there. We went up to the Long Wharf Theater one night and I smelled something, but I thought it was coming from one of the industrial plants in Bridgeport.

Andrew A. Rooney
CBS News
New York City

Air quality jokes aside, Rooney adopts a "know nothing" pose in order to interrogate the utility, the value, even the comprehensibility of the airy and insubstantial qualifications preoccupying the effete intellectuals on campus. Rooney assumes the role of Gulliver, a well-meaning and of course objective fellow, not too large or too small, not too intellectually highfalutin or dumb, who just can't quite make sense of what he hears out there. In a world of confusion, he offers us good fellowship and camaraderie. Anybody had too much of that lately?

We owe Mr. Rooney credit and possibly high marks for his own brand of irony, rendering it impossible to ascertain the degree of his antiintellectualism or his feint. And yet he is also an official of one of the United States' three major independent broadcast networks and is, at least in this writer's opinion, on the staff of a news department that has traditionally gone out of its way to accommodate the incommensurate and the unpopular. His either sincere or pretended dismissal of work at the cutting edge of a redefinition of literacy thus emanates, indirectly, from a vast communications enterprise, one free either to disseminate and enlarge upon the complexities facing public understanding and policy or to repress them. On at least one level, his unsolicited letter performs the role of kitsch, the disarming of the unresolvable in the name of harmony and confidence. His letter could have come from *anyone,* and it may well reflect the opinions of thousands, perhaps even the majority, of readers of Campbell's article. But coming from Andy Rooney of CBS News, the letter takes on an additional meaning, one that each chapter in this book has, in a different way, attempted to explore.

The so-called humanities are of course not the only area of contemporary study that produces neologisms and complex terminologies. Any article attempting to convey the taste of state-of-the-art research in particle physics or biomedical engineering would just as inevitably run into some "high-class" words. In all likelihood, however, these fields would be immune to Mr. Rooney's derision. The humanities are particularly vulnerable to the objections of superfluity, triviality, and excessive refinement implicit in Mr. Rooney's response. Derrida has demonstrated how deeply entrenched these suspicions are within the foundations of our Western heritage. Mr. Rooney would be circumspect in ridiculing the finer points of technological or biomedical research because, however indirectly, he would not want CBS to oppose national security or health.

Still, how could I be so perverse or trite as to challenge Mr. Rooney? With their feigned gullibility and humor, good fellows like him are the pith of society. They restrain us from reaching too high or sinking too low. They somehow manage to negotiate a life-affirming equilibrium between the peaks of human folly and the slough of perversity. With precisely this good-humored, down-to-earth enthusiasm, American culture, for one, has profoundly influenced world events and produced earth-shaking inventions. As we approach the end of a century that has not recovered from the furious pace and complexity of its innovations—nor is it about to—we wonder only at how long this bravado will suffice as the posture we assume to get us through our scrapes.

As this book comes to a close, I realize that I have perhaps overdrawn on my credit as a teacher of languages and literatures to pronounce on issues not traditionally within the compass of my disciplines. The practical dimension of this attempt to define and trace the history of literacy—and the resistances to it—in modern and post-modern culture almost demands, however, that we furnish our elaborated problem with a response. Any prescription I deliver must be modest and tentative, very much in need of subsequent response, refinement, and productive disagreement. In fact, my pharmaceutical program runs only to two items, which are outlined below.

Study of the Implications and Applications of Local Difference

In its widest sense, literacy is attentiveness to the minute particulars of language, artifacts, documents, things, environments, and experiences—and the discernment of their relation to the broader systems from which they derive a certain placement, impetus, context, or meaning. While systems, whether semiotic, social, political, or economic, do not *exhaust* the significance of particulars, their impact, whether described as tonal or modal, is considerable: The process of interpretation necessarily takes it into account.

Reading in a meaningful way involves ferreting out of the context those specific factors that give rise to the unique resonance that a message, artifact, event, or experience carries. While phenomena may arise in *general contexts,* careful reading articulates what Derrida has called the local difference of each instance under consideration. The term "local difference" most immediately evokes images of political and linguistic power relations: the domination of regional jurisdictions and folkways by centralized government; the obliteration of dialect by the established *lingua franca.* And yet the term opens a much broader range of implications: the difference between multiple instances, whether of a word or character in a literary work, between manifestations of a psychological "law," or between the competing enterprises of an economic system.

Rigorous reading accounts, incompletely, for the local difference of the phenomenon under consideration. Readers cognizant of the nuances of language have always protected the position, integrity, and discreteness of signifiers' local differences. At an historical moment, however, when technological advances in communications, cybernetics, and transportation subject local phenomena to increasing dominance by centralized agencies of control, the delineation and preservation of local differences become more urgent (because more tenuous) concerns.

The greatest extension of literacy thus involves the very careful reading of the relationships that configure all organized systems, not only the linguistic and imagistic codes of artworks but also systems of production, distribution, management, communication, education, law enforcement, and social services. We live in a time when it may prove particularly worthwhile to study the status, conditions, and value of the local phenomena either fostered or suppressed within these systems. In a sense, the biggest task and challenge for literacy at the present moment is to conduct a careful reading of *the world in which we live,* deploying methods developed by such writers as Wittgenstein, Barthes, Foucault, Lévi-Strauss, and Derrida. Particularly in the context of the acceleration and totalization that have prevailed over the past generation in science and com-

munications, certain local phenomena—skills, crafts, minor enterprises—that have become unprofitable from the perspectives of production and/or consumption may well warrant revival. Such a close
analysis of systems in accordance with semiological and rigorous
philosophical methods may well unearth other instances of local difference that long ago outlived their welcome.

In some enterprises, the enhancement of specificity through attention to local differences is already under way. This is clearly now
the case in literacy and philosophical studies. "Lacan" does not merely
name an important French psychoanalyst, now deceased; it may
also be regarded as an approach that restores local difference to the
observation, formulation, and treatment of psychological manifestations. The shift in attention in historical studies away from dominant personalities and classes to the lived experience of "common"
individuals also reflects a reorientation to this type of perspective.
In a whole range of other enterprises, however, "independence"—
from the established networks of distribution, from the sources of
capital and authoritative approval—usually implies a kiss of death.
The nearly insurmountable obstacles faced by autonomous producers in film, publishing, television, drama, and the fine arts have
been well documented. The analysis of systematic relations and local differences that I propose will surely inquire into the nature,
modulation, and improved evaluation of systematic "independence."

In certain respects, megaorganizations of production, employment, finance, and information may well provide goods, services,
and information of a higher quality than their local counterparts,
and more in keeping with the needs and lifestyles of the people who
interact with them. The inquiry into the possibility and viability of
local structures that I propose, encompassing such fields as law,
medicine, business, public administration, and the traditional arts
and sciences disciplines, need not at all challenge the operations of
megaorganizations where they are successful. But such an investigation may divulge a set of operating principles more or less ap-
plicable throughout the marginal sphere. It will hopefully assist in
the articulation (rather than disavowal) of the supplemental economies that arise around predominant systems. The most pressing
current challenge to our collective literate skills is rigorous defini-

tion of the margin and its qualities—and the fostering of those productive and existential alternatives that totalizing organizations have obliterated or discouraged.

The Articulation of Literacy as a Public Value

Given the vast investments that the institutions of government, information, and even education have in the maintenance of public tranquility, this brief codicil to a minimalist prescription is far easier enunciated than enacted. It requires that politicians and public servants espouse literate concerns, no simple task if we consider how abstract these issues seem in comparison with the needs, say, of technological and medical research. It involves an extensive reorientation, already under way, in many parts of the United States, of the curricular planning and implementation of primary and secondary schools, colleges, and universities. (We live at a time when the backlog of technical information necessary for professional competence in many areas increases on a yearly basis. The issue is not to "reverse" the technical thrust of professional training in favor of "literate" subjects but to implant the skills of differential literacy within that training. This is impossible, however, without the provision of some purely language- and culture-oriented courses in the preprofessional curriculum.) The thrust and atmosphere of primary and secondary education surely change when they become oriented to a profession of *general* literate skills instead of to a vast, possibly bewildering menu of conflicting demands. A time has clearly come for primary education to become more focused, deliberate, and unrelenting in its commitment to deliver basic literate and quantitative skills. (This will *not,* however, involve teaching reading and writing at increasingly early ages.) Such a retooling is a vast undertaking, requiring an enhanced sociopolitical understanding of the school's relation to its community, but it can be facilitated by an improved transfer of information and services between school systems and universities. The orientation, mission, and implementation of teacher-training is an issue of decisive importance. It must be reoriented to literate priorities if the schools have any hope of shifting their direction and results.

When the facilitating medium of language becomes the focal point and evolutionary access to more advanced study, the territorial claims of exclusivity asserted by the traditional disciplines lose much of their force and justification. At the same time, a foregrounding of the interdisciplinary nature and implications of studies that have perhaps become insular takes place. The interface between the various studies and professional discourses become as crucial as the "contents" of those programs themselves. Advanced studies oriented to the codes underlying all systematic endeavors—and their mutual translatability—require greater emphasis and resources at the "general," and often introductory level. But the beneficial outcome of such interdisciplinarity and synthetic perspectives, even if they enter the curriculum at some cost to professional specialization, will be citizens and practitioners who can place their work in the broadest possible context of sociopolitical interactions and historical precedents. Once the codes of organized activity become the inception and organizing principle of learning, secondary and advanced education will become increasingly interdisciplinary in emphasis and global in outlook. The skills of professional specialization are often job- and task-related and can be transferred once work has begun.

Established educational institutions, however, are by no means the only components of the literate environment. Books such as Gitlin's demonstrate how broadcasting networks, in the interest of ideologically neutral "entertainment," resist upgrading the quality of their programs. In a democracy, any thought of governmental *regulation* of quality raises the gravest ideological as well as logistical considerations. At the same time, I am certain that wonders could be achieved in this sphere if the quality of the literate environment were even a public *value*, not a requirement or a specification. The time has perhaps arrived for ameliorating the *commercial* dimensions of broadcasting executives' decisions by providing some noncommercial support for the basic television channels, perhaps a variation on the user's tax levied in some European countries.

But television is only one of several cultural enterprises characterized by commercial hysteria and an impetus, based on social scientific testing, to adopt the lowest acceptable level of verbal and intellectual complexity. Excessive intellectual toniness is more threatening to the managers of film, theater, and artistic performance and exhibition, as well as of television, than sexual and even political sensationalism. The cultivation of the needs and desires of "specialized" audiences goes hand in hand with our current technological capabilities, which include cable television and easily available video recording equipment. The mere coexistence, however, of different tastes, styles, and subdivisions of the public does not alone constitute an adequate response to the conditions of the literate environment. (Alone, such a pluralism amounts to a cultural "repressive tolerance.") We sorely need a rigorous review of and adjustment to the literate conditions of the programming and artifacts already implanted in the landscape, much of it offered at no cost and allowing little or no selection by its audience.

The dissemination of the wider skills of literacy can only transpire by concerted effort; it is neither a matter of *conversion,* regardless of the religious rhetoric adopted so often in the current debate, nor of indoctrination. The success of this endeavor, joined as it is by academics, primary and secondary educators, independent writers and artists, curators and arts administrators, and journalists, is particularly crucial during an advanced technological age. There will, however, be little impetus behind the vast enterprise of distributing the wealth of human language and culture until literacy, as a complex concept, achieves its explicit enunciation as a value.

Literacy, then, is at once a set of linguistic capabilities, a public issue, and a literary construct that has entered and informed the works of some of the most decisive authors. It is *resolved,* in one way or another, at every historical moment, and our particular response will constitute a telling insignia of our age.

Notes

Chapter 1

1. See Roland Barthes, "Myth Today," in *Mythologies*, tr. Annette Lavers (New York: Hill and Wang, 1972), pp. 109–59. For good general introductions to Barthes' work, see Jonathan Culler, *Barthes*, Viking Modern Masters Series (New York: Viking, 1983); and Stevan Ungar, *Roland Barthes: The Professor of Desire* (Lincoln University of Nebraska Press, 1983).

2. Barthes, *Mythologies*, pp. 117–21.

3. Barthes, *Mythologies*, pp. 88–90.

4. Barthes, *Mythologies*, pp. 81–83, 153.

5. In identifying kitsch as an enemy to rigorous thought and personal freedom, Kundera is following the lead of the Frankfurt School, notably the critique of mass culture furnished by Theodor Adorno in such works as *The Dialectic of Enlightenment* (written with Max Horkheimer) and *Minima Moralia*. Adorno is intensely aware of the collusion between what he calls the entertainment industry and various forms of political repression. For a specific critique of kitsch, see *Minima Moralia*, tr. E. F. N. Jephcott (London: Verso, 1984), pp. 118, 147, 203, 206, 226.

6. Milan Kundera, *The Unbearable Lightness of Being*, tr. Michael Henry Heim (London and Boston: Faber and Faber, 1985). I henceforth identify this work in my text as *ULB*.

7. Milan Kundera, *The Book of Laughter and Forgetting*, tr. Michael Henry Heim (New York: Penguin, 1980), p. 3, henceforce abbreviated in my text as *BLF*.

8. The narrator's discomfort with the blurring effects of pop music again has a precedent in Adorno's criticism. Adorno found in jazz a similar gravitation toward the lowest common denominator of musical discrimination, a point well worth arguing. (One of the endearing qualities of Adorno's work is its sheer grouchiness, its openness with regard to its own arbitrariness, its entertaining the possible mistake.) For Adorno's comments on music, see *Minima Moralia*, pp. 50, 149, and "Perennial Fashion—Jazz," in *Prisms*, tr. Samuel and Shierry Weber (Cambridge: The MIT Press, 1984), pp. 119–32.

9. See Louis Marin, "Disneyland: A Degenerate Utopia," in *Glyph 1: Johns*

229

Hopkins Textual Studies (Baltimore: Johns Hopkins University Press, 1977), pp. 50–66.

10. Todd Gitlin, *Inside Prime Time* (New York: Pantheon, 1984), p. 14. I henceforth identify this book in my text as *IPT*.

11. Albert Camus, *The Plague* (New York: Random House, 1972).

12. Gore Vidal, "On Italo Calvino," *New York Review of Books*, 23, No. 18 (November 21, 1985): 3.

13. For a sense of this estrangement within academic literary departments, see James Alan McPherson's introduction to *The Stories of Breece D'J Pancake* (New York: Holt, Rinehart and Winston, 1982), pp. 4–9.

14. Colin Campbell, "The Tyranny of the Yale Critics," *The New York Times Magazine* (February 9, 1986): 20–48.

15. See, in this regard, Denis Donoghue, "Deconstructing Deconstruction," *New York Review*, 23, No. 10 (1980): 37–41; Robert Alter, "The Decline and Fall of Literary Criticism," *Commentary*, 77, No. 3 (1984): 50–56; Gerald Graff, "Deconstruction as Dogma, or 'Come Back to the Raft Ag'in in Strether Honey!'" *Georgia Review*, 34 (1980): 404–21; and, John Searle, "On Deconstruction," *New York Review*, 30, No. 16 (1983): 74–79.

16. An exception to this trend has been the work of Jonathan Culler, who has consistently illuminated the intricacies of critical theory both for specialized and more general readerships. Particularly indispensable in this regard are Culler's *On Deconstruction* (Ithaca: Cornell University Press, 1982), *Saussure*, Viking Modern Masters Series (New York: Viking, 1976), and *Barthes*. A different effort to broaden the arena for critical and theoretical problems is Geoffrey Hartman's *Easy Pieces* (New York: Columbia University Press, 1985).

17. Italo Calvino, *t zero*, tr. William Weaver (New York: Harcourt Brace Jovanovich, 1976).

18. Italo Calvino, *If on a winter's night a traveler*, tr. William Weaver (New York: Harcourt Brace Jovanovich, 1981).

19. See Jacques Derrida, "The Conflict of Faculties," in *Languages of Knowledge and of Inquiry*, ed. Michael Riffaterre (New York: Columbia University Press, forthcoming) and "Où Commence et comment finit un corps enseignant," in *Politiques de la philosophie*, ed. Dominique Grisoni (Paris: Grasset, 1976), pp. 55–97.

20. See, particularly, Roland Barthes, *S/Z*, tr. Richard Howard (New York: Hill and Wang, 1974), and *L'Aventure sémiologique* (Paris: Seuil, 1985); and Michel Foucault, *The Order of Things* (New York: Random House 1973); and *The Archaeology of Knowledge*, tr. A. M. Sheridan Smith (New York: Pantheon, 1972).

21. A groundbreaking and crucial effort in the application of critical-theoretical constructs in their full complexity to a pressing political problem was the conference on Nuclear Criticism held at Cornell University in April, 1984, part of whose proceedings were published in *Diacritics*, 14, No. 2 (1984).

22. The conflagration takes up Book Three of William Carlos Williams's *Paterson* (New York: New Directions, 1963), pp. 93–145. For reference purposes, I abbreviate the title of this work in my text as *P*.

23. This subject is, of course, a thematic focus of Kierkegaard's *Either/Or* (tr.

David F. Swenson and Lillian Marvin Swenson [Princeton: Princeton University Press, 1971]), one to which its multiple forms of discourse and style are variously calibrated. I have discussed the importance of this concern and its complex dramatization in *The Hegelian Aftermath: Readings in Hegel, Kierkegaard, Freud, Proust, and James* (Baltimore: Johns Hopkins University Press, 1982), pp. 63–70, 110–58.

24. The citation is from Jacques Derrida, *Of Grammatology*, tr. and intro. Gayatri Chakravorty Spivak (Baltimore: Johns Hopkins University Press, 1976) pp. 62–63. In my text, I will henceforth abbreviate the title of this work as *OG*.

25. Ferdinand de Saussure, *Course in General Linguistics*, tr. and intro. Wade Baskin (1915; rpt. New York: McGraw-Hill, 1966). I henceforth refer to this book as *CGL*. For a good introduction to Saussure's writings and their significance, see Jonathan Culler, *Saussure*.

26. Ludwig Wittgenstein, *Preliminary Studies for the 'Philosophical Investigations' Generally Known as the Blue and Brown Books* (Oxford: Basil Blackwell, 1958), p. 45. I henceforth refer to this volume in my text as *BBB*.

27. Ludwig Wittgenstein, *Tractatus Logico-Philosophicus* (1921; rpt. London: Routledge and Kegan Paul, 1961), henceforth abbreviated in my text as *TLP*.

28. Among the most significant works to consult regarding speech-act theory are the following: J. L. Austin, *How to do Things with Words* (Cambridge: Cambridge University Press, 1969); Jacques Derrida, "Signature Event Context," *Glyph 1*, pp. 162–254; John Searle, "Reiterating the Differences: A Reply to Derrida," *Glyph 1*, pp. 198–208.

29. Two of Barthes' most fascinating readings of cultural artifacts are *Empire of Signs*, tr. Richard Howard (New York: Hill and Wang, 1982), and *The Eiffel Tower and Other Mythologies*, tr. Richard Howard (New York: Hill and Wang, 1977).

30. Claude Lévi-Strauss, "The Structural Study of Myth," in *Structural Anthropology*, tr. Claire Jacobson and Brocke Grundfest Schoepf (London: Penguin, 1979), pp. 209–11. I henceforth abbreviate this book in my text as *SA*.

31. Claude Lévi-Strauss, *The Savage Mind* (Chicago: University of Chicago Press, 1973), pp. 71–72. In the text, I henceforth abbreviate the title of this volume *SM*.

32. These essays are translated in Martin Heidegger, *Poetry, Language, Thought*, tr. Albert Hofstadter (New York: Harper and Row, 1971), and appear, respectively, on pp. 89–142, 187–210, and 211–29. I henceforth refer to the volume as *PLT*.

33. Heidegger, "Language," *PLT*, p. 202.

34. Heidegger, "The Origin of the Work of Art," *PLT*, pp. 20, 34, 46–53.

35. See Saussure, *CGL*, pp. 9–15, 76–78.

36. Martin Heidegger, "Identity and Difference," in *Identity and Difference*, tr. and intro. Joan Stambaugh (New York: Harper and Row, 1974), p. 26. I henceforth abbreviate this book, *I and D*.

37. Derrida's own account of the development of the notion of difference is to be found in "Différance," in *Speech and Phenomena* (Evanston: Northwestern University Press, 1973), pp. 107–30. Here, as in "Ousia and grammē," in *Phenomenology in Perspective*, ed. F. J. Smith (The Hague: Nijhoff, 1970), pp. 54–93, Derrida indicates the traces of presence in Heidegger's conceptualization.

38. See Derrida, "Signature Event Context," *Glyph 1* pp. 172–97.

39. See Jacques Derrida, *Positions* (Chicago: University of Chicago Press, 1981).

40. See Friedrich Nietzsche, *Thus Spoke Zarathustra*, tr. R. J. Hollingdale (New York: Random House, 1976), pp. 40–51.

41. Williams, *Paterson*, p. 235; William Blake, "Auguries of Innocence," in *Complete Poems*, ed. Daniel Erdman (New York: Macmillan, 1968), p. 341.

42. For the figure of the *pharmakon*, see Jacques Derrida, "Plato's Pharmacy," in *Dissemination* (Chicago: University of Chicago Press, 1982), pp. 95–119, 134–55; for the figure of the hymen, see Derrida, "The Double Session," *Dissemination*, pp. 201, 203, 207–26, 251–60; for the figure of the heliotrope, see Derrida, "White Mythology," *New Literary History*, 6 (1974): 5–74; for the figure of the tympany, see Derrida, "Tympan," in *Marges de la philosophie* (Paris: Seuil, 1972), pp. i–xxv.

43. John Fiske and John Hartley, *Reading Television* (London and New York: Methuen, 1978), pp. 59, 63–67.

44. Cf. Gitlin, *IPT*, pp. 24–26, 29–30, 54–55, 224–25. Also see Muriel Cantor, "Audience Control," Michael Novak, "Television Shapes the Soul," Roger Rosenblatt, "Growing Up on Television," and Douglas Kellner, "TV, Ideology, and Emancipatory Popular Culture," in *Television: The Critical View*, ed. Horace Newcomb (New York: Oxford University Press, 1982), pp. 311–34, 335–50, 373–85, 386–422; and Martin Esslin, *The Age of Television* (San Francisco: W. H. Freeman, 1982), pp. 97–125.

45. See Walter Benjamin, "On Some Motifs in Baudelaire," in *Illuminations*, ed. and intro. Hannah Arendt (New York: Schocken, 1969), pp. 158–60, 174–75, 184–85, 188.

46. In its own way, conventional American television has addressed the prevalent issue of racism in American society. Initial television representations of racial harmony may have resorted to tokenism, but recent scenarios of shared consumer bliss have been far more even-handed. Through its attention to racism, however, American television has nonetheless made a substantial contribution, if only through the residual effect of positive interactions among diverse ethnic communities in its depictions.

47. Cf. Gitlin, *IPT*, pp. 63, 84–85, 93, 103, 117–18, 175, 333–35. For a perspective on the television industry that confirms Gitlin's view, see Jerry Mander, *Four Arguments for the Elimination of Television* (New York: Morrow Quill, 1978), pp. 134–56, 192–215, 263–82.

Chapter 2

1. All citations of this novel refer to Nathaniel Hawthorne, *The Marble Faun*, Centenary Edition (Columbus, Ohio: Ohio State University Press, 1968).

2. I use the term "moratorium" in the sense applied to individual development by Erik Erikson in *Young Man Luther* (New York: Norton, 1962), pp. 43, 100–104.

3. In Hegel's *Phenomenology of Spirit*, for example, Appearance is the illusion

first of an interior, then of a transcendental domain, that makes abstraction and all advanced works of logic, theology, and art possible. See the chapter on "Force and the Understanding," in G. W. F. Hegel, *The Phenomenology of Spirit*, tr. A. V. Miller (Oxford: Oxford University Press, 1977), pp. 86–103.

4. I have in mind Eliot's "Preludes" and *The Waste Land* and Stevens's "The Man on the Dump." The creative recycling of the archaeological remains of many cultures is a vital preoccupation of modern American poetry and will be discussed in Chapter 4 of this book in relation to Ezra Pound, Wallace Stevens, and William Carlos Williams.

5. See Johann Wolfgang von Goethe, *Faust*, tr. Walter Arndt (New York: Norton, 1976), pp. 178–194, (ll. 7080–123, 7495–549).

6. I refer, of course, to Mann's novella *Death in Venice*, in *Death in Venice and Seven Other Stories by Thomas Mann*, tr. H. T. Lowe-Porter (New York: Random House, 1960), pp. 3–75.

7. Cf. Chapter 27, "Myths," in *The Marble Faun*, pp. 242–48.

8. Replete with the Roman carnival, the premature interment of a baby, a series of poisonings, and a deliriously happy ending, Alexandre Dumas' *Le Comte de Monte-Cristo* must be regarded as the primary literary model for *The Marble Faun* and the romantic genre that Hawthorne attempted to found. Edmond Dantès' injury, revenge, and moratorium may be said to constitute the synthetic stages of a Hegelian personal development. If the thrust of Hawthorne's unification is historical, aligning diverse epochs behind the American present, the emphasis of Dumas' global view is geographical. The island of MonteCristo is the focal point for an international Mediterranean region, whose post- (French) revolutionary history unfolds through the experience of the novel's hero. Dumas' and Hawthorne's novels share a global perspective, a long historical view, melodramatic travails suffered by their characters, moral crises, and endings that struggle to provide a resolution as complete as the circumstances and morals have been muddled. Despite its vast canvas, *Le Comte de Monte-Cristo* is relatively neglected as a work at the very crux of nineteenth-century moral, sociopolitical, theoretical, and technological issues. See Alexandre Dumas, *Le Comte de Monte-Cristo*, Bibliotheque de la Pléiade (Paris: Gallimard, 1981), pp. 53–63, 159–90, 240–49, 421–58, 647–64, 1063–78, 1210–18, 1343–57, 1377–98.

9. This is a chapter heading, claim, and program in Jacques Derrida's *Of Grammatology*, pp. 6–26.

10. This during numerous personal conversations and academic functions at SUNY-Buffalo, 1978–79.

11. Lacoue-Labarthe and Nancy, in *L'Absolu littéraire* (Paris: Seuil, 1978), assemble and elaborate a set of discursive conventions, including the fragment and the image, that dominate early Romanticism. In so doing, they demonstrate how the sublime and enigmatic moods of Romanticism participate within, rather than oppose, the traditions of metaphysical speculation.

12. In recent and forthcoming work, Rodolphe Gasché attempts to distinguish deconstruction from the negativity accommodated by standard speculative procedures. See his "Deconstruction as Criticism," *Glyph 6: Johns Hopkins Textual Studies* (Baltimore: Johns Hopkins University Press, 1979), pp. 177–215.

13. See, for example, *The Marble Faun*, pp. 53, 266, 366, 368.

14. I refer to Hegel's discussion of classical Greek art in his *Vorlesungen über die Asthetik*. See G. W. F. Hegel, *Werke in Zwanzig Bänden*, Theorie Werkausgabe (Frankfurt: Suhrkamp, 1970), 14: 13–30.

15. "Romanticism" and "Romantic" are obviously pivotal formulations in this argument. By no means do I mean to imply that the particular artifacts produced during the era conventionally known as "Romanticism" are devoid of or inherently alien to textuality and linguistic apprehensions, as the works of Goethe, Words-worth, Shelley, Melville, and a host of others amply attest. For the purposes of the present discussion, however, I employ Romanticism in a more general, historical sense, as a rubric for the configuration assumed by speculative conventions at one extended moment in the tradition of metaphysics. Here, I believe, I follow a lead implicit in Lacoue-Labarthe and Nancy's *L'Absolu littéraire*.

16. For example, *The Marble Faun* receives its color symbolism virtually intact from *The Scarlet Letter*. The painted image (of old Colonel Pyncheon, Chapter 2) plays a decisive role in *The House of the Seven Gables*, where marble also figures (Chapter 15). An entire tale, "The Snow-Image," elaborates a figure (snow) that appears merely as the briefest shorthand in *The Marble Faun*. I am suggesting that Hawthorne's work is at least in part organized as a lexicon to itself and that certain texts assume the task of decoding and translating images presented elsewhere as rebuses, out of context and with a minimum of explanatory material. The iterability of Hawthorne's symbols allows him to play the duplicitous role of both the *placer* and the *solver* of enigmas.

17. See John T. Irwin, *American Hieroglyphs: The Symbol of the Egyptian Hier-oglyphics in the American Renaissance* (New Haven: Yale University Press, 1980), pp. 3–11, 18–22, 28–31, 36–37, 45–57.

18. Nathaniel Hawthorne, *The Scarlet Letter*, Norton Critical Edition (New York: Norton, 1962), pp. 27–28.

19. All these descriptions of Miriam and Hilda derive from Wordsworth's *Lyrical Ballads*. Miriam's moods allude to the first line of "Strange Fits of Passion." Hilda, in her modesty, seclusion, and her association with birds and flowers, becomes a creature of one of the so-called Lucy Poems, "She Dwelt Among the Untrodden Ways."

20. See, for example, the cycles of infinity and life in Hegel's *Phenomenology of Spirit*, pp. 99–100, 106–7.

21. See, for example, the tortuous Paris streets superimposed upon the map of Buenos Aires in "Death and the Compass," or the Chinese labyrinth of time that expands toward completion in "The Garden of Forking Paths." Jorge Luis Borges, *Ficciones* (New York: Grove Press, 1962), pp. 96–98, 133–34.

22. The smokescreen by which the novel camouflages its most suspect variables is closely akin to both the false entrance protecting Kafka's "Burrow" and the Freudian notion of the screen memory. The screen memory is a benign memory substituted for a traumatic one. See Sigmund Freud, "The Psycho-Pathology of Everyday Life," in *The Standard Edition of the Complete Psychological Writings of Sigmund Freud* (London: Hogarth Press, 1953–74), 6: 43–52 (henceforth identified as the *Standard Edition*).

23. I am referring here to the complex surrogation by which the counteraesthetic texts comprising *Either/Or* are at least two steps removed from Kierkegaard. The texts, themselves introduced by the fictive narrator, Victor Eremita, are ascribed to one "Esthete A" and one Judge William. I am also suggesting that this fictive distancing device in a philosophical text is already implicit in the Hegelian perspectival division of labor that articulates *in itself*, *of itself*, and *for us*. See Søren Kierkegaard, *Either/Or*, 1: 3–15.

24. See Neil Hertz, "Dora's Secrets, Freud's Techniques," in *The End of the Line: Essays on Psychoanalysis and the Sublime* (New York: Columbia University Press, 1985), pp. 122–43; also in *Diacritics*, 13 (1983): 64–76.

25. For Kierkegaard's reading of *The Clouds*, see Søren Kierkegaard, *The Concept of Irony* (Bloomington: Indiana University Press, 1968), pp. 158–81.

26. See Søren Kierkegaard, *Repetition: An Essay in Experimental Psychology* (New York: Harper and Row, 1964), pp. 61–65.

27. The figure of the eternal-feminine derives from the end of Goethe's *Faust*, p. 308 (ll. 12104–111).

Chapter 3

1. All citations refer to H. Bruce Franklin's edition of the novel. Herman Melville, *The Confidence-Man* (Indianapolis: Bobbs-Merrill, 1967). In these notes, the title will henceforth be abbreviated *CM*.

2. See *CM*, p. 11, where "the great ship canal of Ving-King-Ching seems the Mississippi in parts." The ambiguity (and ultimate indifference) of Black Guinea's color is to be found on pp. 20 and 46.

3. Cf. *CM*, pp. xviii, 180.

4. Also see *CM*, pp. 27, 65, 80, 81, 125, 138, 141, 159, 187.

5. Also see *CM*, pp. 20, 32.

6. For a contemporary version of this kind of utopia, see Marin, "Disneyland: A Degenerate Utopia," in *Glyph 1*, pp. 50–66.

7. See Benjamin, "The Work of Art in the Age of Mechanical Reproduction," *Illuminations*, pp. 217–51.

8. Wittgenstein's language games are hypothetical situations in which the prevailing rules are altered—or at least rendered unusually explicit—for the purpose of illustrating the linguistic structuration of communicative acts and events. For the basic elaboration of language games and their theory, see Wittgenstein, *Preliminary Studies for . . . the Blue and Brown Books*, pp. 77–125. The notion of speech acts explored by John Searle and others is an extension of Wittgenstein's investigations. A superb analysis of *The Confidence-Man* could be written from the perspective of its speech acts.

9. This attitude bears affinities to R. W. B. Lewis's notion of Adamism. See R. W. B. Lewis, *The American Adam* (Chicago: University of Chicago Press, 1971), pp. 9, 41.

10. For role reversals, as well as other forms of reversal in the novel, see John

G. Cawelti, "Some Notes on the Structure of *The Confidence-Man*," *American Literature*, 29 (1957): 278–88.

11. *CM*, pp. 63, 103.

12. *CM*, pp. 138–39, 151.

13. *CM*, pp. 49, 127.

14. *CM*, pp. 66–69, 78.

15. Also see *CM*, pp. 73 (a parody of the beginning of Blake's song, "How sweet I roam'd from field to field"), 150 (a reference to Wordsworthian "passion-fits of nature"), 166, and 225.

16. See Walter Dubler, "Theme and Structure in Melville's *The Confidence-Man*," *American Literature*, 33 (1961): 307–19. Dubler recognizes the connection between the novel's theme of moral indeterminacy and the various types of dialectical relations it sets into play, but he does not consider the dialectic in which the two halves of the novel are involved.

17. *CM*, p. xx. The figure of the confidence-man can be regarded both as a sequence of different characters (as it was in most criticism prior to Franklin's work) *or* as a single composite character who changes guises.

18. The dialectical logic of the novel does not preclude the possibility that the cosmopolitan's "defeats" are pedagogical moves in a strategem that metamorphoses the interlocutors of the second half of the novel into operators as effective as the cosmopolitan himself.

19. Explications of this episode tend toward a moral evaluation of Indians as opposed to Indian-haters and of Melville's intentions, whether he sided with the Indians or their predators. Yet the wider issue at stake is the ideology of confidence and how both groups are encompassed by it. See Elizabeth S. Foster's introduction to her edition of the novel, *The Confidence-Man* (New York: Hendricks House, 1954), pp. lxv–lxvii; and Roy Harvey Pearce, "Melville's Indian-hater: A Note on a Meaning of *The Confidence-Man*," *PMLA*, 67 (1952): 942–48, parts of which are reprinted in Pearce's *Savagism and Civilization* (Baltimore: Johns Hopkins University Press, 1965), pp. 244–50.

20. The connections that Melville observes between language and power are of course close to the tenets and moves described by Machiavelli in *The Prince*. It is no accident that Chief Mocmohoc's stratagem is almost identical to one employed by Cesare Borgia in *The Prince*, when he captures the Orsini and Vitellozzo after bringing them together in council. See Niccolò Machiavelli, "Legation to Cesare Borgia," in *The Prince*, ed. Robert M. Adams (New York: W. W. Norton, 1977), pp. 89–91.

21. See Egbert S. Oliver, "Melville's Picture of Emerson and Thoreau in *The Confidence-Man*," *College English*, 8 (1946–47): 67–72.

22. *CM*, pp. 50–52, 117–18, 180–83, 184–85, 323.

23. For a good discussion of the implications of the narrator's interjections for the novel's fictionality, see Edgar A. Dryden, *Melville's Thematics of Form* (Baltimore: Johns Hopkins University Press, 1968), pp. 150–95.

24. *CM*, pp. 51, 184–85.

25. *CM*, pp. 107, 149, 181.

26. *CM*, pp. 6, 9, 15, 45, 98–99, 140, 146, 148, 154, 160, 167, 169, 184, 186, 189–90, 198, 200, 250, 257, 266–69, 321, 328, 343, 346.

27. *CM*, pp. 11, 26, 27, 61, 105, 168, 185, 228, 239, 265, 317.

28. *CM*, pp. 19, 44–45, 49, 67, 70, 115, 127, 140, 150, 201, 318, 346, 349.

29. *CM*, pp. 3, 19.

30. *CM*, pp. 3, 6, 16, 36, 41, 62, 84, 100, 105, 135, 195, 224, 230, 265, 272–77, 285, 310, 318.

31. *CM*, pp. 84, 150, 224, 293, 315.

32. *CM*, pp. 210, 235–37, 238–39.

33. See Irwin, *American Hieroglyphics*, pp. 18–25, 31–35, 64–65.

34. For Kant, genius is a "natural gift which must prescribe its rule to art (as beautiful art)." Its preeminent quality is originality. It facilitates a "happy relation" among the various faculties of cognition, taste, and artistic production. "Genius is the exemplary originality of the natural gifts of a subject in the *free* employment of his cognitive faculties." Indeed, Kant speaks of the "cosmopolitan disposition" of the author of one of the exemplary passages of verse that he cites. See Immanuel Kant, *Critique of Judgment*, tr. and intro. J. H. Barnard (New York: Macmillan, 1951), pp. 150–66.

35. *Oxford English Dictionary* (Oxford: Clarendon Press, 1937), 4: 113.

36. This is a notion of Richard Klein's that came up in conversation during the summer of 1976.

37. A paradigmatic and, by the way, hilarious depiction of the mass popularization of an initially arcane intellectual school occurs at the end of Jorge Luis Borges's "Tlön, Uqbar, Orbis Tertius," where "the international press overwhelmingly hailed 'the find.' Manuals, anthologies, summaries, authorized reprints, and pirated editions of the Masterwork of Man poured and continue to pour out into the world." See, for this passage, Borges, *Ficciones*, pp. 33–35. I am indebted to Professor James Bono of my department for pointing out its unique power to me.

38. "Hard Language" was the title and subject of a conference organized by Professors Bruce Jackson and Diane Christian at SUNY-Buffalo in 1974. The conference examined that facet of language bordering on and influencing many varieties of behavior.

Chapter 4

1. The initial version of this chapter was written in 1969, in response to a graduate seminar on modern poetry offered by J. Hillis Miller at the Johns Hopkins University. The paper originally centered on Pound and was entitled "Language as/is Currency in the Economy of Poetry." The acute criticism I received both from Hillis Miller and Richard Macksey led me to Lévi-Strauss and whatever larger picture that has emerged in time.

2. See Benjamin, *Illuminations*, pp. 157, 161, 169, 173, 174–80, 186, 192–94, 217–19, 221, 225–28, 229–30, 234–37.

3. See, above all, Adorno, *Minima Moralia*, pp. 15–18, 21–26, 48–50, 57–64, 115–16, 124–28, 190–92, 208–12, 222–24, and *Prisms*, pp. 17–34, 131–32.

4. See Julia Kristeva, *La Révolution du langage poétique* (Paris: Seuil, 1974), pp. 11–14, 61–67, 86–100, 151–71.

5. The literary criticism of J. Hillis Miller has not only explored the dimensions of modernism but anticipated the sequence of theoretical steps necessary for its contemporary assimilation. See J. Hillis Miller, *Poets of Reality* (New York: Atheneum, 1969), pp. 1–12, 217–84, 285–369, and "Stevens' 'Rock' and Criticism as Cure," *Georgia Review*, 30 (1976): 5–33 (part I) and 330–48 (part II).

6. For a seminal application of the insights of contemporary critical theory to modern poetry, one as fresh and instructive now as it was at the time of its initial appearance, see Joseph Riddel, *The Inverted Bell: Modernism and the Counter-poetics of William Carlos Williams* (Baton Rouge: Louisiana State University Press, 1974), pp. 2–99.

7. In *The Pound Era*, Hugh Kenner not only attempts to elucidate Pound's work hermeneutically; he also dramatizes the energy fields of vorticism, Pound's practices of grafting, and the poet's stylistic experiments on the performative level. See High Kenner, *The Pound Era* (Berkeley: University of California Press, 1971), pp. 24–34, 81–93, 143–62, 163–72, 232–47.

8. All citations and allusions to Stevens's work refer to *The Collected Poems of Wallace Stevens* (New York: Alfred A. Knopf, 1954). "The Man on the Dump" is on pp. 201–3 of this edition.

9. Jacques Derrida defines this term and explores its potential in "Freud and the Scene of Writing," in *Writing and Difference*, tr. Allan Bass (Chicago: University of Chicago Press, 1978), pp. 196–231.

10. Stevens, "The Motive for Metaphor," *The Palm at the End of the Mind*, ed. Holly Stevens (New York: Random House, 1972) p. 240.

11. For the notions of allegory and the allegory of reading, see Paul de Man, *Blindness and Insight: Essays in the Rhetoric of Contemporary Criticism* (Minneapolis: University of Minnesota Press, 1983), pp. 135–36, 160–61, 171, 187–208, 222–28, and *Allegories of Reading* (New Haven: Yale University Press, 1979), pp. 188–220, 221–45, 298–301.

12. Cornelius Nepos, c. 100–25 B.C., was a Roman historian, the author of *De viris illustribus*, *Chronica*, and *Exempla*. He is remembered for the simplicity of his writing style.

13. Stevens, "The Sense of the Sleight-of-Hand Man," *The Palm at the End of the Mind*, p. 168.

14. Although metal is not one of his primary materials, Picasso is an originator in this regard. I think of such sculptures as *Violin* (1913–14), *Glass of Absinth* (1914), *Guitar* (1914), and *Violin and Bottle on a Table* (1949). Among many other artistic productions relevant in this respect, Georges Braques' cubist collages occupy a prominent place: *Still-Life with Pipe* (1912), *Still-Life with Clarinet and Violin* (1912–13), *Newspaper 'Le Courrier'* (1913), and *Glass, Carafe, and Newspaper* (1913–14).

15. In Chapter 3 of *Everybody's Autobiography* (1937; rpt. New York: Random House, 1973), Gertrude Stein makes the point, "America is not old enough to get young again."

16. Claude Lévi-Strauss, *Tristes Tropiques*, tr. John and Doreen Weightman (New York: Atheneum, 1974), p. 96.

17. On the front page of *The New York Times* of Monday, July 21, 1969, President Richard M. Nixon was reported to have characterized his first communication

with the astronauts after the moon landing as "certainly. . . . the most historic telephone call ever made." President Nixon also commented: "Because of what you have done, the heavens have become a part of man's world. . . . For one priceless moment in the whole history of man all the people on this earth are truly one— one in their pride in what you have done and in our prayers that you will return safely to earth. On the same front page of *The New York Times* appeared a poem by Archibald MacLeish, "Voyage to the Moon," which begins, "Presence among us,/ wanderer in our skies,/ dazzle of silver in our leaves and on our/ waters silver,/ 0/ silver evasion in our farthest thought—/ "the visiting moon" . . . 'the glimpses of the moon' . . ./ and we have touched you!"

18. See Derrida, "Plato's Pharmacy," *Dissemination*, pp. 66–67, 71, 89, 90– 94, 97–102, 104–5, 109–12, 136–42.

19. Although it is Stevens who composed poems entitled "Asides on the Oboe," "The Man with the Blue Guitar," "Sad Strains of a Gay Waltz," "Poem with Rhythms," and "Notes Toward a Supreme Fiction," the dimension of musicality is inconsequential in neither the work of Pound nor of Williams. I think of such texts by Pound as "Ballatetta," "The Flame," and "An Immortality," from *Collected Shorter Poems* (London: Faber and Faber, 1968), pp. 52, 64, and 88; and of such poems by Williams as "Calypsos" and "Asphodel, that Greeny Flower," in *Pictures from Brueghel and Other Poems* (New York: New Directions, 1967), pp. 56–57, 153–82. I will have occasion to refer again to the latter work, in connection with the textual fabric of its leaves, flower petals, and membranes.

20. Nietzsche's most elaborate musical text is, of course, *The Birth of Tragedy*. See Friedrich Nietzsche, *The Birth of Tragedy and the Case of Wagner*, tr. Walter Kaufmann (New York: Random House, 1967), pp. 33–38, 52–56, 60, 132–35.

21. See Stevens, "Loneliness in Jersey City," *The Palm at the End of the Mind*, p. 153.

22. In a sense, Wittgenstein's practice of formulating propositions and language games may be described as the elaboration of the conditions that prevail within specific contexts. Hence "A proposition, a picture, or a model is, in the negative sense, like a solid body that restricts the freeedom of movement of others, and, in the positive sense, like a space bounded by solid substance in which there is room for a body" (*Tractatus Logico-Philosophicus*, Proposition 4.463, p. 69). Wittgenstein's models, whether propositions or language games, are bounded contexts used, like Stevens's perspectival experiments, for purposes of linguistic testing. Wittgenstein insists on the integrity and value of language models not coextensive with the full range of everyday linguistic possibilities, such as the game of chess played without pawns, just as one can argue for a certain self-containment within Stevens's perspectival poems. See Wittgenstein, *Preliminary Studies for . . . the Blue and Brown Books*, pp. 77, 81, 125.

23. Besides the passages from "Plato's Pharmacy" cited above, see Derrida, "The Double Session" and "Dissemination," in *Dissemination*, pp. 173–366.

24. Cf. Williams, "The Yellow Flower" and "Asphodel, that Greeny Flower," *Pictures from Brueghel and Other Poems*, pp. 89–90, 153, 154–55, 157–59, 165, 176–82.

25. Walter Benjamin, *The Origin of German Tragic Drama*, tr. John Osborne (London: New Left Books, 1977), p. 29.

26. For the notion of superimposition, see Henry Sussman, *The Hegelian After-math*, pp. 7–8, 11, 20–21, 59, 193, 213, 219–20.

27. This discussion of the assimilation of extraneous matter in modern poetry and the consistency of poetic stuff also implicates the organic process of digestion and its byproduct. The poetics of fragments and debris cannot be far from the psychosexual economy of excretion. Freud was most perspicacious in his understanding of the economic and sexual nuances of digestion and defecation. Few poets have been as economically and excrementally oriented as Pound. The digestive process involves different organs and a different sexual economy than reproduction. We will have occasion later in chapter 4 to explore that Poundian economy running counter to the resonance of the poetic hymen.

28. Lévi-Strauss, *The Savage Mind*, p. 3.

29. Hugh Kenner senses the affinity between modern aesthetics and the improvisational, do-it-yourself mentality in *A Homemade World: The American Modernist Writers* (New York: Alfred A. Knopf, 1975), pp. xii–xviii, 11–14, 21–26, 28–29, 38, 77–78, 86–88, 104–8, 158–65, 173–77, 204–10.

30. Lévi-Strauss is again indispensable in coming to grips with the appropriation of mythology in modern literature. One of the crucial outgrowths of his "Structural Study of Myth" is the abandonment of "the quest for the true version" of the myth and its redefinition as "all its versions . . . a myth remains the same as long as it is felt as such" (*Structural Anthropology*, 216–17). Modern literature is particularly rich in the plethora of ways in which it embroiders upon and appropriates mythology. Pound delves into it as a natural foreground for his poetry; Joyce endows it with the form of symbolic and allegoric frescoes inscribed on the outer surfaces of a fictively mundane world; Broch synthesizes the conditions for its prior elaboration through a process of biographical reconstruction; Kafka engages in structural variations on the ostensibly "original" versions; and Faulkner submerges the myth in an all-but-invisible residue of vanished events and characters. If we follow Lévi-Strauss's approach, however, all of these deployments of mythological material fall within the purview and variability of the myth.

31. Benjamin, "Theses on the Philosophy of History," *Illuminations*, pp. 253, 257–58.

32. Pound's debt to—and fascination with—the Japanese haiku was established firmly and eloquently in a seminar paper read and submitted by Ms. Fatima Lim in conjunction with a graduate seminar on modern poetry that I taught at SUNY-Buffalo during 1982–83. I hope that Ms. Lim will make her work on this topic more widely available through publication in the near future.

33. The economic throught in Pound's *Guide to Kulchur* (New York: New Directions, 1970) parallels that evident in the *Cantos*; the epigraph is from p. 35 of this work.

34. See Borges, "Pierre Menard, Author of Don Quixote," *Ficciones*, pp. 45–55.

35. Pound, *Collected Shorter Poems*, pp. 36, 42, 64, 118–19, 127. This volume contains both *Personae* and *Lustra*.

36. All references in this volume to the *Cantos* are to Ezra Pound, *The Cantos of Ezra Pound* (New York: New Directions, 1973). Textual references to this vol-

ume will assume the following form: the number of the *Canto* in question (in Roman numerals), a slash mark, and the page or pages in the New Directions edition.

37. Andrew Parker has recently published an excellent essay linking the implicit economic theories in Pound's writing to his anti-Semitism. See Andrew Parker, "Ezra Pound and the 'Economy' of Anti-Semitism," in *Postmodernism and Politics*, ed. Jonathan Arac (Minneapolis: University of Minnesota Press, 1986), pp. 70–90.

38. The past decade has been particularly fecund in its exploration of the economic dimensions, derivations, and implications of literature. In France, Jean Baudrillard has traced the persistence of long-standing philosophical and speculative traditions in economic ideology and practice. In the United States, Marc Shell has investigated both sides of the coin: the legends and inscriptions incorporated into pieces of money, and the fashion in which economic concepts invade and influence literature. The French sociologist, Pierre Bourdieu, diverts his attention away from the meaning of artifacts and toward their role as signs in the social codes of class and distinction. Aesthetic, as opposed to functional, literacy is for him merely one additional way in which the powerful and socially mobile members of a society display their clout. See Marc Shell, *The Economy of Literature* (Baltimore: Johns Hopkins University Press, 1978), pp. 5–7, 9–10, 79–88; Jean Baudrillard, *The Mirror of Production*, tr. and intro. Mark Poster (St. Louis: Telos Press, 1975), pp. 17–20, 33–41, 88–91, 129–35, and *For a Critique of the Political Economy of the Sign*, tr. and intro. Charles Levin (St. Louis: Telos Press, 1981), pp. 143–63; and Pierre Bourdieu, *Distinction: A Social Critique of the Judgement of Taste*, tr. Richard Nice (Cambridge: Harvard University Press, 1984), pp. 1–7, 11–96, 260–317.

39. Pound offers his literacy lesson with a vengeance, forcing those of us, for whom his poetry is a phenomenon but not a universe, to depend on the scholarly instruments necessitated by the mosaic (or composite-board) of his allusions. Anyone with this reliance is forced into a certain literality in the decoding of specific names and historical and aesthetic references. In the present attempt to come to grips with the *Cantos*, I very often decipher factual and idiosyncratic allusions with the help of Hamilton Edwards and William W. Vasse's *Annotated Index to the Cantos of Ezra Pound* (Berkeley: University of California Press, 1974). These authors themselves occasionally admit to lacunae in their knowledge. My ability or inability to "fill in" some specific details has not, thus far, disrupted the symbolic, historical, psychosexual, or formal poetic economies that I discern to be at work in the *Cantos*.

40. Pound, *The Cantos of Ezra Pound*, Canto XX/89; *Canto* XXVII/129.

41. On this point, no one speaks more succinctly and bluntly than Pound himself. "This book is not written for the over-fed," virtually begins *Guide to Kulchur*. "It is written for men who have not been able to afford a university education or for young men, whether or not threatened with universities, who want to know more at the age of fifty than I do today, and whom I might conceivably aid to that object. I am fully aware of the dangers inherent in attempting such utility to them" (see Pound, *Guide to Kulchur*, p. 6 [unnumbered]).

42. Ernest Fenollosa's work on the Chinese ideogram was of course crucial to Pound's notion of and wish for a dynamic language of process rather than a static

one of substance. Curiously, though, in his poetry Pound is harder put to compose such verse than to demand it. Pound's Chinese translations and imitations come closest to the mark. See *The Chinese Written Language as a Medium for Poetry*, ed. Ezra Pound (San Francisco: City Lights Press, 1983), pp. 9–10, 13–20; also see Pound, *Guide to Kulchur*, pp. 27–28, 51, 80–81, 121–26, 147.

43. Given the pervasive moral, theological, and ideological charge of the *Cantos*, my invoking Edmund Spenser as one of their significant models and forerunners is less frivolous than it might appear. Spenser is the inspiration not only for a certain moral and psychological pitch in the *Cantos*; his allegory also incorporates sequential economic and productive processes. In the House of Pride episode in *The Faerie Queene* Book II, for example, Redcross must see through the disguises of adversaries whose names, at least, are defined by the imaging process and duplicity (Archimago and Duessa). The House of Pride is a palace of feigned wealth and cosmetic beauty built by slave labor. Its nether parts conceal what Pound would call the usury at its basis—the exploitation necessary to satisfy excessive tyrannical demands. In its economic allegory, the House of Pride is described as a factory of cheap and fake art. See Edmund Spenser, *The Faerie Queene*, Variorum Edition (Baltimore: Johns Hopkins University Press, 1958), I: 21, 25–30.

44. For the notion of economic nature and its violation, see Shell, *The Economy of Literature*, pp. 93–101, 111–12.

45. See Pound, *Guide to Kulchur*, pp. 35–38, 47–48.

46. For a broad speculative view of appropriation, see Martin Heidegger's discussion of this term. Appropriation (*Er-eignis*) takes place within the framework (*Ge-Stell*) of the event (*Ereignis*) and entails a taking possession (*Vereignen* and *Zueignen*). It thus entails basic concepts of placement (*stellen*), taking (*eignen*), and property or selfhood (*eigen*). See Heidegger, *Identity and Difference*, pp. 36–40, 100–106.

47. Pound's ongoing interests and concerns intersect with a broad constellation of Freudian concepts and themes. For the symbolic coincidence between money and excrement, see Freud, *Standard Edition*, 5: 403; 9: 168, 173–74; 10: 200. For the basic writings on the Oedipus complex, see the *Standard Edition*, 7: 56–57, 129; 15: 207–8; 17: 119, 186, 192–204, 261–62. For the castration complex, particularly in relation to women, see the *Standard Edition*, 9: 215–19; 10: 36, 100, 105, 121, 131; 11: 95–96, 199, 204–5; 17: 25, 31, 34, 79, 96, 113, 118, 231–33.

48. The image of the sea-mother is accorded a prominent place in the psychology of Sándor Ferenczi, one articulated explicitly in Joyce's *Ulysses* as well as in the *Cantos* and *Paterson*. See Sándor Ferenczi, *Thalassa: A Theory of Genitality*, tr. Henry Alden Bunker (New York: W. W. Norton, 1968), pp. 18–19, 33, 36, 44–52, 54–57, 78–80, 87–95.

49. In approaching Pound's Homeric sources, I refer to Richmond Lattimore's translation, the *Odyssey of Homer: A Modern Translation by Richmond Lattimore* (New York: Harper and Row, 1975).

50. See Derrida, "Plato's Pharmacy," *Dissemination*, 95–102, 134–42.

51. For the most "classical" instance of interloping at the "primal scene," undergone by the "Wolf Man," see Freud, *Standard Edition*, 17: 36–42, 55–56, 61, 67, 70, 77–80, 97–98, 101, 107–9, 120.

52. See Léo Bronstein, *Fragments of Life, Metaphysics, and Art* (New York: Bond Wheelwright, 1953), pp. 3–9, 21–27, 85–92, 96–103.

53. Leo Frobenius, *African Genesis* (New York: Benjamin Blom, 1966), pp. 97–110.

54. Pound, *Guide to Kulchur*, pp. 57–58.

55. Over the past decade, the notion of entropy has received considerable attention, both scientific and fictive. See Thomas Pynchon's 1959 story, "Entropy," reprinted in Pynchon, *Slow Learner* (New York: Bantam Books, 1984), pp. 63–86; and, Jeremy Rifkin, *Entropy: A New World View* (New York: Viking, 1980).

56. For an entertaining and illuminating overview of the critical controversy that *Paterson* has engendered, see J. Hillis Miller, "Deconstructing the Deconstructors," *Diacritics*, 5 (1975), 24–31; and Joseph Riddel, "'Keep Your Pecker Up'—Paterson Five and the Question of Metapoetry," *Glyph 8: Johns Hopkins Textual Studies*, (Baltimore: Johns Hopkins University Press, 1981), pp. 203–31, and "A Miller's Tale," *Diacritics*, 5 (1975), 56–65.

57. See Hegel, *The Phenomenology of Spirit*, pp. 6–8, 15–17, 47.

58. Chief among these Romantic sources is Wordsworth's *Prelude*, whose near-continuous wind and hydraulic imagery and whose rhetoric of mind *Paterson* in a sense never leaves. The "unmoving roar" of the Passaic (*P*, 55) is reminiscent of the unheard melodies of Keats's "Ode on a Grecian Urn." The allegorical landscape of the river and falls shares the carefully constructed geological setting of Shelley's "Mont Blanc." Yeats is both an implicit and explicit "presence" (*P*, 167). Above all, compare passages in *P*, 5, 7–8, 25, 39, 55, 99, 100, with William Wordsworth, *The Prelude*, Norton Critical Edition (New York: W. W. Norton, 1979), pp. 28–29, 42–47, 82–85, 88–91, 216–17, 258–65, 421–27.

59. I think specifically here of how de Man uses the terminology of literary periodization to dramatize specifically moments in the allegory of reading. See de Man, "Literary History and Literary Modernity," *Blindness and Insight*, pp. 142–65.

60. William Shakespeare, *King Lear*, Act III, Scene II, ll. 1–9, in *The Complete Works of Shakespeare*, ed. Hardin Craig (Chicago: Scott Foresman, 1961), p. 999.

61. Elias Canetti, *Auto-da-fé* (New York: Farrar Straus Giroux, 1984), tr. C. V. Wedgwood, pp. 455–64, a translation of *Die Blendung* (Munich: C. Hanser, 1963).

62. Stevens, "Anecdote of the Jar," *The Palm at the End of the Mind*, p. 46.

Chapter 5

1. Italo Calvino, "The Count of Monte Cristo," *t zero*, pp. 137–52. The extract at the head of this section comes from pp. 139–40, 145, 151–52. I henceforth abbreviate references to this volume as *tz*.

2. Italo Calvino, *The Watcher and Other Stories* (New York: Harcourt Brace Jovanovich, 1975), pp. 1–73. I henceforth abbreviate references to this volume as *W*.

3. Robert Pattison, *On Literacy: The Politics of the Word from Homer to the*

Age of Rock (New York: Oxford University Press, 1982). I henceforth abbreviate this volume as *OL*.

4. Jonathan Kozol, *Illiterate America* (Garden City: Anchor Press/Doubleday, 1985).

5. Walter J. Ong, *Orality and Literacy: The Technologizing of the Word* (London and New York: Methuen, 1982). I henceforth refer to this volume as *O and L*.

6. *Literacy and Social Development in the West: A Reader*, ed. Harvey J. Graff (Cambridge: Cambridge University Press, 1981). This highly useful volume includes historical approaches to the problem of literacy from 1066 to roughly 1900 by such writers as Emmanuel Le Roy Ladurie, Elizabeth Eisenstein, Natalie Zemon Davis, Kenneth A. Lockridge, and Harvey J. Graff.

7. *Literacy, Language, and Learning*, ed. David R. Olson, Nancy Torrance, and Angela Hildgard (Cambridge: Cambridge University Press, 1985). This volume is situated at precisely the kind of interdisciplinary node where more research needs to be done. The book includes essays by Elizabeth Eisenstein, Ian Winchester, Michael Cole, Helen Keyssar, Wallace L. Chafe, and Frank Smith, among others.

8. For the particular interaction between the perspectives that can be extrapolated from the Derridean models of the voice and writing, see Derrida, *Of Grammatology*, pp. 12, 17–18, 25, 30, 38, 43, 70–73.

9. See Kozol, *Illiterate America*, pp. 102–31, 204–17.

10. Two exemplary passages that indicate Ong's vision of an intimate and protective oral environment and of its temperamental and cognitive antithesis, a world of print culture, are the following:

> In the absence of elaborate analytic categories that depend on writing to structure knowledge at a distance from lived experience, oral cultures must conceptualize and verbalize all their knowledge. with more or less close reference to the human lifeworld, assimilating the alien, objective world to the more immediate, familiar interaction of human beings. A chirographic (writing) culture and even more a typographic (print) culture can distance and in a way denature even the human, itemizing such things as the names of leaders and political divisions in an abstract, neutral list entirely devoid of a human action context. An oral culture has no vehicle so neutral as a list. (*O and L*, 42)
>
> Primary orality fosters personality structures that in certain ways are more communal and externalized, and less introspective than those common among literates. Oral communication unites people in groups. Writing and reading are solitary activities that throw the psyche back on itself. . . .
>
> Literates often manifest tendencies (loss of contact with environment) by psychic withdrawal into a dreamworld of their own (schizophrenic delusional systematization), oral folk commonly manifest their schizoid tendencies by extreme external confusion, leading often to violent action, including mutilation of the self and others. (*O and L*, 69)

11. It is most interesting to see electronic media such as television treated as modern-day preserves protecting the intimacy and warmth of oral environments.

This oral nostalgia is evident in such a rigorous and helpful approach as Fiske and Hartley's *Reading Television*, p. 15:

> But we live in a society where literacy and its associated skills and modes of thought are valued very highly. This means that the tendency to judge all media, including television, by the prescriptions of literacy is not the result of mere intellectual confusion. Rather it is a reflection of dominant cultural values, instilled during five hundred years of print-literacy. Furthermore, it is a tendency that is not confined to television's critics. The consequent habits of thought have encouraged those people who control and encode the television message (people who are drawn largely from the most literate sections of society) to attempt to preserve literate values within the medium.

Kozol waxes biblical when he promotes oral history as the medium by which "The People Speak Their Word": "From early centuries the Hebrew people have been known as 'People of the Book.' It was 'The Book,' not books—'The Word,' not words—which gave a sacred character to literate tradition" (Kozol, *Illiterate America*, p. 140).

12. Derrida, "Plato's Pharmacy," *Dissemination*, p. 149.

13. See Benjamin, "On Some Motifs in Baudelaire" and "The Work of Art in the Age of Mechanical Reproduction," in *Illuminations*, pp. 166–70, 217–42.

14. See Fiske and Hartley, *Reading Television*, pp. 112–26.

15. See Kozol, *Illiterate America*, pp. 132–41.

Index